THE SECOND GREATEST STORY EVER TOLD – VOLUME 1

An Autobiography

JOSEPH C. THEK, MD

PublishAmerica
Baltimore

© 2008 by Joseph C. Thek, MD.
All rights reserved. No part of this book may be reproduced, stored in a retrieval system or transmitted in any form or by any means without the prior written permission of the publishers, except by a reviewer who may quote brief passages in a review to be printed in a newspaper, magazine or journal.

First printing

PublishAmerica has allowed this work to remain exactly as the author intended, verbatim, without editorial input.

ISBN: 1-60610-903-0
PUBLISHED BY PUBLISHAMERICA, LLLP
www.publishamerica.com
Baltimore

Printed in the United States of America

To all my family members

*Special thanks to Anita Misso,
Harvie Raymond and Jim Davenport*

Preface

I humbly ask that the Holy Spirit bless this book. If there are mistakes either in form or content I ask forgiveness ahead of time.

I suggest you read this with access to a Bible. It may not make sense otherwise. My bias towards the Catholic Church shows. I don't want to give the impression that I am anti-Catholic. I love Catholics. But I know the Catholic Church is in error.

From the beginning I must say that the Bible is the written Word of God. If you disagree then progressing onward may be a waste of time.

Why do I feel this way? What proof do I have?

The two proofs that God gave us. First is the matter of prophecy. (Please read Isaiah 44:28, 45:1)

Truly amazing! The Bible prophesies that Cyrus will overthrow Babylon more than 200 years before it happened using his very name! That would be like George Washington predicting that George Bush would topple Saddam Hussein.

And then there is Isaiah Chapter 53, which predicts the scourging of the Messiah some 750 years before it happened!

Daniel 11:3-4 predicts Alexander the Great 200 years before he came!

If the Koran was able to do that I would sit up and listen, but it doesn't. It can't.

These prophecies are meant as proofs. We ignore them at our own peril.

There are many other prophecies particularly Isaiah, Revelation (Apocalypse in the Catholic Bible) Daniel and in Psalms. Biblical prophecy predicts the near future as well as the distant future. Thus, for instance, there is some confusion regarding Daniel's Antiochus Epiphanes (Daniel 11:21-35) and the Antichrist (Daniel 11:36-45). It is not a question of either/or but of both.

The number of prophecies in the Old Testament about the Christ is numerous. I would refer the reader to the chapter about them in Josh McDowell's *The New Evidence Which Demands a Verdict*.

I scraped the mountaintops. There is so much more in the valleys.

Second is the very existence of the Jews. (Please read Deuteronomy 7:1)

Does anybody remember any of them? No. But we remember the Jews. Why? Because God wants us to. If that's not a miracle I don't know the meaning of the word.

The Jews survived two captivities, the Diaspora and the

Holocaust to regain a homeland in 1948. That partially fulfilled a prophecy made about 2500 years earlier as seen in Ezekiel 37:15-22. When it becomes a spiritual land that's when I think prophecy will be fulfilled.

Now that's a prediction!

It seemed impossible. The existence of tiny Israel amid an ocean of Islamic states is a miracle in itself. But nothing, absolutely nothing, is impossible for God. (Please read Luke 18:27.)

But the preceding is too esoteric for me. You do not come to belief in the Bible through intellectual pursuits. You come to a belief of the Bible through the indwelling of the Holy Spirit. This book is meant to show how that happened for me.

All names have been changed except for my immediate and extended family.

The dialogue is not verbatim. I have written it as it may have happened.

Chapter One
Childhood

Every testimony of a Christian is *The Second Greatest Story Ever Told.* This is mine. You can laugh or cry. I laugh.

I would like to say that's what I chose because it implies some control. Sometimes, I had some, but mostly I didn't. Laughter is part of my nature, like flying is to a hawk. To ask me to wear a frown is like asking a canary not to sing. You may as well ask me not to breathe. As you will see, there is a lot to laugh about.

I was born in Jamaica,—warm breezes, pure water, pristine beaches—Oops! Wrong Jamaica. Jamaica, Queens—tenements, dirty laundry and the shadow of the El—on May 25, 1950. I was the fourth of five children, which was not unusual before the Pill. Everybody had at least five or six kids.

May—the fifth month—25—five squared—1950—'50 twice 25 or 5x5x2—5-25-50. It was a Thursday, the fifth day of the week. Even my initials were multiples of five and each of my names has an "E", the fifth letter of the alphabet. I chose "Peter" as my Confirmation name giving me five "E"s in my entire name. I thought my birthday was special. Everybody should feel that way.

In 1950, trolley cars were being replaced by busses; radios by television sets. Our first house was at Richmond Hill, Queens. The second was at Woodhaven. We played stickball, mumblety-peg and marbles—any game that was adaptable to the street.

Then, my sister, Marianne, was born. It was October 5, 1955. 10-5-55. One day after the Brooklyn Dodgers beat the Yankees in the World Series. I went from the darling to just another kid in the time it took for her to be birthed.

Growing up in New York was an adventure. Like the time Johnny, the brother closest to me in age (4 years), Little Eddie, my cousin, and I, were screaming, "I want a cat," at the funeral parlor next to my maternal grandparents' apartment (My paternal grandparents died many years before I was born.).

"Get out of here!" yelled the funeral director.

"What were you kids up to now?" Grandpa asked when we came to his apartment.

"Nothin'," Johnny replied.

The phone rang and Grandpa answered it. I heard a man shouting than Grandpa hung up. He fumbled in a drawer for pencils and paper.

"Yous want a cat?" he asked rhetorically. "Take these. Go out on the fire escape and copy down license plate numbers."

"Why?" Johnny asked bravely.

"Because I said so!" Grandpa answered. "Now go!"

We clanged on to the fire escape. My hand still gets a cramp whenever I think about it.

He lived upstairs and the ground floor was always dark. Who knows what went on down there? Every time we passed it all of us ran. When Grandpa found out, he concocted this tale. "Little boys disappear from there all the time. I think he kidnaps them".

I was scared. I'd probably run today if I could.

He taught me how to play chess before I could read. It's been a solace all my life. Whenever things were going bad, I could always distract my mind with a game of chess.

Marianne only lived for eight months and was buried on the day Grandpop died. In school they taught us that she was in Limbo. Marianne wasn't in Heaven because that was reserved for people who had reached the age of reason. It puzzled me.

Who are they to say she ain't in Heaven? Don't Jesus love all the little children?

(Please read Ecclesiastes 6:6)

Notice the verse says "one place." Curiously, there is no mention of Limbo in the Bible. Limbo is actually very unbiblical.

The double passing was tough for my mother, but she didn't show it. I never asked how they died. It was an unwritten rule. I learned dying was a part of life. I went on living and strove.

When Marianne passed on I became the youngest again, the baby of the family, the last. (Please read Mark 10:31.)

I adapted to being the youngest.

I was good at math. Give me anything with numbers and I came up with an answer. As I got older, I was always looking for the first principle on which I could hang all other equations, like theorems in Geometry. I failed to realize that the First Principle was God and mathematics is His language.

In 1956 we moved to New Jersey where there were mountains and streams. Trees and lakes replaced city streets. Johnny and I, with some of his new friends, built a cabin. We slept in it whenever we camped. The cabin was strong, but it couldn't weather vandals who burned it. We never discovered who they were. As a result, we went to the mountains without a cabin.

There is only one word to describe my parents—saints. In fact, Uncle Raymond called Mom "Saint Ellen." I never heard her curse and the only things that angered her was when somebody praised the English, or denigrated the Irish. Once my cousin, Lena, made an off-hand remark "We're from the low end of the Kelly gene pool." ("Kelly" with a "y" not an "ey" the way the Protestants originally spelt it). Mom became apoplectic, frothing at the mouth to chew Lena to bits.

She is small, a mere five feet tall; but who ever measured a heart with a ruler? Mom was big enough; her feet touched the floor, at least when she walked.

My dad was an extraordinary man.

"Joey learns by osmosis," he claimed when I was little. "He sits on a book to reach the table."

Dad loved books with cases and racks everywhere. Our house was a library.

Dad made games of everything. Once, he made a lollipop tree in the park. Dad taped them to the branches and we found it by the shimmering light.

"Let's see how many toys you can get in the box," he often said when we had to clean up. A record was established. We were supposed to break it.

Dad made us laugh, and there is not enough laughter in the world.

He used to sit and watch the ants. "They're playing baseball."

Pretty soon we watched too.

"They're not playing baseball," a friend from down the street remarked. "They're only practicing."

Another time, Dad put a pumpkin flower into a big glass jar. As it grew, the pumpkin conformed to the dimensions of the jar. At the end of the summer, he cut it off the vine.

When visitors came they asked, "How did you get the pumpkin inside the jar?"

Dad just smiled and wouldn't reveal his secret.

But, he didn't take into account the rain. Dad inadvertently set the container upright. Water entered and rotted the pumpkin. It had to be discarded.

Dad claimed I loved to talk. When Mom was pregnant with me, the doctor took him aside after listening to her belly with a stethoscope.

"What are you doing?" Dad asked.

"There is something important I have to tell you."

"Like what?"

"Like—he spoke."

After a moment Dad asked, "What did he say?"

The doctor's eyes grew wide, like he possessed some secret key to the universe. As if I said something profound. He put a finger to his lips and hissed, "Shh!" swearing Dad to secrecy. The doctor tugged on Dad's sleeve, pulling him away, and continued, whispering, "The baby asked, 'Who's pitching for the Dodgers?'"

That's the way my dad told it.

Dad too was small in stature until he graduated from high school, then he shot up to about six feet. Dad had red hair, when he had it, and we kidded him about his hair or lack of it. Often, I said, "Wear a hat because you're blinding me."

I gave him a brush and comb one Christmas.

"You must have made a mistake" Dad insisted after opening the present.

"No, I didn't!"

He weighed about one hundred seventy-five pounds if you put another foot on the scale. Dad walked to the store on most days to get the paper. He enjoyed reading the funnies and doing the crossword puzzles.

Then, there was the Christmas tree. We didn't have a place to discard it after the holiday.

"I'm gonna' burn it in the fireplace," Dad began. But that wasn't good enough. He sat us down for a lecture. "Now you should understand about fires before burning the tree. They're very dangerous. Not to be played with."

Everything was fine, except the tree was too big for the fireplace. Smoke filled the entire house; paint peeled off the walls.

"I'll have to get new curtains," a furious Mom said. "And that smell! Aroo!"

"No problem. I'll get a plastic tree next year."

Halloween Eve was called, "Gate Night." Kids could do whatever they wanted to as long as nothing was permanently harmed. It was pure fun. In the old days, the kids left gates to farms open, so, the animals escaped, a form of mischief.

Gate Night *was* an adventure. Once, Bernie Napravnic (a friend of my brother's) had fire extinguishers pressurized and filled with water for us. They could shoot a stream of water about one hundred feet. There wasn't enough room in one car. Two were taken with a person manning a fire extinguisher at each window except the driver's. Everybody was fair game. Danny (a friend of mine) drenched a traffic cop. Mrs. McGuire was carrying two bags of groceries across her front lawn when we opened fire on her. The items went flying in the air as she dove for the ground. Mrs. McGuire looked like a casualty of WWII.

I was a precocious child, always asking questions. One was whether or not God exists. Most of my life, I was unsure. Some things didn't seem to make sense, like children suffering. But, this story is meant to affirm that He is and we have to see the world differently, through His eyes. Ours are imperfect and all we see are shadows.

There is a serious angle to me, like the B-side of a record. If you scratch the humor, you find it. I kept my serious side under wraps because Richard, my oldest brother, suggested I shouldn't talk about religion or politics unless I wanted an argument and I, unfortunately, counted Christianity as a religion.

But I can't keep my big mouth shut. Some things need to be said or else we are doomed for a repetition. If we get wet, so be it. I don't want us to throw the groceries in the air like Mrs. McGuire.

"Betcha can't hit the target with an arrow," Johnny instigated in the yard of the Turner house at the end of our street.

"Can to," I replied and proceeded to shoot an arrow at the target. The shaft carried over it striking a moving car in the tire. The arrow bounced off but I hid anyway.

I can hear the wife explaining to her husband.

"How was your day?" he'd ask at the dinner table.

"All right," she'd answer. "But some kid shot an arrow and hit my tire."

"Did it explode?"

"No. Just bounced off."

"Lucky."

Was it bad luck to be hit or good luck that the tire didn't explode? Actually, luck had nothing to do with it.

My cousins—I had a lot—were like brothers and sisters to me. Tommy Thek was born a month after I was. Eddie Kelly—Little Eddie as he was known, though Eddie wasn't little but heavy—was two years older. I was sandwiched between Lena and Kyle Sprague. It was a treat to go to Tommy's house first in Glendale, then, out on Long Island in Oceanside, or to Little Eddie's—first in Newark, then, in Linden, New Jersey.

Johnny, Little Eddie and I, went to the end of their block where there was a park. It had a nearly frozen lake in winter.

"Stay here and watch me," Johnny commanded as he walked out on the ice. We became distracted on the shore and the ice buckled. My brother kept walking. By the time our attention returned, he stood in the middle of the lake on the honeycombed ice.

"Come on in!" we called nonchalantly, and Johnny did as if it were an every day occurrence. He was a little wet because of it. Big deal.

Uncle Eddie, one of my mother's brothers and Little Eddie's dad, ranted when we returned to the house.

"I can't believe any of you are so stupid as to walk on half-melted ice!"

He smacked his son.

Don't see how that changes anythin'.

Johnny and I were paperboys. I knew everyone who had a dog. German Shepherds, Collies, Weimaraners, Greyhounds, Poodles. You name it; I was an expert. Three times they bit me. Tetanus shots? What were they? I must've been all right because the dogs didn't foam at the mouth or die.

Mrs. Dutt was one of my customers. Her sister owned a Dachshund that looked like a moving sausage. It hid in the bushes to await me because I could outrun it if the dog was in the open. Running away from the Dachshund became a game. He was successful in biting me once.

Mrs. Lord had a German shepherd that bit Johnny. The dog had to be quarantined for ten days. On the first day he was released, the dog bit me.

The third time was by a blind Collie. Now, a blind dog bit how many people you know?

Whenever my cousins came to visit, they were willing helpers on our routes. Once, Little Eddie fell in a puddle because it was icy on the bottom. Usually, ice floats or covers the top of a puddle, but on that day, it rained over it and the ice wasn't visible.

"What will we tell your father?" I asked.

"Oh, I don't know. But it has to be good, somethin' he'll believe."

I thought about it on the whole route. Before returning to the house, I said, "I know what we'll say. There was a car out of control and you jumped out of its way and landed in a puddle."

"That's good. He'll believe that."

Uncle Eddie never gave us a chance to tell the story. He took one look at his son, and his anger rose. Smack!

Johnny, Little Eddie and I, explored on the Raritan River one spring. A log spanned the water.

"Let's cross," Johnny said.

My brother and I crossed easily, but my cousin could not because he was too heavy. Little Eddie tried anyway. It sank beneath his weight and he fell. Uncle Eddie saw red when we came home and he saw his son dripping water. Smack!

Little Eddie died in 1967. I was watching The Beach Boys when Aunt Angie, his mother, called. "Edward's been in an accident" she mumbled sadly, fighting sobs. "He's dead."

His car was a GTO with a big 296 engine. It burped

whenever it passed a gas station. He was supposed to go to Vietnam. At his funeral, his girl friend whispered to me, "Eddie was draggin' through Newark showin' off. You know how boys can be. The light turned green, and he was off. I guess the driver coming the other way never saw Eddie or the red light. They crashed."

Another cousin is Tommy Thek. He always had the latest music: The Who; Buffalo Springfield; Blood, Sweat and Tears. I first heard *Sgt. Pepper's Lonely Hearts Club Band* with him, and many others.

His dad, my Uncle Pete, rented, then owned, a bungalow near Sag Harbor, Long Island, and a sixteen-foot wooden boat. Hundred feet high, sandy cliffs, rimmed Peconic Bay between the fins of Long Island. During one big storm, rain advanced across the bay. It was like seeing a curtain pulled closed. When the wind howled, the parking signs leaned from the loose soil. The next morning, thousands of dead jellyfish washed up on the shore because of lightning strikes the day before.

The bay was rough, but Johnny, Tommy and I went out anyway. We wouldn't let a little thing like the weather stand in our way. I can still see Dad with my Uncle Pete on the shore waving to us to come in. "What are they doing?"

"I don't know," Johnny answered.

We ignored them. The wind ripped a hole in the side of the boat, and water poured in.

"I can't swim!" a scared Tommy shouted.

"Now's a fine time to tell us," Johnny muttered.

We turned around. Johnny, Tommy and I made it back alive. We watched the boat sink from the safety of the dock.

Prior to its sinking, Tommy and I went often to the marina, where the boat was moored, to play Wiffleball. It was an inverted U-shaped inlet with sand on three sides protecting it and an outlet into the bay. He stood on the little dunes and threw a wiffle ball down at me. Tommy made it curve and dipsy-doodle away from my bat.

He liked the Braves. I rooted for the Dodgers before they moved, then later, the Mets. Many times we pretended to be big-league batters, Hank Aaron or Duke Snider. It didn't help my skill because I lost a lot.

Tommy and I fished at the marina with a glass milk bottle, bread and string.

"What do we do now?" I asked.

"Put the bread in the bottom of the bottle, tie the string around its neck and throw it in the water. Soon a fish will see the bread and swim in it. When he does, all you have to do is pull up on the string and you'll get a fish."

"Won't he just swim out?"

"Nope. Too stupid to turn around. I've done it a dozen times. It works."

And it did! That's how these New York City boys went fishing.

Tommy and I used the boat for fun and exploring. We

sped into the wake of the Shelter Island Ferry. The front of the craft rose a couple feet in the air, then, crashed back down on the water. The boat wasn't equipped with life jackets. Tommy and I wouldn't have worn them if there were. We loved to court disaster and to be metal canes in a lightning storm. Plus, he couldn't swim!

Tommy and Johnny tied a rope to the stern of the boat. The free end was placed on an air mattress to be used like water skis. I was elected to go on it because of Tommy's inability to swim. Besides, I was the smallest. At first the air mattress hardly moved.

"A little faster," I ordered.

Johnny increased the speed of the boat. The mattress, with me holding the rope, took off. It was difficult to keep above water.

"Slow down!" I yelled.

"Speed up you say?" Johnny with his hand to his ear put the engine on full throttle. I jerked forward and nearly fell off of the mattress. We buzzed the beach and the swimmers scrambled to safety. I went under with the mattress and fell off. I came up sputtering water. Johnny gave that maddening laugh of his.

Tommy and I didn't figure on the tides, the winds, or anything else. We just went. Whenever the first tank was empty, it was time to turn around. I repeat; Tommy and I loved to tempt God. He was patient with us and for that I am eternally grateful. Our guardian angels worked overtime. We gave them a few scares.

After the wooden boat sank, Uncle Pete bought a new fiberglass one.

"Say, won't it be fun if we slept in the boat? Sort of christened it?" Tommy asked.

No one said not to touch the tarp if it rained. We tried to sleep with the stars going every which way, when it started to get cloudy. Tommy and I lost the stars. Drops followed. Up went the tarp.

At first, the water ran off. Eventually, it pooled at the low point.

Maybe if I hold it up here, I thought as I put my finger up and touched the tarp to help gravity where the rain caused it to sag. That's when the trouble started. It dripped. Soon the tarp was more like a funnel.

"There's no place for the water to go!" Tommy exclaimed.

"What's your plan?"

"Evacuate!"

We both were soaked rowing back. On the shore, waving us in, stood Dad and Uncle Pete again.

We had walkie-talkies. We hid one in the woods across from the bungalow. When a child went by, Tommy, Johnny and I, played a sound effects record of ghosts and goblins into the other one. The noises were emitted across the street in the walkie-talkie. Pretty soon, a mob of kids stood by the trees and found it. We played the record into our walkie-talkie, but the kids weren't scared anymore. Johnny walked outside and took it from them. He held the walkie-talkie up to his ear.

"What's he doing?" Tommy asked.

Johnny pretended to get instructions. He started running with it down the road away from the house. The children went after him.

"Boys, what are you up to now?" Aunt Henrietta asked while poking her head in to see what we were doing. Tommy and I hid our walkie-talkie and replied, "Nothin.'"

"Why is Johnny running down the street, and who are those boys running after him?"

"I don't know," Tommy answered, and I shook my head and shrugged my shoulders.

Aunt Henrietta didn't pursue it further. That was good for me because I heard about the German torture methods to get you to speak—the dripping water, the rack. I was sure she was about to use them on me. I would not be the stool pigeon, the squealer. Or would I?

Johnny outran his pursuers, then, doubled back with the other walkie-talkie.

"Why were those boys chasing you?" asked Aunt Henrietta.

"They weren't chasing me. We was racing."

"It looked like chasing."

"Well, they wanted to know who the fastest boy was and I took off. I won."

Aunt Henrietta looked skeptically at Johnny but then left us alone.

Richard, and my cousin, Peter (One of three sons of Uncle Pete and Aunt Henrietta. They also had a daughter, like our family.), went fishing at four in the morning one day. Both of them were driven over by Noyack Inlet, where Tommy and I played Wiffleball, and dropped off. A boat appeared out of the early morning fog from the deeper waters of Peconic Bay. My brother told me the story.

'Say! What you got?" Richard called.

"Bluefish! And plenty of 'em," a man on board answered. "How 'bout you?"

"Just some blowfish!" Peter answered.

With that, the man stooped over and disappeared. In the fog he was barely seen. Then, he reappeared and threw something to the boys. Richard caught it. There in his hands was a bluefish with hook holes and all! The boat turned and disappeared into Peconic Bay.

"I caught it in the inlet," Richard swore to Uncle Pete upon being picked up.

Well, he had.

Back at the bungalow, Uncle Pete looked closely at the bluefish. There were marks where the hooks had been and Uncle Pete was convinced.

"My nephew caught a bluefish in the Inlet!" he told everyone. He was believed because at one time Peter was the first to sight a seal in Sag Harbor.

Seven or eight years later, Regina, Richard's newlywed, was on line in a fishing store. The man before her asked the cashier what was caught in the inlet.

"Mostly blowfish," the shopkeeper answered. "But once, the Thek boys caught..."

That's how legends are born.

Lena, another cousin, is almost a year older than I. Every year on my birthday, I catch up in age for three weeks until her birthday on June 14. They wave The Flag on her birthday but not on mine. It's unfair. I couldn't wait to be as old as she. I called to say we were the same age. As the years go by, Lena calls me on my birthday and reminds me of how old I've become.

I spoke with my cousins about Heaven and angels. As a boy, I was very religious (I didn't know then that there is a huge difference between 'religion' and 'spirituality.'). We talked about our parents' mortality, never our own. We were fearless, or more appropriately, reckless. But God is everywhere, not Someone we find only in a church. So I fell in love with nature—trees, flowers, mountains, water. The affair still persists. It is all His handiwork.

For me, this is the way toward happiness. But it isn't about us. It's about Him. Always has been, always will be. I've spent my life on Earth to learn that. We can build our cathedrals of sand in the air but they will be washed away by the first terrorist attack.

Then, there was school. Suellen, my sister, attended Butler High. Richard stayed in New York with my grandmother until she died; then he went to Newark College of Engineering (NCE).

Since my parents were ardent Catholics, I was enrolled at St. Mary's, with my brother, Johnny. It is in Pompton Lakes, two towns over from Pompton Plains where we lived. On the first day, I boarded a bus for home.

Somethin's changed since this mornin'.

I stopped in the aisle and looked around. After a minute, it hit me.

I know! The faces ain't the same!

Johnny had followed me.

"It's the wrong bus!" he called up the stairwell. "Get off!

He has come to my rescue ever since.

I was a good Catholic. I went to Mass every day. Father Cyril said it in less than twenty-five minutes. I admit its brevity influenced me. I never let my Catholicism inconvenience me.

St. Mary's is an interesting choice of names. The Catholics revered Mary as much as Jesus. We were taught that she is the "Mother of God". But Dave Hunt in *A Woman Rides the Beast* says quite appropriately on Pg. 438 that, "'Mother of God?' Yes Jesus is God and Mary is His mother, but she is not the mother of Him as God..."

(Please read Mark 3:31-35.)

Every Catholic Church I ever went to has a statue of Mary. Isn't that a form of idolatry? Doesn't the Second Commandment condemn it? (Please read Exodus 20:4 and Jeremiah 44:17.)

Eerily familiar.

Isn't the Catholic Church breaking its own rules?

I was small in stature too. I was always the third tiniest because Charlie Earnhart and Vinnie Oliveci were shorter than I. Being tiny gave me an appreciation of the underdog, but I knew someday I would be big. Look at my dad.

I was forever being punished for something. I laugh at it now, but it wasn't funny at the time. I didn't have a first name. It was "Thek do this" or "Thek do that." Never "Joseph."

The dunce cap was *passé*, but the dark and dreary cloakroom at the back of our classroom became a familiar place, because that's where the "good" sisters put me. I consoled others who were new to the surroundings saying, "Don't worry about it. It's not so bad."

Vinnie Oliveci, with the other students, put his lunch in the cloakroom. I stole and ate the Twinkies from Vinnie's bag while I was there. Maybe the other students were blamed, I don't know. I am admitting I took the Twinkies. Sorry, Vinnie.

I was in many fights. I, being small, was usually on the losing end, but I fought nonetheless. Johnny, as big brother, freed me from the clutches of bullies; then, he beat me up.

I've only had two broken bones. One was after a touch football game.

"I tagged Johnny," I swore.

"Did not," Billy Hipp, a neighbor, countered and laughed. I couldn't let him, could I? I punched him and he, being twice my size, picked me up and threw me on my left shoulder. I knew my collarbone broke as my left arm hung down like an unhinged door.

The cast ran from my shoulders to the waist. Boy, did it itch! I became an expert at stuffing hangers down inside to scratch it and not bleed. I played football with the cast on. Now, they don't even use one.

The second break came from playing "Keep Away" on the macadam schoolyard. I became entangled in the chain-link fence surrounding it and broke my right hand. The nuns made me write with it in a splint, even though I had learned good penmanship as a lefty.

"That's the Devil's hand," the 'good' sister told me.

That was news to me. Wasn't a good southpaw, like Warren Spahn, worth his weight in gold? I think the school desks were solely for the right side. Not that I have a complex or anything. Heaven forbid I should complain! So, I learned to write with my hand in a splint. My pinky was always out to the side because of it.

Everybody was an altar boy. I memorized the "Our Father" in Latin. *"Pater noster..."* Nobody, not even the priest, knew the language or what was said. It didn't matter. God understood. I guess He speaks Latin.

I was thrown out of the altar boys and put in the choir instead, because I could carry a tune. The nuns paraded me around to different classes and encouraged me to sing. Like a parrot, I did—mostly Irish songs. It was a chance to perform. After all, I am related to George M. Cohan. At least, that's what Mom said.

Because I always created trouble, the nuns put me in the back of the class and gave me a book to read. Whether it was *War and Peace* or Charles Dickens, I didn't care. I read and read, and read some more. That was the best thing the nuns did for me. I developed a love of both reading and writing.

Because of that love, I wrote for the school newspaper, *The Gael*, but most of my writing were barbs thrown at Ed Dreifort. He was a big, gangly, uncoordinated kid, who shared my bus and lived three blocks from me.

We went bowling and his ball got stuck.

"Go see what the matter is," I said.

He took off, right down the lane. A man's voice came over the intercom.

"Hey kid, get off the alley!"

Ed looked to me for an explanation.

"He must mean someone else. Keep going."

He did and Ed and I were thrown out, but my sides hurt from laughing. They still do.

We did everything together. Ed and I swam in the streams up the mountains. Whenever I wanted to play sports, which was every day, I called him. His mother had plastic covers on everything while mine let us play golf in the house. He spent a lot of time at my home or outdoors.

At school, Patrick McCarthy was my best friend. He was heavy and not a member of the "in" crowd. I was on its fringe and couldn't admit that he was my friend—another of those unwritten rules. Pat understood, and the pecking order was established.

He was an altar boy. One day, Patrick was wearing his cassock particularly well. He could have been a poster for Boys' Town. Pat looked positively angelic.

There was one thing wrong though—his socks. They were two different colors. It wouldn't usually matter because the cassock covered them, then he knelt.

I laughed from the first row. Pat turned around and wondered what was so humorous. Standing up, the cassock covered his socks again. He turned back to the priest reciting the Mass. Pat knelt again. I pointed to his socks and made sure everyone else saw them.

Then, there was basketball. Everyone on the team had scored that year, except Patrick who was a third string guard. During the last game of the season against our arch-rival Holy Spirit, St. Mary's was winning by a wide margin, so, Pat was put in. I led the chorus from the bench.

"Shoot, McCarthy, shoot!" we shouted.

When Pat finally did, it wasn't even half-court. The ball ricocheted off the supports of the basket.

"What are you doing, McCarthy?" the coach yelled.

"I...I..." Pat stammered.

"You're out! Thek go back in!"
Pat never scored that year.

We had our problems like acne and growing hair in places it had never grown before. I survived. Maybe there were a few bones broken and some scars, but I was always loved. Out of my parents' and siblings' sight, I thought I was alone. I didn't know it, but I was wrong. God was watching all the time.

Basketball. That's how I met Ian O'Grady. I was fourteen and practicing outside by myself down at the lone court in town.
"Can I play?" he asked.
There were only the two of us on the court. "Sure."
We walked home afterwards, and I discovered he lived about three blocks from my house (in the opposite direction from Ed Dreifort's). Ian went to Holy Spirit grammar school. He would be attending DePaul High in the fall and so would I.
Sports are good ways to meet people, like going to church. In fact, they are like religion. One can be addicted to them. My family was. Basketball is a good game for winter. But for us, baseball was the ultimate sport. I looked forward to spring because of it. Stats were used in our house like prayers in others. I memorized everything so they could be brandished like a rapier. No clocks. There aren't any two-minute drills like some other sports.

It's not over until the last out is made. As George Carlin indicated, one is always running home.

Baseball begins in spring, lasts through the dog days of summer and ends in fall. Other games in winter are simply substitutes for it. By March, I was chomping like big league players do on chewing tobacco to go out and play.

The first day at DePaul I met Michael Ventra.

"Keep quiet in the halls," a nun commanded. He let out a low roar.

Turning around, the nun asked me, "Who did that?"

I heard him, but shrugged my shoulders. He and I became good friends, after detention.

He brought out my serious side. I think of it as the boring aspect of me that puts people to sleep. First, we talked about frivolous things. It was a ritual. Laughter eased our minds. Knowing Michael and I were running out of time, in the last five or ten minutes of our conversation, we said whatever was on our minds. But, I didn't want him to snore.

There were many detentions that first year. One Saturday, I was an exterminator of termites infesting the school. The next, I painted the lines on the parking lot. Some spaces were regulation, but most were either too big or too small. I don't think you would have any trouble if you rode a murdercycle, excuse me, a motorcycle to work, and it was crooked.

"Those lines!" the nun exclaimed. "Just look at them!"
"It's the paint."
I was never put on paint detail again.
DePaul had its own set of morals, a silent, unwritten, code. The nuns and priests were its agents. Guilt, the feeling that one is doing wrong even when one isn't, is a learned response. I learned it well. I was inculcated without even knowing it. If you didn't comply, then you were expelled. As rebellious as I was, I still conformed—a little.

Ian O'Grady introduced me to drinking and, boy, did we drink! It's not something I'm proud of. One night, Ian was too drunk to make it safely back to Ogee McGrath's house. Ogee and Vinnie Oliveci put him in a ditch, covered him with leaves, and left him to sleep it off. When Ian awoke, he went to the wrong house. Ian opened the door, went inside and promptly vomited. I heard he was like Mt. Vesuvius.

I can almost hear the married couple in their nightshirts with the husband returning to bed.

"What was that, George?"

"You're not gonna' believe this, Martha."

"Try me."

"Some strange kid just puked up his guts all over our living room carpet."

Anyway, Ian was arrested.

He also introduced me to the Hokey brothers. It was in the fall of my sophomore year. That night, I hung around with Jimmy, the older of the two. He hid several six packs in the trunk of the jalopy that Jimmy took us out in. I sipped a beer.

"C'mon drink up," he teased. "You're drinking like an old lady."

My manhood challenged, I gulped the rest down and popped another can. The world tipped and spun. God looked out for me because I certainly didn't know what I was doing.

Danny Hokey, the younger of the two, gave a new definition to the term "late." Oftentimes, Danny was so late he didn't arrive until the next day.

They had seven other siblings; five had muscular dystrophy and were dead by twenty. There were four "normal" children, if you want to rate them as normal.

Jimmy was the intellectual with a mean streak and Danny just wanted to have fun. I would argue with the elder brother for hours. Then, I'd play a game, or go to a concert or a dance, with the younger one.

When Jimmy and Danny were of draft age, they expected papers in the mail every day. None came. Finally, Jimmy went to the draft board ostensibly to enlist because it would be better for him to go in as an officer. When he gave his name, Jimmy said the recruiting officer was surprised. "According to this, you're dead."

"What?"

"Are you Paul or James?"

"James."

"It's lucky you came down or else you'd have been in the dead pool forever."

That would have been fine by me, Jimmy thought. *What did I do?*

Anyway, Jimmy was drafted. Danny couldn't go until he came back, it being illegal for two brothers to serve at the same time.

Then, there was the night at the drive-in. It was Jimmy's last before going in the army, and he wanted the car. Unfortunately, Danny took it to the Wayne drive-in with Leslie, a girl who wanted to get inside his pants. Michael drove Jimmy and me there.

It was along the river, and the night was foggy. The clients didn't seem to mind. We snuck in through the fence on foot, after parking our car a safe distance away.

The three of us sat then threw pebbles at the back window of the vehicle. We saw a head pop up in the back seat. It was silhouetted against the eerie light of the projector beam in the mist. Jimmy, Michael and I, stopped. The head couldn't see us in the fog. It disappeared, going down, so, we threw pebbles again. This time, two heads popped up. The three of us quit again. After a brief time, the door opened and they exited the car.

"Wait here," Jimmy ordered.

I had a sinking feeling in my gut as he disappeared into the mist.

"I know you're out there!" Danny shouted. "Where are you?"

Michael and I held our ground about thirty feet behind the car, while Danny and Leslie circled the car in the fog. Suddenly, Jimmy slid in and locked the doors behind him.

"Very funny!" Danny remarked. He fumbled in his pockets for the keys. Jimmy took them out of the ignition, smiled and held the keys up to the closed window for Danny to see.

"Give me those!"

Jimmy put the keys back in the ignition. Turning the engine on, he revved the motor; then, Jimmy pulled away. Danny tried to get him to stop by playing "Chicken" with him. But, Jimmy had the car. As it approached, Danny jumped out of the way.

Jimmy left Danny and Leslie without a means of transportation in the mist at the drive-in.

"Wait 'til I see him!" Danny said between clenched teeth as we snuck out.

"Now just calm down," I said. "It won't do any good to pay him back."

"I'm gonna get him for sure," Danny continued angrily.

Leslie fell in a puddle on the way.

"Now, I'm really gonna get him," Danny said.

"I'm okay," Leslie said. "It was nothin' but a little accident."

Danny seemed placated.

"This is a story you can tell your grandchildren," I mentioned while we avoided puddles. "On second thought, that's not a good idea."

After taking Leslie home, we drove to the Vatican (the Hokey house). Danny spied Jimmy reclining on a couch.

"Why you..." Danny began as he pulled him off, and they started to wrestle on the floor before we could intervene.

After we had separated them, I said, "You two shouldn't be together tonight. Danny can go with Michael and Jimmy can be with me."

From his corner, Jimmy said, "All right. C'mon with me in the car. The night's still young."

After we took the flags away from some pins on a nearby golf course, Jimmy nonchalantly said, "We can go for something bigger."

"Like what?"

"Just follow my lead."

Uh-oh.

Friendly's, an ice cream parlor in Wayne, had a six-foot sign tied to a column welcoming their patrons. There were two leaves to the sign with writing on both tied to a pillar. We "borrowed" it.

Now, Jimmy and I were in a car with this big sign covering the back seat.

"We have to get rid of it," Jimmy said.

"Where?"

"C'mon."

I suspect he planned the whole thing from the beginning. At least, that was my excuse.

We placed the sign in front of Bond's, a competing store.

Without our knowing it, Jimmy and I began a feud between the two establishments. You see, the Bond's manager blamed Friendly's for the sign in front of his store. Little did he know, there were other parties involved in the escapade. I certainly never told him that we robbed the pillar.

During the summer between my sophomore and junior years, Ian O'Grady took me to his "camp" in upstate New York by the 1000 islands. It was a cottage by Clear Lake near Alexandria Bay. We went by bus and met his parents there. His dad, J.A., sold real estate in town and took his vacation during the slow months of summer.

We jumped off a cliff across the lake.

I hope the water's deep enough.

It was and Ian and I swam away.

Ian's dad took us to Mass. J.A. sat in the first row. Then, for some reason, he stood up. We followed his lead unconsciously. Everybody else in the church sat. There we were, standing in the first row unable to see everyone else in the church sitting. Finally, J.A. turned around. He sheepishly sat; Ian and I did too.

The service was very ritualistic. I didn't realize then that there was another way, another Christianity. We were taught that you could only get to Heaven by following the laws of the Catholic Church. If you left, you would go to Hell. We weren't even allowed to read the Bible. It was way above our understanding and only the priest could interpret it. What a bunch of hooey!

I think there is another motive. If one reads the Bible, one can see how wrong the Catholic Church is. They want us submissive to them, not God. The Church doesn't want us to read Matt. 23:2-10 but especially Matt. 23:8-9.

J.A. wanted to drop the "Big One" in Vietnam. He ranted about it every day. J.A. must have dreamt about bombs. The next minute he could be making hamburgers on the grill.

On the morning of my 18th birthday, Patrick McCarthy picked me up on our way to Yankee Stadium along with twenty others. Ernie Valli found Kevin Quinlan in Mass receiving Communion at the altar when he should've been in the car.

Ernie wasn't going to let Communion slow him down. No sirree bob.

"Quinlan!" he bellowed in the church.

The red-faced Kevin slinked away from the altar and followed him like a whipped dog to the auto. I should've known it was going to be a bad day. Letting lunatics loose on an unsuspecting public should be a crime.

By the third inning of the first game (it was a double-header), I was drunk and asleep. I awoke to see Michael Knight barf on the person in front of him.

"Take Me Out to the Ball Game," the policeman in the right-field stands sang as he led us, his body swaying from side to side. "Take me out with the crowd. Buy me some peanuts..."

All of us stacked our empty containers of beer. There were over two hundred cups. We didn't know people in the left-field stands would take this as an affront. They started piling their cups too. Our stack became higher.

The cups, some half-filled, tipped, forming a big C. Gravity, and you can see the "gravity" of the situation, cannot be denied. The cups fell, some on the people in front, a few on us and some on the field. Beer sloshed out. The game was stopped. We were astounded. The cop, who had led in song, approached us.

"Out, boys!" He shouted with an out motion of his right hand. Hearing that, Ernie ran around the mezzanine. The cop chased him. It was the ninth inning of the second game, so, we had our money's worth, in more ways than one.

I don't know where public drunkenness became an ideal. It shouldn't be, ever. I can attest that I am crazy enough without it.

On the way home, we stopped at a Laundromat to sober up and to clean Knight's clothes. Our parents never found out; at least, I don't think they did. Maybe they were watching the Mets on TV.

Life was full, but there was one thing missing: a girl.

Chapter Two
ADOLESCENCE

It's funny how someone comes knocking on your door when you least expect it. Her name was Valerie. We met at a dance in St. Mary's basement, one of those weekly things to get the teenagers off the streets.

"She's a slut," a red-haired caddy informed me, pointing toward a tall, beautiful girl.

That appealed to me because I was looking for one.

I strolled over to her, trying to be cool.

"Say, want to dance?" I asked.

She looked up at me with green eyes blazing, "Sure."

It was a long song, The Doors' *Light My Fire*. I looked carefully at her young face, my arms akimbo. "Say, how old are you?"

"Almost fourteen."

"I just turned seventeen."

The music blared. I thought I'd use a particularly romantic line. "Say, want to go outside and make out?"

"I hardly know you," Valerie replied angrily as she walked away.

Maybe she's not a slut, I concluded belatedly.

Later that night, Valerie approached me. "Will you walk me home?"

"Of course," I answered and thought that Valerie was the rain after a drought.

"Those poor McCarthy girls," she said as we walked down the street from their house. I was surprised. Everybody made fun of Pat's sisters, but Valerie referred to them as normal people. I was impressed and fell in love. You cannot deny its primal force. Love is the most powerful thing on Earth. You can have your gravity and relativity. They do not inspire.

I kissed her when we reached her front doorstep. It was the sweetest kiss I've ever had—innocent yet inviting. If she was a slut, it wasn't important anymore.

I'm in love and that's all that matters.

But, her mother stood inside the doorway, watching. Elated, I didn't notice and left. Valerie was grounded.

However, her mother couldn't stop her from going to the church picnic at Seaside Heights.

"Say, want to go down the shore?" I asked casually during one telephone conversation.

"Sure would. Anything to get me out of this house."

Valerie packed a lunch, but who thought of food? When Dad drove me to the church to get on the bus, we passed her carrying a picnic basket. Until then, I had not seen her in the daylight. She was so graceful, walking like a deer.

On the bus, we passed a supermarket.

"'Grand Onion?' What's that?" Valerie asked.

I looked out the window. "I think it's 'Grand Union'."

"Oh."

"No 'U.'"

"Oh."

"Never mind."

The day was sunny when we went to Seaside Heights. Valerie and I donned our bathing suits and splashed in the ocean. I held her hand while the waves nearly knocked us over. Then, we retired to a blanket on the sand. She filled out her bathing suit admirably and I ogled her. Valerie had short brown hair, beautiful skin and was sexy.

Is this me? How do I deserve this?

"Want some lunch?" she asked.

"Why not?"

Anything to be near you.

After the beach, Valerie and I walked on the boardwalk, where I proved I had money by spending it. The sound of the calliope followed us everywhere.

Dusk approached.

"Want to go on the Whirly-Gig?' I asked knowing full well she would have to be pressed up close to me.

"Sure."

Well, all right!

Afterwards, Valerie and I went under the pier, and lay down by each other. We played Burt Lancaster and

Deborah Kerr until the waves came up and lapped our feet, making us late for the bus. All things considered, it was a great day, one of those top ten you will never live again. If only we could discard the others and just keep these. On the other hand, maybe God wants us to experience killing time so that we'll come to Him.

Talking of killing, I was and am troubled by it. I think that we should leave it up to God. After all, He gave us life and only He can take it away. When someone tries to kill you, we should let them. I know that's not a popular response, but aren't we, like Saul, trusting in the weapons of humanity to destroy our enemies? We should trust God to do that. To retaliate is contradictory. Christ could have but didn't. The church was built on His blood. If we resort to violence then we become like our enemies. If they want this world, let them have it. This world is only temporary anyway. Christ was perfectly clear. (Please read Matt. 5:44.)

Notice He doesn't say to kill them. There is no asterisk in Matt. 5:44. Nor is there one in the Ten Commandments where the Father instructs us not to kill.

Our leaders of both parties are misleading us. We need some of them to pray like King Hezekiah in ancient times, out of desperation.

All of us are desperate. If we don't know that, it is unfortunate.

Yes, I went through a deep valley between my childhood

and my maturity. Now I'm back on top of the mountain looking up with outstretched arms and finding the first principle. However, I'm getting ahead of the story again.

I was off to Montreal to see Expo.

"Wait 'til you see where we're staying," Dad bragged for months.

We (Johnny, Dad, Mom and I) went with cousin Tommy, Aunt Henrietta and Uncle Pete. It was my first glimpse of the Adirondacks.

All of us arrived at this 'magnificent' place to stay the night. It was a trailer park and one RV was ours.

"You have to sit on the toilet to take a shower," Dad said. The trailer tilted. "Oh, it's just your Aunt Henrietta moving," he continued without flinching. "The sofa and kitchen table convert to beds, and your room has two sets of bunks."

Oh great!

"You get to sleep up there," Johnny pointed to the top.

What could I say as Tommy and Johnny slept below?

Putting me above was fine, except I didn't fit. Big by then, I scraped my head on the ceiling or slammed toes against the wall. The next morning, eggs rolling underneath the sliding partition door and into our room awakened me.

"What's going on?" I wondered.

"It's only the door to the refrigerator," Dad explained. "It came off when your Aunt opened it. No problem."

When we went to Expo, the lines were so long that Tommy, Johnny and I, took the Metro (subway) to Montreal. We became lost looking for Notre Dame and stopped a priest for directions.

"*C'est un cartier tres chic*," Johnny began then spoke to him in a facsimile of French for over five minutes.

"I'm Episcopalian. I don't understand a word of French, only English."

I wrote a love letter to Valerie saying I'd be home soon.

After I arrived in Pompton Plains, I met with Ian O'Grady and a friend of his at the lone train station in town.

"Lovely Rita, meter maid. Where would I be without you?" they sang.

How am I gonna call Val?

Two girls stopped by, so I became a fifth wheel. I retired down the tracks. About three miles away, I found a telephone booth and rang her.

"It's me," I began. "I'm back safe and sound."

"Good!" she exclaimed. "My mother is driving me crazy!"

A couple nights later, I took Ian O'Grady to the Milk Barn, a local teen hangout, where the two of us joined Valerie.

"Say, why don't we double date?' I suggested.

"How about Ringwood Manor next Sunday?" he asked.

"It's all right with me," Val chimed in.

Ian took a blonde named Sharon, and I went with Val.

It was a lousy time. Ian and Sharon didn't get along. We dropped her off, and then went bowling. Val went to the ladies' room in between games.

"She wants to go out with other boys," Ian said.

"Doesn't Val like me?"

Before he could answer, she returned.

After bowling, I dropped Ian off and went to take Val home. It was still early, so, we went for a ride. When it was time to turn around, I hit a big rock on the side of the road.

"Where are you going?" Val asked as I pulled off on the side of the road and prepared to exit.

"Want to see the damage."

There wasn't even a dent! When I re-entered, the car motor wouldn't turn over. *Something must be wrong because I hit the rock. Oh Lord, let the car start.* I looked down and noticed the gear was in Drive. I put it in Neutral, and it turned over. I sheepishly took her home.

On the way there, Val said, "I'm like a little girl in a toy store who wants everything on the shelf."

I thought I heard a brush-off. I was too stupid to realize I was one of the toys. When I took Val home, I thought I'd never hear from her again.

Weeks later, I was flabbergasted when Val called. It was like a dream.

We went to a dance together but both of us were so absorbed with ourselves that we each forgot about the other. Adolescence can be difficult.

I went to climb Mt. Marcy in the Adirondacks. One of the other campers wore a sweatshirt with his college name on it. It was the same as Val's last name—St. John. Every time I looked at him, I thought of her.

That was my first time mountain climbing. Going to the campsite, we passed mounds of snow on the side of the road with poles in them.

"What are those poles for?" Dave Triolo, another hiker, asked.

"So the plowmen know where to put the snow," Johnny answered.

As hikers, we should've turned back then. Being stupid, like fish caught in milk bottles, the expedition continued.

After Christmas, in December, it was cold, less than ten below. Preparation? What was that? The first rule of climbing is to always respect the mountain. We broke it. A plastic tarp placed in front of the lean-to for warmth didn't work.

Johnny awoke with a start. "I can't feel my feet! They're frostbitten!"

His feet were only asleep, like we should have been, but there was no rest after that.

It started to snow. I put my boots, with my feet still in them, directly on the rocks around the fire. When I talk about boots they weren't mouse boots or anything that resembled expedition footwear. They were simply big green boots with laces. Our cheap sleeping bags didn't keep us warm either.

In the morning, there was about sixteen inches of fresh snow. The hike was postponed—the only smart thing we did. We were alive. That's the most important thing. There are priorities.

Yes, there are. Virtues can conflict (like mercy and justice). When they do, you need to go back to the priorities. If you know the first principle all others will follow it like water flowing downhill. That's why I searched for it.

The First Principle is God Himself. The second is faith in the First and the third is to do the right thing. Many people (e.g. Buddha, Confucius etc.) go to the third step and ignore the first two. You can't. You may answer that life itself is the third step. After all, you must be alive to do the right thing.

Aren't there issues worth dying for? Yes, an absolute exists and all relativity is dispersed. The Theory of Relativity is for physics, not morals. When morals become relative, it leads to confusion. Our goal is to find the absolute and when we do, relay the information to others so that lives or souls are not wasted.

My whole life on Earth has been consumed by that quest. The answer has been Christ all along.

1968 was an interesting year.

It began with the Tet offensive. President Johnson asked Congress for another quarter of a million troops. When he was refused because of the Tet offensive, LBJ decided not to run. In late March, he informed the nation.

I was going on a date to see The Temptations. Beverly, my date, was a little late, so, I sat down to watch TV with her dad. President Johnson came on the air.

"...I shall not seek, and I will not accept, the nomination of my party for another term as your president."

I sat upright as if I'd been shocked by an electric wire. "What did he say?" I asked Beverly's dad.

"That he's not running again."

It was tantamount to a resignation. I was ecstatic! Beverly bounced down the stairs.

"LBJ's not running," I said.

"So?" To her it was about as useless as a colorblind Irishman (can you imagine a Kelly who can't see green?) or an allergic bee.

She and I went to the concert. Val watched from the balcony.

A couple weeks later, I took Val horseback riding. (I say it was horseback riding, but it was the horse doing all the riding.)

Afterwards, I took her to Child's State Park, one of my favorite places because it has three big waterfalls. Spring was in the air. So was love. I held my breath on one of the bridges and kissed her.

On the way home, I asked, "Will you go with me to the prom?"

She answered, "Yes", and I was restored to the sky. I almost felt a good blue. It was another of those Top Ten days.

On another date before the prom, Val and I went to the movies to see *Bonnie and Clyde.* Afterwards, I took her to the Milk Barn. While we were there, she asked, "Want to go steady?"

I didn't know what to think and was caught off guard. Now, you have to understand that going steady was a big deal. It was like being married, kid style. There would be a ring and…

Val stood up, thinking that my reticence was a "No". She went to the lady's room. When Val came back, I ecstatically gave her my ring.

We're married. There's no going back.

"You sure you want to do that?" she asked.

"Yes."

"Even with my mother?"

"Yes, yes," and we sealed it with a kiss.

Youth knows no limitations. I woke Ian O'Grady up to tell him the good news before going home.

The day before the prom it rained more than six inches. There was no place for the water to run. Northern New Jersey is a huge parking lot with every square inch paved.

The day of the prom, there was a flood. Pat McCarthy

said, "I can't get home. Can I change in your car?" I acquiesced, but Pat took my tuxedo by mistake, and I took his. Neither of us knew.

"This darn shirt is too big," I said that night as I kept pushing what I thought was **my** tuxedo shirt down, as I ate the tasty roast beef, baked potato and vegetables.

"That's funny because mine is too small," Patrick told me. "And the pants are too long."

"That's really weird because mine are too short."

Val was so concerned with her appearance that she never noticed. All night long, none of us connected the dots. I just thought that was how tuxes were. Val was with me and I didn't care about anything else.

On our way back the radio blared music. I could still smell the roast beef, baked potato and vegetables from dinner as some of them were stuck between my teeth. Her house was also by the Pompton River and it was foggy. I was in Pat's tuxedo, and Val in her gown.

If she gets any closer, I'll lose it.

Suddenly, the car stopped.

"Say, what's going on?" I exclaimed. "I didn't use the brakes!"

Before I could get an answer water poured in under the doors. I slammed the car into reverse and, miracles of miracles, the engine responded.

"What happened?" Val asked hysterically.

"The lakes joined the river and flooded! I didn't see it and drove right in!"

I had visions of dragging her out of the front seat in her gown with me in a tux. Drowning never entered my mind. God has plenty of experience with water. Remember the partings of the Red Sea and the Jordan River?

Val smoked, so I had to, didn't I? Getting started was hard. On television, everybody finds it relaxing and easy to do. Smoking wasn't that way at all. I had to work at it. I coughed whenever I was near smoke. I practiced. It's difficult to be cool.

On April 4, 1968, I went out with Danny Hokey. He always had a car even if something was wrong with it, like not having reverse. We pulled into a station to get gas.

"Can you back up a little?" the attendant asked.

The jalopy couldn't. Danny pulled around the island instead. Out he went on the road and back into the gas station again. The attendant's jaw dropped. Danny acted as if everybody didn't have a gear. Maybe they don't.

That night, he and I made a "run" to Suffern—on the border of New York and New Jersey. The drinking age was eighteen in New York and twenty-one in New Jersey. We went to Suffern on winding roads to get beer along a stretch called "The Run". I think Suffern owes its existence to the drinking age.

That night Martin Luther King, Jr., was assassinated in Memphis.

"That was a shot in the dark," Danny quipped.

"Not funny. He was a great man. We cannot afford to lose him."

You were supposed to sacrifice something for Lent, so, I did. I gave up going to church. A big mistake. At the time, I equated "The Church" as the Catholic Church. I thought there were "us" and "them." Either you were a Catholic or you were going to Hell. I didn't know any better. Now I do. There are many "churches," but we should all be Christians.

I like to think as if each church is a farmer. One grows apple trees and offers God apples. Another raises orange trees and gives oranges to God. A third peaches, etc. There is only one God who receives it all. All the produce has to go through a farmer's market called Jesus first before it is acceptable to the Father.

The Catholic Church is about 'religion,' rituals, traditions.

"Tradition" makes me think of Tevye in *Fiddler on the Roof*. Jesus degrades traditions. (Please read Matt. 15:1-6.)

Islam is steeped in traditions too as are all the religions of the world, invented by humans. That's what they all have in common. They each are an attempt by humanity to reach up to God. By doing the right thing, saying the right prayer or mantra, they teach we can achieve Heaven or nirvana. In varying degrees, they are all attempts to reach up to God based on works.

Christianity is very different. It is God reaching down to humanity, not us reaching up at all. Christianity is not really a religion. It's the Way. That's how both Paul and Luke describe it in Acts 9:2, 18:25, 18:26, 19:9, 19:23, 22:4, 24:14, 24:22, and 1 Corinthians 12:31. In the Old Testament I would cite the following verses Isaiah 35:8, Jeremiah 2:17 and Malachi 2:8. (Please read them.) Jesus describes Himself like this in John 14:6.

Pretty strong stuff.

(Please read Ephesians 2:8-9 too.)

We cannot earn our way to Heaven. It is His gift given to us. All we have to do is believe.

Saying Christianity is a religion on a par with all others is very demeaning. It doesn't come from man, but from God.

Returning to my life, except for weddings and funerals, I didn't go back to church until I started dating Sharon, over twenty years later. At the time, I figured my mother was going to Heaven. It was designed for people like her. I figured she would never be happy if I went to Hell. *Ergo* (Do you like the Latin? Twelve years of Catholic school was not in vain!), I must be headed for Heaven! I was and am stupid. I didn't realize that each person is judged on his or her own merits.

Homeroom was a crazy carnival. I had nuns after the first year. On the last day of school in my sophomore year, my homeroom teacher draped her body over the doorway.

"You will stay for detention!" she screamed at the class.

Understand that my family couldn't afford for me to take the school bus home. I hitchhiked after class in my sophomore year. It was an art. As soon as the bell rang, there were hordes of hitchhikers in front of the school. You had to know every trick to survive and didn't want to get stuck for hours with the others.

Mrs. Napravnik was waiting in the parking lot outside for her son, Mark, (my age, but in a different homeroom). Every afternoon, she took me about one mile away from the school, *and* the other hitchhikers. I depended on that ride.

There was Mrs. Napravnik waiting for Mark. If I were late, she would leave with her son, and I would be with my thumb out all day. And, there was the homeroom teacher, filling the doorway. What was I to do?

I can't use the door. I thought for a moment. Then, it was like a light bulb went on in my head. *The window!*

I went out the window (my homeroom was on the ground floor). Mike Pierre followed my example. He became stuck in the window frame because Mike weighed over two hundred pounds. There he was with his feet dangling in the air, upside-down defying gravity, when the "good" sister pulled him back inside. I made it to Mrs. Napranik's car leaving the nun waving her finger at me as if to say, "I'll get you next time, Thek."

I had Father Grauel for Religion class. The priest wore a raincoat everyday that he put in the closet. One day,

Joey Angelides, a classmate, hid in it. When Father Grauel went to put his slicker away, Joey jumped out, surprising the priest with a big, "Aha!"

A week or more went by. Joey was absent, but Father Grauel didn't know it. The door of the closet didn't reach the floor, so, Mike Pierre placed his foot under it. Every time the priest turned his back, Mike rattled the door against his own desk. "What was that?" Father Grauel asked.

"Nothin," Mike replied.

Father Grauel moseyed over, to put his coat away, opened the door and shouted, "Aha!" as he did. There was no one in the closet.

Another time, all of the class (thirty people or so) hid on the down staircase, except for one student, Charlie Westerman. When the priest arrived, he didn't see us.

"Where is everybody?" Father Grauel asked Charlie when he saw the vacant classroom.

"Out sick," Charlie answered.

"All of them?"

"Yup."

"I don't believe you," Father Grauel said. "I'm going to get Sister."

While he went for the principal, we filed into the room and sat. When the priest returned with the head nun, the students acted like they had been there all along.

After that year, Father Grauel never taught again. In fact, he left the priesthood. If we had something to do with it, I will not accept congratulations.

I wonder about the term "Father." I would refer you to Matthew 23:8-10 again.

How can the Catholic Church explain them away without self-condemnation?

The homeroom nun for junior year, Sister Mary Edward, always changed my desk every day. I never knew where to sit. "Thek," (my first name was never used. It was like it had been erased.) "sit up here," the nun would say one day. The next day, she'd say, "Thek, sit back there," and I'd go as far away from her desk as possible. If I didn't know better, I may have gotten a complex.

Sister Mary Edward was also my French teacher. I couldn't understand *The Little Prince* so I made a shortcut and copied the English translation under the French in the book. I had the misfortune of getting my picture taken while asleep pretending to be reading the French book. The picture wound up in the yearbook and received an award. I didn't know anything about it.

The next day in homeroom, Sister Mary Edward, went on a tear.

"I've never been so humiliated in my life! Thek get up here!"

Uh-oh, what did I do now? I exited my desk in the back of the room and approached her in the front.

"I'm so angry with you!" she shrilled. "It's not bad enough that you were asleep but you wrote in the book too! A week's detention!"

I was just happy the sister didn't hit me. Some others had red imprints on their faces for days.

I tried to avoid homeroom by going to Mass every day. Monsignor McHale, the spiritual head of the school, (whom we called "Spud" because he was bald and Irish) started with the serenity prayer over the intercom. "Lord, lend me the serenity to accept the things I cannot change; the courage to change the things I can; and the wisdom to know the difference."

Mass is a curious institution. In 1 Corinthians 11:24-26, Paul very clearly states that The Last Supper is a "remembrance" or a "commemoration." Luke says the same thing in Luke 22:19-20.

The fact that those words are left out in the accounts of Matthew and Mark does not provide any proof of transubstantiation. It only means they didn't use them. Please don't add to Scripture.

Notice the memorial is both body and blood. Yet, we only receive Communion in the wafer form—no blood. (Please read Hebrews 9:22.)

Is man creating practices that go against the will of God? If so, they are doomed to fail.

God told us through David in Psalm 16:10 that the Holy One's body would not decay. Why then does the wafer get moldy or maggots if left for a couple days? I would think that would be enough evidence that there is no transubstantiation.

And by attending Mass we are saying that Christ's

sacrifice wasn't quite enough, we have to help Him along. Nobody knows how many Masses are needed to get a soul out of the supposed Purgatory. Yet, we take the same Christ's sacrifice, which wasn't enough to get a soul to Heaven to begin with, multiply it a gizzillion times, and presto, we have enough indulgences to release a soul from Purgatory. If you believe that, I have a bridge in Brooklyn I would like to sell you.

(Please read Hebrews 10:10.)

No wonder we were not allowed to read the Bible. If I had, I would have discovered the deception.

In my senior year, the World Series was the St. Louis Cardinals against the Boston Red Sox. I rigged up a transistor radio to the inside left pocket of my suit. Simultaneous to the opening ceremonies of the Fall Classic was our class trip to Stratford, Connecticut to see a Shakespearean performance.

I wasn't going to let some verse interrupt baseball. This was the World Series! I ran an earplug from the transistor inside my jacket. The wire appeared at my collar and I plugged it in my left ear, listened, and hid the wire with my hand. Somebody else must have brought a radio to Stratford because when the Star Spangled Banner was over, the whole row whispered, "Play ball!"

The nun, sitting to my right poked me. "Tell them all to be quiet!"

There I was with my left hand always by my ear and she tells ME to keep the others quiet! That's rich!

I communicated with elaborate hand signals after the noisy beginning because I was the only one who knew the score.

"What ARE you doing?" the 'good' sister asked in a low voice. "You look like you have St. Vitas' dance."

"An itch." Any qualms I might have had about lying to a nun were overshadowed by the perceived importance of the ballgame.

I managed to report every half inning without getting caught, a minor miracle.

We had retreat that last year. It was supposed to be spiritual. Each student was assigned a room and we weren't allowed to bring books or games. In other words, the retreat was boring. So, I made a deck of cards out of paper with Ian O'Grady.

"And what, may I ask, are you two doing?" asked the priest who caught us. "Get rid of those cards," he ordered then left because someone else was playing with a fire extinguisher.

Then, there was what was termed a 'riot.' Monsignor McHale made an intercom announcement the day before.

"I want you all on your best behavior because the bishop is coming tomorrow."

That was like waving red flags before us.

"Can I have some of your Twinkies?" I asked of Vinnie Oliveci in the cafeteria the next day and I put out my hand.

The request seemed innocuous. There should be a warning label on Twinkies saying they could be addictive.

"No! They're mine."

With that a food fight started.

The nuns panicked.

"The penguins locked the doors!" Tom McCall, another student who became the ringleader of the rebellion, shouted. "Outside!"

We followed him amid flying food. The bishop's car was parked in front of the school.

"What are you gonna do?" I asked.

"Let's show him!" Tom McCall shouted as he let the air out of his tires. Big deal! They called it a riot! Monsignor McHale didn't forgive us, and the bishop never visited again. Blame it on the Twinkies.

"Bobby Kennedy was shot and killed after winning the California primary," blared over my clock radio one morning awakening me. I didn't believe my ears. *There has to be a some kind of mistake,* I thought groggily. *They must mean his brother.* A couple of weeks before, I pretended to be Bobby Kennedy and gave a speech in history class. I am a liberal in some things, like he was.

When I went downstairs, I saw Dad hunched over the radio. It was one of two times I saw him cry.

Bobby Kennedy was the last hope for the peace movement in America. When he died, the movement took to the streets. What a bitter struggle. All the good men were dying. In Vietnam, in America—everywhere! Then, I graduated.

Chapter Three
Camping and the First Trip Out West

I wasn't born into money and worked. I caddied all the way through high school and college, sometimes being the greens keeper. I mowed the greens in the morning and carried bags in the afternoon.

The summer of '68, being a presidential election year, there was a convention in Chicago. Martin Luther King and Bobby Kennedy were dead. LBJ was not running again. Eugene McCarthy (he had won in New Hampshire) carried the torch.

Mayor Daley had other ideas. When the hippies camped out in Lincoln Park across from the hotel where the delegates were, he let in the goon squad. The longhairs had their heads beat in and McCarthy lost. Hubert Humphrey, the vice president, won.

Nixon ran against him in November, but his campaign was really directed at the policies of LBJ.

Is it important? Not really. God has a plan for us regardless of what happens in the political arena.

At the end of the summer, we decided to climb Mt. Marcy again. There were seven campers, necessitating two cars with the camping gear in ours. I drove to the Adirondacks with Mike Ventra and Dennis Dirk, who was a center on our high school basketball team and a year behind us.

They were both big. Michael had been a tackle on the football team and Dennis was over six feet, five inches.

On the way up the Northway to the Adirondacks, three girls in a Volkswagen bus passed us. They slowed down, went behind us, and then whizzed by again. This time, the girls posted a sign in the window.

"Want to go to Lake George?" it asked.

The girls pulled off the road and stopped.

"Stop!" Dennis shouted.

"But we have the camping gear," Michael said.

"And I'm going steady," I added.

"It's just for a talk."

So we stopped.

"Want to go with us to Lake George?" a gangly girl said.

"Some other time," I insisted. "Can't we just swap phone numbers?"

I don't know who was more disappointed, the girls or Dennis. I had to be faithful, didn't I? We kept going and I didn't look at Dennis.

Once there, I was the first in the group. Along with my backpack, I carried a crate of oranges from the produce department where Johnny worked. Not a bag, but a crate!

Other campers coming down the trail laughed when they saw me. I replied, "You think this is funny, wait till you see what's next."

Dennis toted a quarter keg of beer on his shoulders!

When we arrived at the campsite no lean-tos were available.

"We can camp under the stars for now," Johnny said.

Dennis set the quarter keg down and inserted the nozzle. Trying to remove some beer, he exclaimed, "Hey, it's all foam! There's not a single drink in it!"

"Don't worry," Michael said. "I carried along bottles of hard liquor too, just in case. I have sherry, brandy, and Southern Comfort."

Really roughing it!

In the morning, despite hangovers, the ascent of the mountain began. About two thirds of the way up, Michael remembered he left his camera somewhere along the trail.

"I borrowed it from Pete, my brother-in-law," Michael whined.

Somebody had to get the camera. He was too big and heavy to go down the mountain, get it, and return all the way back.

"You're a caddy, why don't you go?" Michael said.

"But it will take a miracle to find it in these woods!" I countered.

"Look especially where we stopped."

"And where is that? It's like looking for a needle in a haystack."

"Pretty please," he begged using those big eyes of his. It was strange to see this football player pleading.

What are friends for? So, I went. I couldn't find the camera anywhere.

Have to admit he lost it, I figured turning around to quit the search. As I did, I spied the camera sitting on a rock. Coincidence again? Now, I think not.

The arduous hike to the top of Mt. Marcy was resumed, but we made it harder than it had to be. Life is that way too.

That night, there was a lean-to available. I don't know why, but the ranger dressed up as a bear. He tried to scare us by rustling some branches.

"I'll get him with this." Dennis pointed to an axe.

"Wait a minute!" I screamed. "That's a bear out there! You could get hurt!"

"I'll get him!"

Before I could say another word he was gone into the woods.

A few minutes later the ranger emerged minus the bear outfit.

"He's gonna kill me!" he shouted. "I was only joking!"

We sat in a circle and played "Old Maid". Richie Drink, one of the produce boys from where Johnny worked, claimed, "I don't know which card to choose because I can't see the other side."

That was all Johnny needed to hear.

"Put your cards down, face up, so everybody can see them."

Richie did. We laughed. That was the end of the Old Maid game.

During the night, a chipmunk entered his sleeping bag. Richie panicked. Being a city boy, he mistook the stripe. Jumping out of his sleeping bag, Richie screamed, "It's a skunk! There's a skunk in my sleeping bag!"

We laughed again, but couldn't fall back asleep.

In the morning, Michael, using his big, bellowing voice, yelled at people in another lean-to across a pond from us. "Stop the noise! Or else I'll have to come over there!"

What noise? I haven't heard a peep. This trip better end. Maybe we should've gone to Lake George and sinned.

Sinning is a good topic. The Catholic Church teaches that there is a difference between sins. Some are venial and others are mortal. But are they to God? (Please read James 2:10.)

To Him, sin is sin and I find the Catholic interpretation to be very unbiblical. How was the doctrine of mortal and venial sins begun?

Dennis and I became good friends. One time, when he was at my house with Danny and Jimmy Hokey, I distracted him while my dad placed a car bomb in his engine. It was supposed to screech and smoke, but not hurt the car. The car bomb would go off when Dennis started the engine.

Dad, Jimmy, Danny and I, waited a long time for him to go home. The Hokey boys crouched behind a bush on the left side of the house, while Dad and I hid behind one on the right. Dad was as excited as we were to hear the loud noise and see the smoke rise from the engine.

Dennis must have seen us. I can hear him wondering, *Why are they in the bushes?*

He put the keys in and turned over the engine. We expected the car bomb to explode and plugged our ears with our fingers. It must have been dependent on the heat of the engine. Anyway, it didn't go off. Dennis pulled away.

When he approached downtown, near his house, the car bomb erupted. Smoke billowed out from the engine amid a loud screech. It's a wonder no one was hurt.

An amazed Dennis pulled over and hurriedly exited. The car was towed.

The next night we received a phone call from his irate dad, state-trooper Mr. Emil Dirk, with his bull neck and crew cut. I heard him yelling at Dad but couldn't understand what was said. Dad just said, "Yes, Emil," and hung up.

"What did he say?" I asked.

"The car was his, Dennis just borrowed it. He was mad at me for allowing this to happen. The car has to be tuned up and he's gonna give me the bill. No more car bombs."

That summer, I became enamored with Dad's book about the national parks. It was published by *National Geographic* and had pictures of mountains, waterfalls, geysers, deserts, caves, cliffs, canyons—everything. I wanted to see them. There had to be a way.

Life is too confusing here. Out West, all my dreams will come true. I can see Haight-Ashbury.

It was the Greenwich Village of the West Coast—the pinnacle of the counter-culture. Although Greenwich Village was nearby, its proximity detracted from its allure. Haight-Ashbury was far away—exotic. *San Francisco here I come. Everything will make sense then.* I made the decision to go.

But there is no greater fool than one who believes his own lies.

First, we (Johnny, Tommy Thek and I) were to climb Mt. Washington in the White Mountains of New Hampshire to prepare for the bigger trip the following summer. We packed the car for a weekend stay. Being late in the year, plus the highest winds on Earth were recorded at Mt. Washington, didn't faze us. We were going.

Johnny was driving in Troy, New York, Tommy and I were grooving to Steppenwolf's *Magic Carpet Ride* on the radio. My brother asked, "Why are all the traffic lights facing the other way?"

We found out when we turned a corner. All the cars were coming right at us! We were traveling down a one-way highway the wrong way! Calling us stupid is an insult to stupidity.

Johnny quickly pulled into a side street to save our lives.

We continued driving and after a couple hours the White Mountains finally loomed on the horizon like specters. Their summits were obscured by clouds, as if God had erased them. There was no one, not a soul, there.

It started to snow, and the car became our sleeping quarters. We couldn't go into town if we wanted to. There wasn't any town! Conway was on the other side of the mountain. To get there we probably would wind up in a ditch or down the side of the mountain in a frozen stream. Most people would be frightened and act accordingly. Not us. This was an adventure and we couldn't turn around.

"Let's park on the hill," Johnny said. "We may not be able to get here in the morning."

"Turn the heater on," I said. "It's cold in here."

We had nearly a full tank of gas so Johnny acquiesced. When the car warmed up, he shut off the engine. The expedition wasn't canceled.

In the morning, we began the ascent. Initially, everything was easy. At timberline, there was a sign reading that above that point was the worst weather in America. At the first indication of inclement weather, you were supposed to turn around. I guess a smart ranger put it up.

"Can you imagine that?" I said. "These are the White Mountains we're talking about."

We pressed on.

Tommy twisted his ankle. The flakes flew again. The black, rubber boots we wore merely had buckles. No expedition boots, no mouse boots. We never thought about death. Wasn't that meant for others?

It had been a long trip, but one of the rules of climbing is that you never split up.

"What should we do?" I asked.

"The top can't be too far off," Johnny answered.

"Go on. I can't go up," Tommy said. "Leave me on the trail and pick me up when you come down."

To our shame, Johnny and I decided to hike on and leave Tommy momentarily on the path. In reality, the top was nowhere nearby.

The snowing increased, flying into and biting our faces. We couldn't see. It covered the rock cairns that marked the trail. Johnny and I were lost in the middle of a white out. Everything was cold—our hands, feet, ears, noses. We became walking blocks of ice. Johnny and I finally quit and turned around. We thought the mountain had won.

"Where are you?" I shouted down the mountain to Tommy.

"Over here," came the reply out of the mist, his voice quivering through chattering teeth.

Johnny and I retraced the trail by calling to Tommy. Without him there, we would have died. It was lucky that we had left him on the trail. Actually, luck had nothing to do with it.

We followed his voice through swirling snow and wind battering our faces. God was taking care of us even if we didn't know it. The flakes stopped once the trees were gained and we warmed up on the hike down.

On the way home, there were signs directing us to The Flume. None of us knew what it was so we stopped and walked. I asked the first person I saw, "What is The Flume?"

"It's a big," the hiker answered.

"A big what?"

"Just a big." Followed by the dreaded words, "You can't miss it."

Well, we missed it. I never heard "big" used as a noun before. Tommy, Johnny and I hiked and hiked and never saw "the big". Maybe it was the wrong trail. I don't know. I really wanted to get home. I never discovered what The Flume was.

At Christmas time, Ian O'Grady returned from Marquette University, where he was matriculating. We went down to the Jersey shore in his sister Anne's brand new Volkswagen bug the day after Christmas to visit his grandmother and drink some brandy there.

On the way home, we were in the fast lane going down a big hill when the driver two cars ahead stopped. The next one hit the brakes too. So did Ian. He turned to me and remarked, "That was close, ain't I a good driver?"

The car behind didn't stop, though. He was trying to get

into the middle lane and didn't see the brake lights. The wheels shrieked as the driver rammed us at full speed. The sound of crashing metal still haunts me. We plowed into the car in front and the windshield popped out when I hit it.

I was thrown forward against the dashboard. Then when we hit the stopped vehicle in front of us, I was propelled backward. I broke the front seat and wound up in the rear.

When it was all over, I picked up the smashed Volkswagen windshield and started walking down the road.

A cop stopped. "Are you okay?" he asked.

I was in the middle of the highway with a windshield under my arm and he's asking me if I'm okay!

"Yes," I answered.

He believed me and left. It's a good thing God was there. I would not have survived if it were left to that policeman.

Our car, Annie's brand new Volkswagen, looked like an accordion. It was totaled in the four-car collision.

When I finally made it home, I tried to take a bath. I couldn't raise my head. My parents took me to the ER in town. Ian O'Grady was there with his dad.

"You wrecked Annie's brand new car!" J.A. shouted.

The insurance man gave me three hundred dollars as a settlement. That was my money for the trip out West. I wouldn't recommend it, but I had the three hundred and was alive.

That November, Nixon beat Humphrey in the presidential election. 1968 was an unusual year, a bookmark year. Vietnam would become Nixon's war.

Nixon was on the right and Humphrey was on the left. Both supported the war. It didn't make any sense especially if you had any Christian values. I don't see how a Christian can ever shoot another. The Ten Commandments says, "Thou shall not murder." According to the American Heritage Dictionary "murder" is "The unlawful killing of one human being by another, especially with malice aforethought." In other words, it's a planned or plotted killing. That's very important. In practical terms, if someone is raping your daughter, it's okay to kill him because it was not planned. But to bomb somebody is out because it is. "Collateral damage" is unacceptable. "Pray all you want, but keep your powder dry," is an affront to God's power. The story of Gideon corroborates this as well as that of King Hezekiah and the Assyrians. I don't see any asterisk or amendment. Yet, war goes on with people who call themselves "Christians."

(Please read the standard Matthew 5:39 and Matthew 5:44.)

Seems pretty clear to me.

I don't like the term "pacifist." "Non-violent activist" is more appropriate. It implies that something is being done about violence, and people are not sitting on their hands while others walk all over them. Why does fighting back or organizing have to be violent? Shouldn't it be nonviolent?

I admit that I was angry with the Muslims for blowing up the WTC (zooming ahead for a moment). I was raised in NYC and wanted revenge. (Please read Romans 12:19.)

We should lay all our burdens at Jesus' feet, including revenge.

The reason why David replaced Saul was because Saul trusted himself and not God (1 Samuel 15:12).

Aren't we doing the same thing when we send our airplanes to bomb?

In Acts 5:1-10, both Ananias and his wife, Sapphira, are struck down and die not by the hand of Peter, who cut off the ear of the servant in the Garden of Gethsemane, but by God. In sharp contrast to the Old Testament where Samuel is used as God's instrument to kill Agag king of the Amalekites.

The message is to put your trust in the Lord and not in guns or anything else.

I do not understand why we insist on being the most powerful nation on Earth. If we believe in God, we don't need firepower. That can get us in trouble as Saul and David exemplify. To believe in God while carrying guns around is an affront to Him.

I think Christ died for our salvation and freedom. No, freedom isn't free; it comes with a price—Jesus' blood.

With all that said, maybe God is using the soldier as His instrument. There are verses that seem to support the other side. (Please read Ecc. 3:8 and Nehemiah 4:7-9, especially verse 9.)

According to me, you would not post a guard because God protects you. Obviously, I'd be wrong (wouldn't be the first time). Maybe He uses us to protect ourselves or simply to scare others away. That's puzzling and I have yet to answer it. I have to be careful. My own ego could be involved. We have to do what God wants, not necessarily what we want.

You might say, "Those examples are Old Testament. We are not under law now." In the New Testament in Acts 23:20-21, Paul's nephew informs Paul's jailer of a plot to kill him. Why did Paul use his nephew? I don't know. It remains a mystery to be solved when we see Jesus.

My conclusion is this: for me, personally, to condone violence is wrong. For someone else, I'm not sure but I lean away from advocating violence. "Let God's will be done on Earth as it is in Heaven." We all have to listen to that Inner Voice and follow Him.

I thought 1969 would be a quiet year. It wasn't.

It started by the Jets upsetting the Colts in the Super Bowl. You have to be from New York to really appreciate that. It was like Notre Dame beating the Dallas Cowboys.

Then, came the Mets. More on them later.

During all that time, I dated Val. I stayed at home to attend school at Newark College of Engineering (NCE) because I couldn't afford Villanova and Lehigh, even though I was accepted. Sticking around meant I would be close to her, which was what I wanted anyway.

In early 1969, Valerie was going to school, when a car struck her. Her leg didn't heal right, so, it was going to be operated on in the near future. She would be on crutches for a couple weeks. *Gives me a chance to go out West. Plus, I'll see Haight-Ashbury.*

At the time, I expected Haight-Ashbury would provide the answers to life. Jefferson Airplane was from there. It had to be cool.

We used the Yellowjacket for our trip, a Dodge Dart that looked like a bumblebee. I don't know how the car made it. Getting to the corner with it was a trick.

I departed with Dave Triolo, Johnny, and my cousin, Tommy. He and I were nineteen. Dave and Johnny were older, twenty-three. My parents knew better than to argue because we were going in any event.

It was late June. The three traveling companions and I drove through the mountains of Pennsylvania, Maryland and West Virginia, to Skyline Drive in Virginia. Gas was cheap, a little over a quarter a gallon. I was never west of the Delaware Water Gap; everything was new to me.

The mountains I saw gave me food for thought.

Those peaks remind me of Val's breasts. Have to think of something different. I'm off to Haight-Ashbury!

Before Woodstock, Haight-Ashbury was the acme of the counter culture. It was the West Coast's Greenwich Village, reported to be "in."

Once you entered the east end of Skyline Drive (which becomes the Blue Ridge Skyway in North Carolina) there was a problem, once on it you couldn't get off. So, we drove up and down, up and down, up and down. We went slowly on the long ride because it could be steep.

At the west end are the Great Smokies. Mount Mitchell is there and is the highest peak east of the Mississippi. We decided to climb it.

"It's too late to climb now," Johnny said.

"Where will we camp?" Dave asked.

Johnny looked at the map. "Here," he said pointing to a spot on it. "Near the top."

We drove up Mount Mitchell to the campsite.

"How do you cook spaghetti?" Tommy asked.

"I guess you put it in boiling water," I answered.

"All of it?"

"I think so."

He cooked the whole box. It expanded out of the pot. We ate, and ate, and ate spaghetti until we were sick.

In the morning, we drove to the bottom and climbed the mountain by foot. There were no views. The mountain is so far south that it's not above timberline. At the top, there was a little girl in a dress. Dave, who was clad in khaki with a Bowie knife, whispered, "**Don't** get her in any pictures."

I tried; I really did. But, you know how kids get when they see a camera. She was EVERYWHERE. No matter what I did, the little girl entered the picture. We tried to look appropriately fatigued for the photos.

On the way down, there was a big snake on the trail

sunning himself. Dave was scared of the slithery things so he stopped. When Johnny yelled, "Snake!" Dave ran. I think he still is running.

Johnny injured his knee going down. Not enough to stop the expedition though. When all of us were at the bottom, we drove up it again to the campsite.

Nobody told us about the road to the summit or the spaghetti either. We were disasters waiting to happen.

The next day the fellows and I left. We were supposed to visit St. Louis to see the Mets play the Cardinals, Seaver against Gibson; but the best made plans...

It took us most of the day to go through Tennessee and Kentucky. It was getting windy at dusk when we were getting ready to cross the Ohio River from Kentucky to Illinois on a bridge.

"What is it?" I asked the toll collector.

"Just a tornado."

I didn't know what was coming, but knew it was bad! We were on the bridge when we heard a loud crack! The entire bridge became illuminated!

"What was that?" Dave yelled.

"Lightning!" I exclaimed.

The strike was followed by an eerie stillness.

Dave turned to me and asked, "What's happening?"

"The calm before the storm."

If the coffin wasn't nailed shut, it was now. After the bridge, there was a below ground level bar.

"Pull over!" Johnny commanded. "We'll go inside there!"

We stopped to wait the storm out. God was looking out for us because we heard that a person was killed in it.

Alongside of the road was a drainage ditch filled with water from the storm, and trucks.

"What happened to them?" Dave asked.

"Tried to weather the storm, I guess," I answered.

The wind from the semis going in the opposite direction nearly put us in there too.

We arrived in St. Louis at two in the morning. We missed a day game by over twelve hours. I repeat; calling us 'stupid' is an insult to stupidity.

From there, our path took us through the endless cornfields of Kansas on our way to Colorado Springs and the Garden of the Gods.

"Get a good night's sleep because tomorrow we climb Pike's Peak," my brother commanded.

The four of us rented a motel room.

In the morning, we hiked.

"It says here that there's a tramway to 9500 feet," I said pointing to the map

"That's for sissies," commented Johnny standing up straight and puffing out his chest. "Real men hike all the way."

We hiked up the trail.

"Say, it's thirteen miles to the top," I noted.

"I know," my brother replied. "But some Indian guy goes up and down in a little over two hours every year. If he can do it, so can we. We have all day."

I agreed and followed along; I was wrong.

Above timberline, all of us could barely breathe. Then, we were caught in a hailstorm.

"We have to get out of this!" I shouted after being pelted with quarter-sized hailstones a couple of times.

"Go under that big boulder for shelter," Johnny pointed.

Our stopping threw us off the time schedule. When it was over, Johnny told us, "We'll take the cog railway down another side of the mountain. It leaves at four."

A little while later, Dave pointed and shouted, "The train's coming down! Now how do we get down?"

"There's a road down the other side," my brother said. "We'll hitch on it."

After walking on the trail that crisscrossed the face of the mountain, Johnny directed, "Let's go straight up and save some time."

Sounds good!

Heading directly up for what we thought was the top; we arrived and discovered our error. We had hiked to the Cirque instead, with an impassable cliff on the other side. All of us went down and around it, to get back on the trail.

"I—can't—breathe! My—lungs—filled—up!" I managed to sputter out in halting gasps when we neared the summit.

"Get on my back!" Johnny exclaimed. "I'll carry you!"

He did, bad knee and all! Once I stopped hiking, the mountain sickness left me. We didn't know how close death was.

We reached the top at seven. There was a snack bar with pay toilets.

That's ridiculous! I come all the way from New Jersey to Colorado, and there are pay toilets on Pike's Peak! Now who hikes up here with change in their pockets?

I snuck under the door without giving anything. If you can find the janitor, I will pay now.

It was near closing time. We hitchhiked down a dirt road on the other side. A family from Missouri picked us up.

"Climb in the back," ordered the driver.

"There's a skunk in there!" Dave exclaimed before he got in.

"That's just Sammy. He's our pet," the driver explained. "Get in!"

"How do you know he's a he?" Dave asked.

"No little skunks."

We didn't have another choice, so we got in.

The dirt road was treacherous without a guardrail. I thought we might go over the side and involuntarily scrunched up.

"I don't see how cars can race up this every year," I said.

"We climbed it," Tommy said.

"The drivers must be as crazy as we are," Dave observed.

They drove around the mountain to our car where we parted.

My thoughts were of home and Valerie. They were like magnets drawing me back. I phoned her.

"It's me," I explained.

After a moment, Val asked, "Where are you?"

"In Colorado."

"Oh."

"It'll only be five more weeks."

"It's only been one week! Seems longer."

"I'll make it up to you."

"How?"

"You'll see."

With that I hung up and bought her some souvenirs.

The next morning, our group was off to Rocky Mountain National Park, north of Boulder. The roadway was steep and zigzagged back and forth across. I couldn't drive. I sat with closed eyes while the others did.

"Tell me when it's over," I moaned through clenched teeth.

"As a mountain climber, that's pretty bad," Johnny taunted.

"Oh, yeah!" I answered. "When I hike, at least my feet are on the ground!"

On the other side, we passed the Continental Divide and decided to go riding. I figured the first time horseback riding was a fluke. Why not try again?

I rode out of the barn and my feet fell out of the stirrups.

Maybe if I kick the horse, he'll know who's in charge. Who am I kidding? I can't do it.

The horse knew who was in control and broke into a gallop back toward the barn. I held on to the horn of the saddle for my life, which may not be worth much, but to me it is.

He went under trees I couldn't possibly make sitting erect, so, I ducked. When the horse came up, I went down, and he nearly killed me. I didn't go riding again and never will. Talk about getting back on the horse that threw you is crap. Are people crazy? They must have a death wish.

The next day, we tackled the Rockies. There was a traffic jam and I watched as a tow truck lifted a car out of the valley below. Seeing it didn't help my fear of the big mountains.

"What are they doing?" Dave asked.

"I guess that driver was looking for a shortcut," Johnny answered.

"He found one!" I shuddered.

Maybe going to Haight-Ashbury wasn't a good idea. I should've looked at the map!

All our gear wouldn't fit in the trunk; so, some things went on the roof, covered with a plastic tarp. Tommy was good at packing. He knew all the knots.

Somewhere in Utah, it ripped; the tarp flapped in the breeze. A herd of cattle started to run.

"What are they doing?" Dave asked.

"Stampeding," I answered.

"Why?"

I shrugged my shoulders while Tommy pointed to the flapping tarp. "Must be spooked by the noise."

Everywhere there were disasters, some of which we caused. The tarp came off. God didn't let it rain on us.

We were dirty and grimy.

You never see sweat in commercials.

We booked a motel room in Utah.

"What's that?" asked Dave pointing to a hanging object outside the room.

"A bat," Tommy answered.

Dave ran into the room. Upon entering, he noticed something crawling. "What's that?" he pointed again.

"A scorpion," Tommy replied.

That was it! He and I played chess on a magnetic board at two-thirty in the morning in the bathroom, so Johnny and Tommy could sleep. At least the light worked.

We continued on to the Grand Canyon.

"Let's hike to the bottom," I suggested.

"No time," Johnny answered as he shook his head.

Instead we watched a movie that the ranger showed about the Havisupi tribe who live on the canyon floor.

"Brand new houses were flown in for the Havisupis a couple of years ago," he informed the audience. "They used them for their cows."

We washed our clothes at a Laundromat and even took a shower at the room we rented but water was at a premium. Our trail led us back to Utah where we camped at Lake Powell. The desert was hot.

The desert has spawned many different beliefs. When fatwas are issued by imams, they have gone too far. Can you imagine a Baptist leader telling any followers to kill someone if they don't agree with you? I can't. It's a question that needs to be raised. Why isn't it? I don't believe God wants us to kill our enemies, but pray for them. Can He be any clearer?

On to Bryce Canyon.

"What are those signs? Dave asked.

"Flash flood warnings," Tommy replied.

Dave looked up at the overcast sky.

"You worry too much, you know that," and Tommy was off down the canyon. We followed. The rain never came or we would have experienced them firsthand.

We saw The Minarets and Queen Victoria, figures made of orange rock. A tree grew out of the side of the canyon. It held on tentatively to its position. I guess all of us do.

Afterwards, we went to Zion. The roadway tunneled through the crags. There were occasional outlooks.

"Where are we?" Dave asked.

"On the side of a cliff," Tommy answered. "Aren't you ever quiet?"

I couldn't look the whole way.

"Isn't it spectacular?" Johnny egged me on.

"Take good pictures," I said. "It's the only way I'm gonna see this place."

After setting up camp, a trip to town followed. Tommy and I met two blonde girls who asked, "Want to see a movie?"

"Sure," I answered. "When?"

"Tonight around 7."

Tommy and I went back to the camp.

"Why us?" I asked.

"Isn't it obvious?" was his reply.

"No."

"They're hot to trot."

"But I'm going steady."

"We're on the other side of the country," Tommy rationalized. "She'll never find out."

"But I'll know."

"Oh brother."

Tommy duded up in the tent and I followed suit to my shame. We returned for the girls in the evening.

Does morality have anything to do with getting caught? Not really, but I went anyway. We are all sinners saved by grace. I'm not trying to excuse my action. Even after all these years I still feel guilty and asked His forgiveness many times.

"What the movie about?" Tommy asked.

"Joseph Smith."

"Are you Mormons?" I asked.

"Yes."

"We're not," I answered beginning to become upset.

"What did you expect?" one of the girls asked.

"Well, er..." I stammered.

"Well er, nothin! Goodbye!"

I wasn't crazy about seeing the girls in the first place. It took only a little nudge to get me out of there.

That's it! A stupid religious movie! They were trying to convert us!

We and they left.

The tent was next to the Virgin River. That night, it rained, and the river swelled. In the morning, our air mattresses served us as rafts.

"Why did you bring a bow and arrow?" I asked Dave.

"Just in case," he answered.

"In case of what?"

"Just take it along so I can get a picture," Johnny said.

That night, we visited Lost Wages, excuse me, Las Vegas. "You're too young to come to the casinos with us," Johnny said to Tommy and me. "Why don't you walk around a bit? We'll meet you back here around 1:30."

There we were in our bell-bottom pants in the nearly one hundred-degree heat at midnight.

The city is unlike other cities. It's mostly one strip. When you've seen that, there is nothing more. I got the distinct impression we became the grand attraction as people stared at us.

Numbers, ninety-five % of the people believe in God. Five % don't. But the existence of God is not a numbers game. We can't vote on it. Even if it were a billion to one and the one is God, He will rule. Just ask Elijah.

Where did we come from if there isn't a Creator? Even if the Big Bang Theory were correct, scientists don't have an answer of what came before the Big Bang. What made matter itself? Scientists, and I counted myself one, can rant about not taking "a leap of faith." I ask you, isn't that what they are asking us to do with regard to the Big Bang theory? I'll take my "leap of faith" elsewhere, thank you. Can the clay ask the potter about existence? (Please read Isaiah 45:9)

The teaching of religion can be just as bad. Everybody once believed that the Earth was flat. Now, everybody is aware it's round. (Somebody wasn't reading his Bible. Please read Isaiah 40:22. Lest you think that a circle can be flat too, but a sphere, or globe, would look like a circle if viewed from Heaven.) All the evidence is not in and it never will be. We are taught that to come to any conclusion is premature. The logical end is to lift our hands to God and admit we humbly don't know. You may try to take shortcuts, but I don't know if we will get any closer to God. We are too prone to errors.

That's why people rely so much on direct experience. There isn't enough time to know God in any other way. What I am saying is that I think God wants it that way so we come to Him by faith.

Dave drove through Death Valley. Johnny, Tommy and I were asleep. He opened the window to try to stay awake. The wind blowing through my hair wakened me.

"Say what's..."

CHPLUNK!

Off the road we went! Dave had nodded his head and drove into the sand on the shoulder! Dirt spewed forth everywhere. Suddenly, he became alert and stopped. Nobody was hurt.

"Let me drive!" Tommy said, now awake.

"No! I'm okay now!" Dave insisted. "I can drive." Despite our protests, he did. God protected us again.

In the morning, the route took us near Bakersfield.

Finally California. I'll be in Haight-Ashbury soon.

We drove up to see Sequoia National Park, and then camped near a raging waterfall. The trees were big enough to drive a car through.

"What are you doing?" Tommy asked Dave.

"I'm writing a letter to Kathy."

"On scented letter paper?" Tommy asked angrily. "Don't you think you could spend that money better on the trip?"

Dave shrugged his shoulders and continued to write.

After Sequoia, there was Yosemite. At one end, stood El Capitan and at the other was Half Dome, big rocks with huge cliffs.

Down in the valley ran the Merced River, its water, sparkling clear. At the bottom of Half Dome, the Merced formed a little lake with a big rock in the middle. We went swimming in the shadow of the cliff. The water was cold, but who cared? All of us were young and stupid, two almost synonymous terms.

We **had** to go up Half Dome. One doesn't come to California and not climb it, does he?

"I can't go," Johnny said. "My knee's too bad. But there's no reason you can't go."

I suspect that he didn't want to go, pretty smart if you ask me.

Dave, with Tommy and me, trekked along the nine and a half mile trail. The path took us past Vernal and Nevada Falls. Both are big. Vernal forms a perfect curtain of water, while Nevada thunders over the rock and cascades several hundred feet. It's like a huge faucet.

Before long, Half Dome approached. We had to climb up Jacob's Ladder to get to the summit. There were two steel parallel wires imbedded in the cliff, held above the rock by iron supports about four feet long. At the base were wooden planks nailed to the rock, perpendicular to the wires at about every twenty feet. Jacob's Ladder was about a quarter mile long and nearly straight up.

At the time, I thought it was named after the builder and not a biblical name.

"We have to go up that?" asked a frightened Dave.

"If you want to get to the top, you do," Tommy answered.

"How do we get down?"

Tommy started to climb and I followed.

"Hey, don't leave me alone!" Dave shouted.

Tommy and I kept on climbing. Finally, Dave joined us.

We reached the top but had to go down eventually. If one went face forward, the advantage was seeing where you were falling. Tommy faced the rock as he went down, resting on the planks. I went down next. I chose the less dignified, but surer way, of going down on the seat of my pants. I grabbed the steel wires and hoped they held. I still remove splinters from my rear end.

It became Dave's turn; he chose my method. Tommy and I laughed safely at the bottom.

"What's so funny?" Dave asked.

Looking at him coming down, we laughed harder.

Not satisfied with the nine and a half miles back to camp, I insisted, "There has to be a shortcut. Let me see the map."

A map? What's that? Only softies carry one. **Real** men blaze their own trail.

From Nevada to Vernal Falls, there was a 'trail' on the other side. We should have had our heads examined instead of the map. The 'trail' went vertically down over rocks and other debris from Nevada Falls. It felt like going down monster stairs.

"These rocks are huge! Who's idea was it to come this way?" Dave asked.

"Oh, shut up!" Tommy snapped. "Quit complaining and just climb down."

And that we did. We **couldn't** talk and climb simultaneously if we'd wanted to because we were always out of breath. I think Tommy was thankful for that. The three of us descended all afternoon. Down, down, down—reaching camp just before dark.

That night, I was sick of the tent, so I said, "I'll just take my sleeping bag out under the stars."

After awhile, the camper next to us shouted, "There's a bear!" I didn't hear him, but Johnny did. He shone a flashlight at me. There was the animal close-by. God was watching out for me because the bear ran away. Mom must pray a million times for us. I jumped out of my sleeping bag and tried to go back to the tent.

Before I could the bear returned on the other side for the garbage.

"He's over there!" Johnny yelled.

Johnny, Tommy and I, hurried to the car and, for some reason, locked the doors. Why were they locked? It's not like the bear could open them. We weren't thinking straight.

The three of us looked around. No Dave! He was stuck outside with the bear!

Dave banged on the door.

"We can't open it now, or else we'll all get mauled!" Johnny shouted.

"WHAT ABOUT ME?" Dave screamed.

"Look, he's going away!" I exclaimed. "Now we can unlock the doors."

As we did, Dave scrambled inside.

"That was close," he said. "What would you have done if he hadn't gone away?"

"Wished you good luck," I laughed.

Dave was crestfallen.

"But he did go away," I added.

Jesus gave His life for us. Voluntarily! (Please read Romans 5:8.) Truly amazing!

We don't need priests now. We have Jesus as our intercessor.

(Please read Hebrews 4:14-15 and then to Hebrews 7:26-28 to 8:1.) And He in the order of Melchisedek, not Levi. (Please read Hebrews 7:11.)

We have a high priest, an ombudsman and his name is Jesus. We don't need a priesthood any more. (Please read John 14:6 again.)

In fact, having a priesthood contradicts that verse. When Jesus was sacrificed on the cross the curtain separating the people from the Holy of Holies was torn in two. God was now approachable. (Please read Luke 23:45.)

This eliminates the need for a priesthood. We have Jesus now. Why do we have one?

We returned to the tent. It never looked so good.

I started reading Gandhi's autobiography and Joan Baez' *Daybreak*. I was looking for an alternative to violence and thought I found it in the ethics of nonviolence. Gandhi proclaimed, "The world is my church." He could go into any house of worship and kneel. I added the footnote, "And my life is my prayer." I have tried to live that way ever since.

Now I look at it and realize Gandhi was expecting his works to pave the way to nirvana. Although his works were good they are still "filthy rags" according to Isaiah 64:6.

The First Principle, upon which everything rests, is God and He wants us to do the correct thing. Humanity is condemned to think. God wouldn't have it any other way. Free will is a burden as well as a gift.

The question becomes "Is killing people ever justified." By us, I don't think so. If we plan to kill, don't we become murderers too? We should avoid and work against circumstances where violence can occur. No easy task. What is someone to do when it seems all attempts for a peaceful solution are exhausted and she/he is surprisingly attacked? Is killing justified? No! God will resolve it. We make a mess of it by doing it ourselves.

On our money, we claim, "In God we trust." I submit that we do not trust Him enough. One can't love his neighbor in one instance and kill him in the next.

In the morning, we were on the way to Monterrey. We stayed in a motel and watched television as Neil Armstrong took one giant leap for mankind. Back on Earth, Teddy Kennedy drove a car into the Chappaquidick.

We saw the Pacific Ocean at Big Sur.

"I'll climb out there and get a picture," Johnny pointed to a rock that jutted out into the Pacific. There was a hole in it that we didn't notice. As he positioned himself a wave came up from behind and knocked the camera from his grasp. It lies corroding somewhere at the bottom of the Pacific. Don't go swimming in the water.

We were halfway done. I expected to find the secrets to life. What I found was that I missed Valerie. I called her.

"It's me," I said.

After a pause, she asked, "Where are you?"

"California."

"I thought you might be in New Jersey."

"Wish I was."

"Me too."

"Don't have much money, have to hang up. Will see you in three weeks. Just wanted to hear your voice."

Here we were going on a trip of a lifetime and I was absorbed with Valerie. I thought the secret to life was between her two legs. What a fool I was. I'm a different kind of fool now.

We went to San Francisco. Needing a place to camp, the four of us traveled across the Golden Gate into the mountains, pitched our tent, and returned to the city.

We visited Haight-Ashbury and Golden Gate Park.

Finally, people like me. I'm home.

I could almost hear the "Establishment" singing *Where Have All the Children Gone?* wondering if all of them ran away to "crash" on filthy, bare mattresses in some tenement and do drugs. The Mommas and Poppas were modern day Pied Pipers with the flute on *California Dreamin'* inviting us to come there. The hippies were iconoclasts, breaking the sacred images of wholesomeness, industriousness, and cleanliness. One generation called the other "freaks," while they in turn were called "pigs," which was a measure of how demented both sides were.

However, reality seldom lives up to expectations. All we saw were a few dopers in doorways otherwise the street was vacant in the afternoon. We wanted no part of them, so we left.

Doesn't the counter culture have something better to offer than this?

After the party is over, there is another side. I was disappointed with the real Haight-Ashbury. One dream became a nightmare. *Surrealistic Pillow* was really surreal. All I wanted to do was go home and see Val.

Dave walked with Johnny, while Tommy and I went on foot to Fisherman's Wharf. The two of us became lost and wound up in the dingy side of town. Par for the course.

After we retraced our steps and located the car, Johnny drove up through the fog to our campsite.

"Now, will you look at this?" Johnny said as the moon occasionally peeped through the clouds.

I nervously tried to avoid looking down on the fog but my eyes behaved differently. I have to admit, it was beautiful.

In the morning, we rode to Sausilito to see the boats.

"Get out of here!" a policeman coming down the road yelled.

"Us?" I asked as I pointed at my chest.

"You're—you're—vagrants!" he claimed and escorted us out of town. Maybe we were, I don't know.

Off to Mt. Shasta. The mountain was shaped like an upside down cone, an extinct volcano.

"Let's buy a camera," Johnny said in the nearby town.

We stopped at a local shop but the sign in the window read, "Hippies not welcome."

"I don't think they want our business," Tommy said. "Let's go someplace else."

The whole town was that way. We left without a camera.

So, on to Oregon and Crater Lake, the runoff from the snow fills the bowl of another extinct volcano. The water is as clear as the sides are steep.

"What's that sound?" Dave asked

"A siren," Tommy answered. "Pull over."

I did and rolled down the window. The statey exited his car and walked to ours.

"Where's the fire?" he asked.

"Was I speeding?" I asked in reply.

"Going 50 in a 25 zone is speeding."

Oh great! Is he going to lock us up?

"I see you're from New Jersey. When you get home, this ticket will be waiting."

No jail!

You can take a boy out of the city but...

We stopped to get something to eat in Washington's Yakima Valley. A man joined us.

"Have any drugs?" he asked Tommy and me.

"What?" I replied.

"LSD or pot."

"Absolutely not!" Tommy said.

The man walked away.

Johnny headed east for the first time.

I'm coming home.

We stopped at Glacier National Park in Montana on our

way to Yellowstone and the Badlands. We traveled The Highway to the Sun on the way into the park. It was above timberline and we saw some rangers chasing an animal.

I closed my eyes. I white-knuckled the whole way.

"Tell me when it's over," I said.

"Say, what's that?" Dave asked pointing to the animal.

"A grizzly bear," Tommy replied. "I read in the paper this morning that he mauled some people."

Dave gulped.

Oh great! Another bear!

While Tommy and I lounged on the air mattresses in the river, Johnny and Dave went for a hike on the glacier. Johnny slid down it in shorts.

On the water, we watched bald eagles nest—about two-dozen of them.

"Will you look at that?" I said while staying at a curve in the river.

"We would have missed it if we went on the glacier," Tommy observed.

He was right. Sometimes you have to slow down or else you'll miss things.

Maybe eagles are endangered now, but they weren't on the river that day.

Glacier is on the border of Canada. When the park, crosses the international line, it becomes Waterton Park. When Tommy and I went there, we met an Indian who asked, "Do you have some whiskey?"

"No," I answered. I looked him over. He was not a proud

Indian on a horse, just a bum asking for alcohol. We were too young to buy him any, so, he left.

On to Yellowstone.

The first night, the campgrounds were full, so, we booked a night in a motel outside the park. While going to it, we saw God's rainbow. A kid flashed us a peace sign through her back seat window. Children sometimes have more sense than their parents.

The second night, the Park was not as congested.

"Want some trout?" a voice came from a nearby campsite.

"Us?" I asked.

"Yup. Have enough for the Russian army."

I went into the woods with Tommy. The voice belonged to a twentish man in bell-bottomed jeans, a corduroy shirt and a bandana on his head.

"I'm Marty," he said, offering his hand. A young woman that could have been his twin sat on a rock.

"I'm Lisa."

We shook hands, introduced ourselves and ate plenty of fish.

"Want some Mary J?" Marty asked.

I thought I heard him wrong because I had no idea who Mary J was.

"Excuse me," I replied.

"Some grass, man," Lisa said.

We can't digest grass.

"Some weed," Marty continued.

Now which is it, grass or weed?

"Some marijuana," Lisa finally said realizing neither of us understood.

"Sure. Why not?" I answered. "There's always a first time." *I'll be just like a real hippie.*

Marty passed me a lit joint. I tried to smoke it but found it very difficult.

"You have to toke it," Marty instructed. "Inhale deeply."

I finally did then held on to the joint.

"Now pass it on," Marty said.

With each go round, smoking became easier until Marty had the roach. With our bellies full and our minds in the clouds we returned to our camp.

But my first experience with marijuana was disappointing. I'd left home weeks before with a sense of guilt from Catholic school. I expected to gain some new spiritual insight into everything. Simultaneously, I wanted to escape. I had been seeing America and some of it was not so pretty, like the downtrodden Indian or Haight-Ashbury. When I woke up, things were just as they'd always been except now I had a craving for more marijuana to eliminate the hangover that the marijuana caused in the first place.

Who's the real dope?

My world was no longer spinning but I was hung over. *I never want to feel this way again. If that's what the counter culture is offering, count me out.*

I was back to normal in a few days.

The next day, we saw Old Faithful, the hot springs, and the two waterfalls on the Yellowstone River. There was a sign saying not to hike beyond a certain point or else you could fall off a cliff.

"Why don't we go?" Johnny said.

"Out there?" Dave was bewildered. "Can't you read the sign?"

"What's the matter? You're not scared, are you?"

"Me? Of course not." He went out on the rocks to prove it and we followed. They might as well have put up a marquee with blinking lights telling us to 'Walk.' We were attracted like magnets to anything that was dangerous.

Then we went to the Grand Tetons where all of us ate at a restaurant in Jackson's Hole. Tommy, Johnny and I, had big, juicy, steaks.

"Give me some money, please," Dave pled.

Only Tommy had some extra. He shook his head.

"Pretty please."

"Remember the scented letter paper? This is why we save our money."

Dave ate a hot dog. Tommy waited all that time to zing him. Personally, I think it affected Tommy more than Dave.

Next were the Badlands and Devil's Tower. We saw the nearly finished Crazy Horse and Mount Rushmore.

"I see five heads up there," Johnny claimed while looking through his binoculars.

"What!"

"The four presidents and Charley Brown."

"Charley Brown? What's he doing up there?"

At that time, Johnny swears a little kid poked him in the side and said, "Say, who's that up there with Charley Brown?"

I was impressed with the debris at the bottom, which they never bothered to cart away. Cameras never focus on the garbage.

After my dreams had evaporated in Haight-Ashbury like Carly Simon's clouds in her coffee, I just wanted to return to New Jersey. I was clawing my way out of the abyss, clutching at a straw and its name was Valerie.

"What's that smell?" Dave asked somewhere in Ohio.

"What smell?" I asked.

"It's like a dead fish."

Dave put his nose in the air and sniffed. Pointing at Tommy, he exclaimed, "It's you!"

Tommy blushed.

"Did you use deodorant today?" Johnny asked.

"Well, no," Tommy confessed.

"Why not?"

"Ran out. Dave's still mad about the hot dog."

"Why you..."

Johnny put up his hands before they came to blows. "Hold it! We're almost home. One more day."

It's good we're going home tomorrow. We're getting on each other's nerves. Now we're fighting about BO.

When things calmed, Johnny said softly to Tommy, "Tomorrow you can borrow my deodorant."

It was time to go home. The four of us had seen what God created—mountains, waterfalls, deserts, wildlife, lakes, oceans, islands, trees, geysers, cliffs, canyons and glaciers. We also saw what humanity had created—Las Vegas, Haight-Ashbury, the whiskey-craved Indian, the seamy side of town and knew loneliness. Is there really any comparison? We've messed it up. Tornadoes might be an example of God's awesome wrath. What is He angry about? Wouldn't you be if you created everything and then someone has the gall to say you don't exist?

At the time, I was just happy to be home. Now I could see Val.

It's a big country. Like Dad said, we stole it fair and square. To all those who had a hand in building her, I give special thanks.

The trip matured us.

Doesn't life do the same thing? Isn't it a journey? Along its path are many peaks and valleys. When I am tired, I know that God will take me home.

I looked at God's creation and wondered if He existed. I was so consumed with Valerie that it tainted my judgment. Looking at this great country and its natural beauty, I should have reached a different conclusion than I did. All the theories of how it all began cannot escape that we have to postulate Someone or Something at the beginning. Only Christianity provides the answers to "Why?" I was oblivious to that.

Everything considered; I had a grand childhood and adolescence. I had good, dependable, parents, and my friends supplied me with a cross-section of America. My brothers, cousins, and sister, provided me with relief from the miseries of life—most of the time.

I was back in New Jersey. I had to call Val.

Chapter Four
AFTERMATH (THE SECOND AND THIRD TRIPS OUT WEST)

I picked up Val. She was off the crutches now.

"Your beard tickles me when we kiss," Val claimed.

I hadn't shaved on the trip and sported six or seven weeks' growth. I grew my hair long before going out West, and now I looked like a real hippie.

But I'm not a hippie! Better get my hair cut.

So, the next day I removed the beard and went to the barber's. He took one look at my long hair and proclaimed, "That'll be extra."

When I went home, Dad was furious. He took me back to the barber's and loudly asked, "Shouldn't my bill be a little less because I'm bald?"

The barber was not impressed, but I was.

Danny Hokey came over.

"Do you want to camp out in Upstate New York at a place called "Woodstock" for a three day concert?"

I've had enough camping out and counter culture. Besides, I'm in a wedding party for Diane (Val's older sister). Danny went without me.

Richard married Regina Ruskin (a shortened form of Rusniaczek.). Mom was upset because Regina is Polish.

Then, Suellen wedded a Protestant named John Edwards of English descent.

"English!" Mom screamed upon learning. "Anything but that!"

"But, I love him," Suellen replied.

My mother fell silent but glared at Sue. In the vernacular of the day, I thought my mother would have a cow when they wedded. At least, Regina was Catholic. But, Mom grew to love John too because he was a good man.

My sister became a nurse. Sue met John when he was hospitalized from an accident where he hit a telephone pole.

They bought an old house around the corner from us. One Christmas Eve, after she was married, Suellen was working at the hospital. While she was out, John figured to improve the kitchen by installing some new linoleum. He couldn't do it alone. "Can you help?"

"Sure," I volunteered.

We couldn't lay all the linoleum before Sue returned from work.

"Now what am I gonna do for tomorrow?" Sue was

furious when she got home. "I can't cook or have people over because the floor is a mess!"

They bought a hutch the next year. The problem was John didn't measure it. It didn't fit in the dining room.

"Can you move a doorway?" John asked me.

"I don't know how but maybe Richard can."

We never discussed purchasing a different hutch.

This is the story I heard. John and Richard moved the doorway between the dining room and kitchen. Sue pulled in the driveway after work on Christmas Eve.

"What did the two of you do?" she screamed. "There's sawdust everywhere!"

"We're not done yet," John said sheepishly.

"Obviously," Sue laughed sarcastically. "I'm never having Christmas dinner here again! There's no tellin' what you will do."

(Please read Ecc. 3:20.)

Even if geological records, archeological digs and carbon dating seem to support Darwin's idea that we evolved, we have to remember that we are mere potsherds. If God says He created us then He created us. On the other hand, He would not lead us astray. It's a mystery to me and one that can only be solved in Heaven.

Are we are being tested? Are we passing or failing the test? All we can do is pray to God for better discernment and study His Word.

On a routine chest x-ray, a radiologist discovered that John's mediastinum (the place in the middle of the chest where the great vessels and root of the lungs are) was wide. He had an aortic aneurysm. The aneurysm formed because of his accident. Now, with marriage, two boys and several years later, John needed a graft.

"John is going in for an operation," Sue told us sadly. "He needs your prayers."

It was a success. John was one of the first to have a plastic aorta. We breathed a huge sigh of relief.

Then, there were the Amazin' Mets! We had followed them throughout our trek out West. Every day my companions and I bought a paper to look at the box scores. They were lousy before, never finishing above seventh place. I would have been happy if the Mets won half their games.

Seaver and Company won the pennant and World Series against the powerful Baltimore Orioles.

I thought the upset of upsets was the Jets against the Colts. I learned a valuable lesson from them. You can never lose, if you don't give up. If the Mets could win, anybody could. I mean anybody! Including me!

I was back in college. On the weekends, I dated Val and took trips to New York City with Danny to see Michael.

I went over the Nolan house (cousins of Danny. Sue Nolan, about our age, had just broken up with Roger, who was in the army stationed in Germany.). They put me under a blanket and pretended I was in the desert. I removed all my clothes under the blanket. The Nolans laughed. After I dressed, Sue giggled, "The first thing in the desert is to get rid of the blanket, not your clothes."

The next day when I related the story to Val, she retorted angrily, "You aren't supposed to take off your clothes for anyone but me!"

On one date, as we made love in the front seat of Dad's car, the moon shone. I saw her smiling like the Mona Lisa. Val was enjoying it! Girls weren't supposed to delight in sex, were they? I thought she was a slut after all. So, we broke up. I don't know if Val understood. I don't know if I did. God was looking out for me again.

After that, I went out with Sue Nolan. "Thinking of Val?" she asked when I didn't hold her hand.

"Yes," I answered honestly, realizing it was a "no-no" on a date to think of someone else.

"Maybe, you should take her out and try to settle matters".

"Thanks."

"It's easy to understand."

Val and I dated again for a while before we broke up a second time.

Around then Jimmy came back from Vietnam. When he asked Val out, what was I to do?

I went out with Jimmy, his brother and another cousin of theirs, Cheryl Coin. She was a singer and loved to perform. The church where Cheryl and the Hokeys were members was putting on *Guys and Dolls*. She and the boys' dad (he was called "The Pope" because of being so Catholic) were to sing. Danny volunteered to help backstage with the props. I did too.

One night, I was alone on props.

"Where's Danny?" I asked Cheryl.

"Not coming. Took off somewhere and won't be back."

Some friend. Gets me involved then leaves.

That was the year the Knicks beat the Lakers for the NBA title. I listened to the radio while setting up. I remember Willis Reed playing with a gimpy leg and Marv Alert yelling, "Yes!" into the microphone.

Danny took me down to the Jersey shore many times. I saw the sunrise over the ocean with him. What a magnificent sight! Most people look at the sunset. But it is usually boring as the sun disappears. However, the sunrise is like an explosion, as if someone detonated the beach and ocean.

Once we went to the shore with three others.

"Where will we change into our suits?" Danny asked, not having enough change for the bathhouse.

I scratched my head for a moment. "I know. We'll make a big hole in the sand on the beach and change in it."

Singly, four of us put on swim trunks in it. Danny followed us, the last one. When he removed his pants, we pushed in the hills of sand around the sides of the hole.

"Not funny! Get me out of here!"

We left him naked in the sand. All that showed were his head and hands.

"What if the tide comes in?" Danny panicked.

We returned and dug him out.

One night, the Hokeys, Cheryl and I, went for a milkshake. Jimmy slipped some LSD or something similar in it because the milkshake started talking to me.

"I thought I was going to write books, now they will be written **about** me, not **by** me," I said trying to be profound.

We sat on someone's lawn, and I heard the trees talk. When I entered home, I called Michael. "I've reached nirvana."

"Huh? What did you take?"

The experience lasted a couple of days. On the way to school, I thought I heard the bricks speaking to one another.

Another night, Cheryl called around eleven P.M.

"Hello?" Mom answered the phone.

"This is Cheryl Coin. Is Joe there?"

"Which one?"

"The younger."

Mom gave me the receiver.

"Hello?"

"My parents left me alone in this big house and I'm scared. Can you come over?"

"I'll be right there."

"Where are you going at this hour?" Mom asked as I prepared to leave with a blanket in tow.

"Over the Coin's. I'll see you in the morning."

Who knows what she thought.

"I'll sleep on the couch," I said as I entered the Coin house.

"Oh," Cheryl replied.

She kissed me on the cheek in the morning. "Thanks for coming over last night," Cheryl said on her way to work.

"Don't mention it."

I went back to sleep. When I awoke, I let myself out carrying the blanket. Who cared about the neighbors?

Not sleeping with her reminds me of abortion. Is it always wrong? Matters of rape and incest are a "sticky wicket". We should pray about it and leave the matter in God's mighty hands no matter how much I am personally against it. Here my emotions and judgment conflict.

One has to take the wide view into consideration. Doesn't the mother have some say? Isn't she a person too? Like I said, it's a "sticky wicket".

There are good people on both sides. We need God's guidance.

Yet, He forms us and cares for us. This country has a lot of lives to account for. Greater than forty million. The number is staggering. Some might be arguable, however, most are just a matter of supposed convenience.

Abortion, alone, will not solve the problem. It should

not be used as a means of birth control. It is killing a person. The unborn have rights too. There are those that argue the fetus is not a human being. What is it then? A pig?

I'm sorry. Anybody who has seen the products of conception in the birth canal could attest, the fetus **is** human.

If past history is an indication, we can expect conditions to worsen. Leaving things up to us is not a good way to solve a problem. We need God and His wisdom. We must remember that this world is only temporary. (Please read 2 Cor. 4:18.)

That Easter, I was supposed to travel to the shore with Michael. On the morning we were to go, something went wrong with the Yellowjacket.

"Don't drive the car down the shore," Dad said.

"But I told Michael I would drive."

"The idiot light keeps going on. It's losing oil."

"But..."

"Under no circumstances."

I picked Michael up ostensibly to tell him we wouldn't be going down the shore. The idiot light blinked on.

"Let's check the oil," he said.

By mistake, I examined the transmission fluid. "The dipstick says we're okay." *What's Dad talking about?*

The two of us took off for the beach.

The idiot light came on again. We pulled off the highway.

"Maybe we should turn around," Michael suggested.

"Ignore it. I've already checked the dipstick. There must be something wrong with the wiring."

We started up again. At first everything ran smoothly and I felt vindicated. Then, there was a loud clunk followed by black, billowing smoke pouring from beneath the hood. The engine froze. We were about seventy miles from home.

"What do we do now?" I asked. "Dad will kill me."

"We hitch back. Next time, pay attention to the idiot light. That's why it's called that."

"How do I explain to Dad being down here?"

"Kidnapped," Michael said sarcastically.

"Kidnapped? Be serious."

He shrugged his shoulders.

We left the car in a gas station to be fixed and hitchhiked to the house. I was in no hurry to get home.

Two girls in a little Volkswagen Beetle with Delaware plates were motoring in the other direction. Seeing us, they turned around abruptly.

"Get in," the driver told us.

They took us to a park where I procrastinated in going home. The girls' company distracted our minds. Finally, Michael said, "I have to be home tonight."

Before we returned to Pompton Plains, I looked at Michael and said, "Maybe he won't get mad if you're there." That's an old ploy. Have your best friend over when you expect punishment and maybe you'll get a lighter sentence.

"And where's the car?" Dad asked angrily when we arrived.

So much for that idea.

"In Eatontown," I replied sheepishly.

"What's it doing there?"

I stood before The Grand Inquisitor not realizing there was One grander than he. I related the story and as I did Dad's face flushed.

"Joey, what am I gonna do with you?" he asked throwing his hands in the air and leaving the room.

No punishment could hurt more than seeing the anguish on his face.

The Yellowjacket was towed back to Pompton Plains.

God must've felt the same way when Adam disobeyed Him. We've been living the consequences ever since. Perhaps you can blame Adam for his disobedience. But would we have done any different? Forgiveness is in order. Thank God there is a second Adam.

The student strike of 1970 affected Rutgers, across the street, first. Eventually, conservative NCE joined. I was one of the ringleaders going back and forth to Rutgers to attend different meetings.

"Of course, we could be arrested," a wide-eyed radical said.

"That's crazy!" I interjected but was shouted down.

There are fanatics in every organization.

The war had come home. It was everywhere.

"We could blow up the Route 46 bridge," Danny suggested one night.

"WHAT?"

"It's only a little bridge."

"Won't that hurt someone?"

"It could."

"Count me out."

"Forget it."

"Forgotten."

I would like to say that was how it happened. It would exonerate me from feeling guilty. Actually, the idea to blow up the bridge was mine. If you can imagine, reverse the roles. Danny was the one giving me second thoughts. Which makes me realize we are all sinners saved by grace. (Please read Romans 5:8.)

We had become fanatics! I went from avoiding being arrested to planting bombs in a couple of weeks. This country was falling apart with butterflies coming out of the cocoon and flying off tangentially in every direction.

We finally discarded the plan. That was a measure of how crazy everybody was. Even in mowing the lawn, a position was taken. You could cut the right side first, or the left, or try to stay safe with the center.

Everybody became a radical. The war polarized the nation. Either you were for or against it. There was no middle ground.

"Billy Hill from down the street got drafted," Dad announced one night at the dinner table while reading the news.

"This war is wrong," I said raising my voice.

Dad put down the paper. "God is on our side."

"I'm sure the Nazis felt the same way."

His clenched fist came down on the table. The china rattled. "Don't you ever compare what we're doing to the Nazis!"

"Why? We're killing people just like they did only now it's napalm instead of gas chambers!"

Dad got up and looked like he was about to throttle me.

Mom got up, her little body quaking. "Aroo! You will be the death of me. Both of you just calm down!"

We were so surprised by her outburst that both of us did.

"I'm sorry, I raised my voice to you," I began. Mom raised her hand telling me to stop.

"He knows," she said. "What we need now is peace and quiet before someone says something they'll regret later."

The referee had spoken. No further words were said.

School, especially NCE, had become irrelevant. Val didn't encumber me, and now, I was arguing with my parents. I decided to leave home. It was time to go.

On my first trip out West, I read Joan Baez' autobiography. I decided to go to Palo Alto, California, and visit her Institute for the Study of Nonviolence. My cousin, Bobby, lived nearby. I boarded a bus and stowed my carry on things including my poetry overhead. My heavy luggage was put in the cargo receptacle down below.

When we were in Utah I asked, "Can I have a sweater in my luggage?"

The driver looked and looked, but couldn't find my heavy luggage.

"That's funny, it's supposed to be here but I can't find it."

"My camping gear and my tent are there! What am I gonna do when we get to San Francisco?"

"They must have been shipped to San Antonio by mistake," he continued nonplussed.

"That's just great!"

"Well, we were close."

"Yeah, they both begin with 'San' and end in 'O'."

"No need to get nasty."

"But they're 1500 miles apart!"

All I owned was on my back and what I carried on. Everything else was on its way to Texas.

I arrived at San Francisco at about six in the morning. I took what I had and hitchhiked to my cousin's house. I knocked on the door before seven. Vera, Bobby's wife, (who was from Berlin and didn't speak any English at the time) answered the door.

"*Yah?*" she asked

I didn't know a lot of German.

"I'm Bobby's cousin," I tried to communicate. *Think. Think. What is the German word for cousin?*

"*Yah?*" she asked a second time.

There I was at 7:00 in the morning standing before the

screen door with Vera barring my entrance. Finally, Bobby arose to let me in.

Bobby tried to locate my luggage. Nothing we did worked.

I stayed there for two weeks baby-sitting for their daughter, one-year old Natasha.

Bobby taught German history at Stanford. He got in trouble and was fired for displaying the flag with a peace sign where the stars usually are. The claim was that Bobby defaced it. Technically, he bought the flag that way. The real reason for the firing was his political stand.

Bobby took me to the Institute for the Study of Nonviolence where I helped to cement the cellar. I learned of a seminar that was scheduled, and I applied. The course cost more money than I had, so, they awarded me a scholarship.

The seminar was led by Joan Baez' guru, Ira Sands. He walked with a limp because, as a child, Ira had polio. He sported a gray goatee and was a Gandhi expert. Ira was like a third father to me.

He lunched with Martin Luther King, Junior, at a restaurant in the Midwest a couple of weeks before King was assassinated. Ira noticed there were reporters at the other tables watching Martin's every move. "What are they doing?"

"Waiting."

"Waiting? For what?"

"For me to die."

He related to me the story of a Freedom March in Mississippi. A policeman took him from the march to his office.

"Sit!" the policeman commanded.

Ira sat on the lone chair in the middle of the room.

Then the cop started to beat him. Left then right. Left then right. Ira turned his head from right to left as if he were being slapped. Taken aback, Ira finally fell out of the chair on to the floor.

"You're not nonviolent are ya'? Are ya'?" The policeman screamed as he kicked him.

Ira tried to form a protective ball.

The policeman kicked again. Ira felt a rib crack. Finally, he stated, "Look, if you keep it up, I'll either die or I'll get so angry that I'll hit back. Can't you see I don't want to do that?"

Ira was amazed when the policeman didn't hit him again.

"I'm sorry," the redneck cop claimed in a lowly tone.

He politely put Ira back on the chair. That town will never be the same. Nonviolence can work.

The seminar was held outside in the mountains for about two weeks. Each session lasted from nine in the morning until around four in the afternoon, and about twenty of us met every day.

We discussed everything in those two weeks, especially the farm workers' boycott that was to become such a big part of my life.

I was estranged from the world. Ira challenged me to rejoin it.

No human has the answers: not musicians, nor actors, nor politicians, nor ministers. Religion tries to deal with why there is suffering. Adults are easy because they deserve it (a simplistic answer). What about the children? I think that's a mystery that only God can answer.

For the seminar, I stayed above in a gazebo on the side of a hill. It was beautiful. One night, a comet came down the valley. I saw a lot of shooting stars that were magnificent.

I still wondered about the first principle. What Aristotle called The First Cause uncaused.

Joan Baez descended from her mountain home one afternoon. With her sparkling eyes and long black hair she could have been a movie star. Her husband, David Harris, resisted the draft and was in jail. The facade of a righteous war was crumbling. Even newscasters doubted. Every night on TV there were the infamous body counts. The U.S. probably killed every Viet Cong twice according to the record. But, they weren't dead. They were just practicing.

"Want to see a movie at my house?" Joan asked.

Of course we said, "Yes." It was an anti-war flick.

Ron, one of the seminar's attendees, had a van. Six of us piled into it and took off one morning. When he turned coming down the mountain, the backdoor flew open and

Anne fell out. She disappeared over the tall grass on the side of the road.

"Stop the van!" I pounded on the wall.

When he did, I jumped out of the back.

Coming up to a confused Anne, I asked, "Are you okay?"

She sat up and felt each joint. "I think so."

The others appeared. I was worried about her. One doesn't fall out of a moving car and not get hurt. Does one? "Better go to the hospital for x-rays."

God was looking out for her because she was all right.

On our way back, a car behind us pulled up at a red light.

"Want to go to a birthday party"?" the driver asked.

"Sure. Far out," came the reply and we were off to play Wiffleball. California can be a friendly place.

On another afternoon, I went to Palo Alto to eat. A sign in the window read, "Don't walk in on bare feet."

I couldn't let the opportunity pass. So, with assistance, I walked in on my hands. I don't know why, but they threw me out!

There were four people from Connecticut: Denise, Kathy, Peter and Howie. Kathy immediately caught my eye. She used to sing and play *The Circle Game* and was like a younger Joan Baez. I couldn't help but fall in love with her.

One night, Ron drove nine of us to San Francisco to see a Hot Tuna concert.

"I'd rather see the city," Kathy said. "There will be plenty of other concerts."

"I'll go with you," I said.

We walked around San Francisco. Love was again in the air. Up and down the hills we went. We saw Alcatraz and the Bay in the distance from the tops.

Have to act like a gentleman, I reminded myself continually.

She was a vegetarian so Kathy and I ate spaghetti at a local restaurant. I was in Heaven, another one of those Top Ten days.

Don't mess it up. You're good at that. Don't talk about love.

"I saw a bumper sticker coming over here that said, 'My country right or wrong'," I said trying to retain my composure.

"I'm sure the Nazis felt the same way."

How can I talk of love? I'm too scared. I wonder what she's thinking.

"Another one said, 'These colors don't run'." I laughed at the memory.

"What are you laughing at?"

I paused and stared at her. *Oh, I love the way you look. The long, black hair. The dungarees.*

"The colors on the bumper sticker," I whispered.

"What about them?"

"They ran because of some rain."

Keep the focus on politics. That's safe.

"I don't know how Joan can be so courageous about her husband," I said. "If it was me, I'd probably be wailing."

"Oh c'mon. You would not. People come from all over the country because the jail-time is shorter in California. You'd be happy if you were sentenced here."

"He could've avoided going to jail altogether by going to Canada."

"He could not!" Kathy retorted. "There's a big difference between running away to be up there with the dodgers and staying here to be a resistor."

"Your life is messed up either way," I said realizing that talking politics was not such a good idea. *But she is beautiful when she's angry.*

"Dodgers are cowards. They don't stop the killing."

"That easy for a woman to say," I snorted before I censored my remarks. I wished I hadn't said it as soon as it was said. James is right; the tongue is like a rudder on a ship and full of deadly poison.

"Oh, it's a man thing? They should have babies. Then they'd have more courage."

This is not the way I wanted it to go. How do I get her to shut up?

Taking advantage of her mouth temporarily stuffed with spaghetti, I said, "It's getting late. Better get back."

"Listen up!" Ron shouted as we climbed into the van after walking back. "I don't have enough room for you to sleep if all of you put your heads against one wall. So, to make more room, you should alternate with every other person putting their heads against the other wall. I think we'll fit. If you look to right or left, you'll see feet beside you and not heads."

We were like college kids who pile into a phone booth. We couldn't move but we did fit.

When we approached the top of the hill before the highway, Ron exclaimed, "Oh cripes! I just lost first and second gears!"

We stopped and pulled over to the side of the road. All of us got out and sat by the sidewalk. After sitting for a long time on the curb, Howie asked, "Can't we let the hill and gravity give us enough speed to get us to third and on to the highway?"

Ron thought about the suggestion. "As long as we don't stop, we can go all the way to Palo Alto. Get in!"

We started at the top of the hill, pulled on the highway at the bottom, and drove thirty miles home in third gear. It was like being on a roller coaster.

The next day, Ron fixed his van.

The killing continued. Something had to be done about it. My companions and I held a luncheon outside of Lockheed. We expected arrests, but it didn't matter any more. Shows you what a difference a few months can make.

My friends and I held up picket signs inviting people to come. "Can't you quit?" I asked one engineer. He did.

It was time to come down from the mountain and rejoin

the world. Those two weeks changed my life. I arrived a mixed-up teenager, and I came out a man.

Vietnam was tearing apart the country. The Russians didn't need their missiles; the U.S. was self-destructing.

I went to the airport to fly back to the Big Apple. They had just raised the rates. When I reached the Port Authority in New York in the middle of the night, I didn't have the change for the bus home. I couldn't cross the Hudson River. I called home collect.

Johnny answered, "Hello?"

"This is Joey. I'm in the Port Authority, but I'm out of money."

"I'll be there as soon as I can."

No mention of the time. He just came. It's good when a brother loves you.

My thoughts were of California and Kathy. I was going to return.

"Say, want to come along?" I invited her in Connecticut one night later that summer.

"Not now," she answered. "Too close to graduating."

Another rejection. Oh well.

If Kathy accepted, I might not be writing this book.

When I had enough money, my parents took me to Vermont and dropped me off at Ian O'Grady's. He was now attending St. Michael's near Burlington. It was summer, but he was working at a local gas station there. Ian gave me a Gibson guitar on which I tried to play Bob Dylan songs. Wasn't everybody strumming them?

After Ian's, I hitchhiked to Boston to visit Michael, who was living with Lea. He went to the movie house.

"But I thought you don't have any money," I said.

"I don't."

"Then how will you get in?"

"Watch me."

Michael walked backwards through the throng of people exiting the previous showing. It appeared that he was leaving, not entering. When Michael was inside, he sat down. It worked, and Michael watched for free.

Then, I hitched to Connecticut to see Kathy. I stayed at her house in Stamford with my guitar and case. They were like a flag because it seemed everybody played.

"Say why don't we go to a movie?" I said while she drove.

"*Catch 22* is playing. But what will we do with your guitar?"

"Leave it in the car."

"What if someone sees it and breaks in?"

"They won't."

When we parked I made a point of leaving the guitar in the unlocked car. Keys were for *them*, not for *me*. I thought leaving it unguarded was a statement. What it was, I don't know. Later, the guitar was stolen in New York City.

I hitched back to New Jersey. I saw New England well before the leaves changed. It was beautiful but it was also time to go back to California.

I needed someone to share the expense and the

driving. Kathy wasn't going, so, Pat McCarthy came with me. We took the repaired Yellowjacket (after being towed from the shore, the engine was rebuilt in time for the trip).

Pat and I were outside Cleveland in a campsite.

"What are you doing?" he asked exiting our new tent.

"Painting the car with watercolors. I wrote some of the words from Buffy Ste. Marie's *Universal Soldier* on the trunk. I put a peace sign on the roof in case a plane flies over."

That night it rained heavily. Pat laughed when he poked his head out of the tent the following morning.

"What's so funny?"

"Look at the car."

The watercolors ran all over it!

"Can't go like that," I said.

"What'cha gonna do?"

"Start over."

We picked up an old man hitchhiking in Illinois. He wore an American Legion uniform and carried a box with him. I wondered what was in it. The old man was going from Boston to Portland, Oregon, for the American Legion's yearly convention, which explained his uniform. Clear across country. Nothing daunted him.

When Pat and I stopped for gas, the Legionnaire asked, "Can I have a cup of water?"

What's in the box?

When I saw a beak come out of the top of the box, my curiosity was really piqued!

What's in there?

"Can I have another?" he asked.

That did it! My bubble burst.

"What's with the box?" I pointed to it.

"I'm hitching cross-country with the national mascot for the American Legion. It's a duck named Kilroy."

"A duck! Isn't it hot in the box?"

"I don't have nothin' else to carry him in."

I thought that somehow made sense and we were off.

We pulled in again for gas. "Can I have another drink of water?" the old man asked. He held the paper cup near the cardboard box. A beak appeared and slurped up the water. Filled, we left.

The water should have gone in the radiator because the car overheated somewhere in Nebraska. I stopped. I saw two hippies, one with red hair the other with black, walking down Route 80 on a distant hill behind us by a few miles. We waited for the engine to cool down and they came closer. By the time we were ready to leave, the hippies were upon us.

"Do you want a ride?" I offered.

"Sure," the redhead answered.

"Where you from?" I asked as we pulled away.

"Canada."

"Why are you walking?"

The hippie with long black hair perked up. "This dumb redneck cop told us it was illegal to hitch in Nebraska."

"So, we were walking across the state," the redhead chimed in.

"But Nebraska is a big state. It's not like New Jersey," I informed them.

That was news to them. Every time I think of Nebraska, I remember the endless cornfields or the mileage markers alongside the road. It's nowhere to be stuck. That cop was laughing somewhere.

The back seat was crowded with the Legionnaire, his duck and the two hippies on either side of him.

"I have to get out in Salt Lake City," the old man, said. "Thanks for the ride."

We were driving through Nevada when Pat noticed the idiot light flashing. "We better pull over."

"No way'" I answered. "It will go off when we go downhill. It only comes on when we go uphill." I was an expert by now. "Besides, we're in the middle of a desert!"

We reached California but the Sierras are big mountains. No matter how Pat and I pressed, the car wouldn't go faster than thirty miles per hour.

We finally reached Oakland. The Yellowjacket chugged across the Bay Bridge.

I looked in the rear view mirror. There were red flashing lights!

Oh great! What now?

"License and registration," the cop said after I had pulled over and rolled down the window.

"Why were we pulled over?" Pat wanted to know from the passenger seat.

"Going too slow. This vehicle is dangerous."

I was afraid the cop would ask for my draft card because I didn't have one. There was a draft lottery in the past fall. Twenty numbers at a time were broadcast at the bottom of the television screen. If you had a number of 150 or less, you could expect a one-way ticket to Vietnam. No more deferments. I was late and missed the first twenty numbers.

Johnny's number came up 157. He was on the cusp. 200 came. Neither mine, nor my cousin Tommy's, appeared.

Am I in the first twenty?

At 300, the birthdays still were not called.

I must be in the first twenty.

320 and 340 came and went. Still no birthdays. Then, 341 through 360 flashed across the screen. I saw Tommy Thek's number. He was 353 and in the clear.

But still no May 25th.

Oh well, I'm going to 'Nam. Better pack my bags. This time, I won't take a bus. I'm gonna die.

Then, the telephone rang. It was Val. "I've been watching Channel 5 and I saw your birthday."

"What is it?"

"361."

I'm gonna live!

I was elated. I was free!

I sent my card in anyway. Someone sent it back. They could have arrested me. Somebody at the draft board had some sense.

I sent it again, with a letter, but the card returned. They weren't allowing me to resist; so, I threw it away. I thought and think that Vietnam was a disgrace to this great country and to all our fighting men and women. For what were we giving our lives? So rich people could party? What would Jesus do? I can't see Him in Vietnam sporting a US uniform.

The cop never asked for my card; and we made it to the Institute bunkhouse in the hills near Palo Alto, where we slept.

"I'm exhausted," Pat admitted. "I'll fly home."

The Canadians left, and I was in California, alone with a car that couldn't go over thirty.

What am I gonna do?

I went to a used car lot.

"How much will you give me for my car?" I asked the salesman.

He must have seen me coming. "Seventy-five dollars," he answered after inspecting the vehicle.

Oh well. Beggars can't be choosers.

I took the cash.

Behind the car dealer's place was an empty lot. I knocked on the door of the house adjacent to it. A sixteen-year-old blonde girl answered. "Yes?"

"I couldn't help but notice the empty lot next to your house. Do you know who owns it and do you think he would mind if I pitched my tent there?"

"That'd be the same person we rent from and, yes, he would mind."

"But I've come all the way from New Jersey and I just sold my car," I said desperately.

"Maybe you can pitch your tent in our backyard. Let me ask." Then she yelled, "Mommy!"

The mother, Mrs. Greer, angrily came to the door. "What do you want?"

"This young man wants to know if he can camp in our backyard."

Mrs. Greer took her time looking me over as if the fate of the world was in the balance. "Sure. Why not?" she finally answered.

Cindy, the daughter, was one of nine kids. The mother ran an electric light to my tent. There was a faucet just outside my doorway. I had a Coleman stove in my camping gear. Not exactly all the comforts of home, but it would do.

On the first night, a friend of Cindy's commented in an off hand way, "I'll be out around midnight."

I knew very well what was on her mind.

I'm glad she finds me attractive, but can't she find someone else?

Her boyfriend, Cindy's older brother, was in prison, but he was getting out that night. To make matters worse, the brother was married and his wife was at the house, too.

Oh great! I'm a sitting duck in this tent. How did I get involved in this soap opera? He's gonna shoot me, I know it.

The boyfriend was freed. God was looking out for me again because he went right back in when the boyfriend tried to rob a liquor store at gunpoint. I breathed a sigh of relief, and the girl never came at midnight.

I did odd jobs around the Greer house like fixing bikes. I went inside for the bathroom, otherwise, I stayed in my tent. The kids were violent towards each other, but never to me.

I was celibate the whole time. Not by choice, that's just the way it was. The Catholic Church forces celibacy on its priesthood. I find that stance very unbiblical. (Please read Genesis 2:18-24. And in the New Testament, 1 Corinthians 7:1-9.)

One has only to read an account of the promiscuity of Rome, especially its priests, to see the truth of that statement. The popes had mistresses and children. They were proud of them. Not allowing marriage is blasphemous.

My cousin, Bobby, was fired from Stanford for displaying his peace flag and hired by USC in the History Department that included Herbert Marcuse and Angela Davis.

I was hired in a local hamburger place. The money I made, all $1.35 an hour, burned holes in my pocket.

I was offered a place to stay with four people. There were Claudia, Ellen, Ben and Steve.

"You're welcome, but we don't have a room," Steve said.

"I'll sleep on the floor."

And it was settled.

Before Steve broke it, he loaned me his motorbike to go to work. Afterward, I went to work by bicycle.

The Institute had another seminar with Ira Sands so I attended. The course was at a different location from the previous one I attended. It was not as intimate.

Through Ira and the Institute, I met Kit Bianca, who was the Palo Alto director of the grape boycott. About that time the farm workers' union won the boycott. It took years, but they were victorious. Through Kit, I became involved in the lettuce strike in Salinas.

"You're putting non-union lettuce on these hamburgers," I said to the manager one day after inspecting a box.

""So?" he asked.

"So, I quit," I answered and I walked out.

The war kept going on and on and on. People—men, women and children, old, young—were dying. At home, good people were getting assassinated. Everybody was fighting all the time. It was fatiguing. The anti-war movement didn't have answers and was against everything, not *for* anything. I needed a revolution in my thoughts and ways. The farm workers' union afforded me one. They offered me hope.

You could say, since I broke up with Val, any woman or

cause would do. If I could not have her, then I would use a substitute. There is an element of truth there, but it is not so simple.

The farm workers' union was more. It inspired me when I was groveling in the mire. The union had a method of fighting, and winning, without the use of violence. So, I hitched to Salinas. That move must have pleased God.

Chapter Five
THE BOYCOTT AND A WEDDING

In the middle of a hot labor camp in Salinas, I knocked on the door of a building covered with a sheet metal roof.

"Hello," Cesar Chavez answered from his rocking chair. Cesar suffered from a bad back. "Come in, come in."

"I'm Joe Thek." I went inside hesitantly. *What am I getting into?*

"We need you on the boycott in New Jersey. Isn't that where you're from?"

"How did you know that?"

"Your information folder," he answered. "Plus your accent."

Cesar explained how the lettuce workers went on strike. "Other crops are grown, but lettuce is the major one."

Cesar was a master organizer. He mesmerized me and wove a tale like a seamstress does a tapestry.

"We need help. Everybody does."

It's up to me.

Before I knew it, I was hooked and on the picket line despite my fear.

After a plane flew by and sprayed a foreign substance on us, I asked, "What's that?"

"It's only a crop duster," Manuel, another picketer, answered. "They're dropping pesticides on us."

Oh great! Just what I need! Chemicals on my head!

It was mighty lonely and becoming dangerous out there in the middle of nowhere. So, the lettuce boycott was born.

If a strike can't be won, a boycott can, even if it takes years. My companions and I traveled all over the U.S. and Canada, to where lettuce was sold.

The union couldn't afford anything more than five dollars a week plus room and board. It was a comfort to know Cesar received the same stipend. Everything was for *La Causa.*

I drove cross-country with Richard Nappi and Jose Gonzalez, the head coordinator of the Jersey boycott. The three of us were supposed to run it there. We accompanied the boycotters from other cities and states.

"Drive," Jose commanded.

"But I don't know how to drive a stick shift," I pointed to the one in the car.

Jose shrugged his shoulders. "Drive."

I learned by trial and error, hoping not to get stopped on a hill.

In Ohio, we were pulled over for speeding while Richard was driving.

"I won't pay the fine," he muttered to me.

Oh great!

"License and registration," the cop demanded when Richard rolled down the window.

"I want to know why we were pulled over," Richard replied from behind the steering wheel.

Here we go!

"I will ask all the questions," the policeman answered.

"You work for me and don't forget it," Richard continued.

But he has the ticket book!

The next thing I knew we were in some Ohio jail. Finally, Jim Drood, a minister who owned the vehicle, paid the fine. Richard, Jose and I, proceeded to New Jersey.

No one would house us, so we had no lodging. I stayed with my parents while Richard was in New York City, and Jose looked for an apartment.

He found an office first, in Belleville near Newark. Jose put me to work on a mailing. I printed (which taught me how to use a mimeograph machine), addressed, and posted it. At last, Jose rented an apartment in Newark.

There were four rooms on the second floor, small and filled with cockroaches. The apartment was in the middle of the ghetto. I was the sole white for blocks around. There was a bunch of kids living above us with their mother, who was too poor to afford a rug. Every night they played marbles, which, to me below, sounded as if the kids were bowling.

Then, the mother took up with a man. One evening, I heard a yelling match above us. The door to her apartment slammed, and I heard someone on the stairs. The man appeared on the street below.

"You jive turkey!" the woman yelled from the window. "Now I knows why your eyes are brown! That's because you're so full of crap!"

The man, below, screamed back, "Oh yeah! And you must have two a**holes to get rid of all yours!"

That did it! She threw his clothes out of the window. A crowd gathered on the other side of the street and goaded the woman.

"Here's your mattress!" she screamed. Out it came. I thought I needed a helmet.

The crowd clapped for her and booed the man.

We continued with our organizing amid the noise.

Richard arrived from New York to live with us and I bet he cursed the day. Chris Shields joined us too. She owned a light blue Volkswagen bug. She used the room with a door as a girls' bedroom. Jose and I shared a room, and Richard had his own. The fourth one was the kitchen.

Now there were four boycotters. We eventually shared an office in Jersey City near Journal Square with the ILGWU (International Ladies Garment Workers Union) whose secretary was named Pilar.

"You're *mucho loco*!" she exclaimed pointing her index finger to her head.

Maybe we were.

I did store checks to see if they carried union lettuce. The produce managers hated to see me coming.

"Let me see your lettuce," I'd command.

If the union label, an Aztec eagle was on the wrapper, everything was okay. If it wasn't, then the supermarket chain went on our black list.

Initially, I picketed alone. Soon, there were supporters while I stood outside of the supermarket and gave shoppers leaflets asking them not to buy there.

"*No compre lechuga!*" (Don't buy the lettuce) I'd scream.

We couldn't boycott everywhere that sold nonunion lettuce, so we chose one chain of stores. When they capitulated, my companions and I sent them shoppers and blacklisted another company. The plan worked well and people cooperated.

I fashioned myself as a young Saul Alinsky, an organizer. Any day, a revolution was expected and I was ready. I even carried around Mao's little red book. I grew a beard and thought it was chic because the beard was red too.

One supporter, David Ruprecht, had been a Peace Corps volunteer in the Philippines. Jose had been in it in Brazil, so they related well. David and his wife, Joan, threw a party for us where we met many contacts. I always carried my pen and notebook for telephone numbers.

Then, Edie Campbell and Barbara Kaufmann, both from Philadelphia, joined us. Edie arrived first.

I answered the doorbell wearing a silly green hat, an African vest, and was singing the Star Spangled Banner. There stood Edie and her parents.

"Come in, come in," I said from beneath my bushy red beard.

"There must be some mistake." Edie's dad viewed my outrageous wardrobe.

"No, this is it" I replied nonplussed. "This is the farm worker house."

All Edie's mother saw were the mattresses on the floor.

I looked at Edie's eyes and fell in love. She was about five foot two, 105 pounds, had long, brown hair, matching eyes and was dark skinned. Many people mistook her for a farm worker.

When Chris' mother came to visit, she was introduced to me.

"Edie and I are gonna be married," I announced.

"Oh. When?" she asked.

"Edie doesn't know it yet."

After a little pause in which Chris' mother determined that I was serious, she offered, "Let me give you some advice about marriage. For it to work there are different combinations of one hundred percent. If it's fifty-fifty, that's perfect. But most successful marriages come when you give sixty percent and expect forty in return. Seventy-thirty, eighty-twenty, ninety-ten and a hundred-zero don't work."

"What if both people give a hundred percent?" I asked.

I didn't listen to her answer because I was

remembering Val. I couldn't get her out of my mind so I broke off my budding relationship with Edie. I had to find out what happened to my ex.

Val was dating Jimmy Hokey. If she became my steady, I would betray a friend. If Val didn't, I would go crazy. I didn't know what to do, so I tried to compromise and be her friend. When she broke up with Jimmy, Val asked, "Can you fix it up with Jimmy and me?"

"I'll try," I answered while thinking she should be with me. *This is crazy.*

Later, I said "Goodbye." I couldn't be just her friend.

I gave lectures too, reading from a prepared paper. I was afraid to trust my feelings and thought I might omit something. On a visit to see Kathy, I read in a coffeehouse from a canned script. It didn't capture the audience's attention, so I discarded the paper and spoke extemporaneously.

"The farm workers don't work for the farmer, but for the labor contractor. He's like a tax collector, a social vampire; lower than the belly of a worm. They pay him for food and lodging. After a day's work you're thirsty, hungry and sweaty. You pay him for your soft drinks, snacks and showers. The workers wind up in debt, which is paid off with more work. A vicious cycle is begun. I know a man who after two years of work still owes the labor contractor. I thought slavery was abolished in this country. I guess not."

I glanced up to see the audience hanging on every word.

By now, there were many people on the boycott and the apartment in Newark was too small. There were wall-to-wall beds. The boycotters had to move.

Jose wanted to go to Cuba on the Venceremos Brigade.

"Say, our mail's been opened," I indicated.

"Some dimwitted FBI agent must be reading it," Edie remarked.

"Don't they have anything better to do?"

Brian Webster, a supporter, gave us the FBI's credit card number. "You can make long distance calls on it."

"Won't they catch us?" I asked.

"Nope. Too stupid."

An agent was stationed across the street from our apartment. He was supposed to be incognito, but the agent was white and stuck out like a lone pitchfork in a haystack. I guess they considered us dangerous, mainly because *El Jefe* (Jose) wanted to harvest sugarcane in Cuba. We could picket all we wanted, but Cuba was *verboten*. It boggled the mind. Jose went anyway, I think to spite them.

By this time, Edie was living with Brian who had his own apartment. She was nearly independent of us. Then they had a quarrel.

"I think I'm pregnant," she explained. "Brian doesn't want the baby."

"What are you gonna do?" I asked.

"Nothing I can do but raise the baby myself."

"I admire your courage."

Her best friend was Barbara Kaufmann. My favorite Barbara story occurred after our second move. Ben-G, a fellow boycotter, had a sculpted head he considered bad luck. So, he gave it to Barbara (Nice, huh?). Edie and I (am I giving you information out of sequence?) shared a closet with Barbara. It had two doors: one to our bedroom, the other to hers.

She set the sculpted head on her bureau. I hid in the closet and waited for Barbara to leave. When she did, I exited the closet and went to her bureau where I turned the head and then escaped through the closet into my bedroom and then out into the hallway.

Then Barbara returned. "The head! The head!" she screamed pointing to the sculpture. "It moved! Honest, I swear!" She thought for a while, "I have to bury it."

By now the entire house was in an uproar. Larry Hawley, another boycotter, insisted, "If you bury that head, a piece of your sanity will go with it."

When Larry wasn't looking, Barbara buried the head in the backyard. I think it's still there.

Edie and I cried on each other's shoulders after my break-up with Val and hers with Brian.

During that time, I met Dennis, "Dino", Lowe through David.

"You can stay with us if you organize," I offered.

"Sounds good."

He was a black poet who studied with Leroi Jones (Imamu Baraka). I wrote poetry at the time, so we had something in common. Dino and I went to local coffeehouses and did 'Guerilla Theater'.

Through him, I met his friend Willy who had been a pimp in Newark. Willy joined the union, too.

At the office, I met Norbert Hecht from Germany and Stefan Robinson, his black friend.

"Say, why don't you join us? We could use you both," I frequently invited. I nabbed Stefan eventually.

His white girl friend named "Oogie" was always on the picket line. Once Oogie and Stefan were in his bedroom upstairs when I heard a crash.

"What was that?" I asked.

"I don't know," Ben-G answered.

I discovered that Stefan put his foot through the windowpane. I wonder what he was doing?

Oogie liked Seals and Croft because they were of her faith, the Ba'hai.

"Won't you come and listen?" she asked.

"I'm confused enough already," I replied. "If I want to convert, I'll let you know."

At that time, I was an avowed agnostic.

I became angered if God was even mentioned. I should've listened more to Cesar, but didn't. He was definitely plugged in to God. I wanted a peaceful world and thought I could get to one without Him. We could create one if only we were more loving. I believed we were at the center of the wheel.

But what if God does exist? Wasn't He responsible for all the suffering in the world? Wasn't He our enemy? Therefore, we had to get rid of Him, even the idea of God. That was the way I thought.

I didn't realize He wants the same thing. It's the Devil that disrupts and deceives. When I became a believer at first I wanted Him on my team. Now, I want to be on His. God is at the center of the wheel and we are its spokes.

The boycott attempted to reach up to God through good works. It can't be done. (Please read Isaiah 64:6 and Ephesians 2:8-9.)

This is not to say that good works are unimportant. (Please read James 2:17.) In other words, faith comes first. Works are an indicator of what is going on inside a person but cannot, by themselves, merit salvation, no matter how good or how many.

In January, 1971, I was arrested for the first time. We orchestrated a boycott of Two Guys, by setting up a picket line in Jersey City. The supermarket didn't capitulate; in fact, they called the police.

When they arrived, Richard insisted, "I'm not gonna move."

Great! Here we go again!

Then it was Jose's turn. "This is public property. As part

of the public we have a right to picket and pass out leaflets here!"

We were arrested and imprisoned in the Jersey City jail.

The cell was sparse with wooden slats for beds. At the end of the bed was a toilet. Some inmates spent many months in there awaiting trial because they could not afford the bail. A pregnant woman on the ladies' side went into labor while I was incarcerated. Her jailers thought she was faking.

Then, there was the fingerprint man. I was booked with a Vietnam veteran who had a flair for this kind of thing, which is more than I can say for myself.

"I don't believe it!" the forensics man claimed while fingerprinting me. "You've got a closed whorl on your right thumb. I've never seen it before!"

That was news to me.

"You could never be a thief because your right thumb would give you away! It is one in a million!"

He removed some mutilated fingers from formaldehyde in a jar setting on the wall shelf. They swirled around in the acrid gunk.

"I was called in to identify them," the forensics man claimed. Lifting a finger out and holding it up for us to view, "A train hit this criminal and his finger was the only thing left."

The veteran ate it up, but I felt like heaving. This mole of a man, enthused over a jar of reeking fingers in formaldehyde in the jail basement.

"Well, he'd been arrested, all right. And I identified him from this finger!"

I just wanted to get out.

When I finally made bail, they let me go. I spent the night in the jail and got a first-hand education. How do people survive there? The jail was a nuthouse. Who is more mad, the captors or the captives?

We discovered Richard was a spy for the growers, an *agent provocateur*. They were crazy to select him even if there was nothing to hide. If something were secret, Richard would never uncover it. *El Jefe* fired him.

Then, there was Ben-G, who was black too. I met him through David Ruprecht.

Ben-G had already received a subpoena stating he had to testify against the guy with whom Ben-G robbed a train station. On the day of his testimony, the judge rocked in his chair. Ben-G, on the witness stand, did too in imitation. I thought His Honor would have apoplexy.

"I'll send you to jail!" the judge exploded.

"I've already done my time," Ben-G calmly replied while continuing to rock in the witness chair.

Earlier, during his own trial, the court offered Ben-G an option: either serve time or go in the Marines. He chose the Corps, but was thrown out, so Ben-G went behind bars.

Before doing his time, he and his accomplice obtained

the combination for the railroad safe at a bar from a third person. One weekend morning, Ben-G and his fellow thief went to the railroad station. They thought the trains were not running. The accomplice dropped him off and waited nearby in the car. Ben-G had to crawl to get to the safe.

However, there *was* a train coming. Someone tapped on the window, while Ben-G crept on the floor toward the safe.

"Say, what time is the 11:30 train arriving?"

He answered, "11:30", then kept crawling toward the safe.

I never said Ben-G was smart. He was caught while the other thief disappeared.

Back in the second trial, the judge asked, "Do you recognize the handwriting on the paper with the combination on it?"

Of course he did, it was his handwriting!

"No," Ben-G lied. "I can't remember."

The judge was furious and threw the case out of court. The accomplice went free and Ben-G wondered why he had spent time in jail.

Now, if Ben-G returned to Bayonne (his hometown), he was afraid of being murdered himself or of killing the guy with whom he robbed the train station in self-defense. The white accomplice hadn't served any time yet.

"I need a sponsor," Ben-G said. "It can't be just anyone. He has to come from a different county besides Hudson where Bayonne is."

"Does Montclair count?"

"Yes. That's Essex."

"Can it be me?

"Sure can. Will you do it?"

"If you will help us organize, I will." *Seems like a fair exchange.*

So, I became his sponsor. By this time, the boycott apartment moved from Newark to Montclair. I pretended to be a minister married to Chris in order to rent it. The apartment was the second and third stories of a house. It had an outdoor staircase, eight rooms and a porch.

"I'll take the smallest room for a bedroom," Ben-G said.

"Why?" I asked.

"Because it reminds me of my cell."

After Jose went to Cuba, David Lawless became the director of the Jersey boycott. His wife, Peggy, was from Yakima Valley, Washington. When she first arrived, we were driving in Jersey City. Peggy looked down to the end of Montgomery Avenue. Not seeing the Hudson River, she asked, "Say, isn't that The Statue of Liberty?"

"Sure is," I answered.

"I didn't know you could get to it by land."

I looked at her as if she were crazy. Peggy didn't know it was in the harbor. Eyes can trick you.

Daniel and Hoppy came to New Jersey with them. One evening we were stopped at a red light in Newark's Ironbound section. A truck pulled up next to us. The driver, asking for directions, bellowed, "Hey, Buddy, how do you get to..." From then on, everyone that Daniel greeted was, "Hey, Buddy."

We needed money, so I organized church collections. A letter from the bishop could be helpful, so I met with him. I barely saw the bishop because when I walked into his office he aimed a light at me and I was blinded. The room was darkened. I didn't expect The Inquisition.

A note was mailed, but not to every parish, just those with liberal pastors. No trouble, it was better than nothing. My companions and I made our collections outside the church wearing our placards.

In New York I met with Ira, the Gandhi expert.

"This new demonstration in Washington in the spring will end the war," he tried to convince the skeptical me.

In our minds, everything was connected: the war, the boycott, women's lib, civil rights. After a church collection, we went to Washington to protest the war on May Day 1971. All the members of the Jersey boycott and a Princeton student named Fred Sawyer, slept in St. Stephen's church. Early in the morning, we went to DuPont Circle. On the way there, I saw a policeman hit a protester on the head with his Billy club. Finally, my friends and I approached the rotary.

The war was going on; people were being killed. Something had to be done.

I sat down in the road in front of a bus. The connection is fuzzy, now, but it made perfect sense to me, then. Edie sat down beside me. Soon, others joined us.

A cop drove his motorcycle to where I was and commanded, "Move!"

I didn't budge, so I was arrested and forced to sit by the fountain in the circle. It was pepper gassed. I was loaded on a bus with the gas burning my eyes. They booked all of us.

While I was fingerprinted, my toe cramped because I was tired. I dropped to the floor, took off my shoe and repositioned the toe.

The policeman leaned over the counter to stare at me still on the floor holding my toe. "What are you doing?"

"I'm putting my toe back in place."

"I think you're afraid to get booked."

"I am not!" I insisted; my integrity now impugned.

"Then get back up here and I'll call the 'toe' truck."

"Very funny," I said from my position on the floor.

Afterward, they conducted me to a one-man jail cell. So many people were arrested that day that the cubicle contained nine people. It was so small that my cellmates and I took turns standing to fit.

Fred Sawyer and I were shipped to another jail. He made a desperate call to Congressman Dellums' office. Fred exited, but I didn't. What happened? I still don't know.

I was arraigned before a D.C. judge. Michael Ventra was in the audience.

"What are you doing in there?" he questioned me, a la Emerson.

"And what are you doing out there?" I asked a la Thoreau. "Shouldn't all people of conscience be in jail?"

I was shipped to Occoquan Penitentiary where the inmates, all protesters, debated whether or not to fast. There were so many of them that I had to pick a spot on the gym floor for my sleeping bag.

"Let's vote on whether to fast or not!" a bearded hippie yelled amid the chaos. Makeshift ballots were passed out. Several people talked in hushed tones very seriously with furrowed brows.

They act like everything depends on them.

The votes were tallied amid the din that ensued. The bearded hippie exclaimed, "It's been decided that those who want to fast, can; and those who don't, don't have to!"

Democracy at work!

Edie went to RFK Stadium because the jails in D.C. were filled. They opened RFK to put the overflow there. Abbe Hoffman was there, too. The prisoners knew he was in, but the police didn't. While Abbe Hoffman was in RFK, the FBI looked for him outside. They didn't know the police had him in custody. It was not a secret, he even was married there: but the FBI couldn't find him. I wonder why.

I spent three long days at Occoquan penitentiary lying on the floor in my sleeping bag. Then the guard yelled, "David Lawless!"

"Boy, am I glad to see you!" I said when I reached him. "Do you have that money from the church collection?"

"Yeah. So what?"

"We'll use it for bail. Don't worry we'll get it back."

When we were released from prison, David and I went to his friends' apartment before leaving D.C.

The police held the city under martial law and arrested everyone in the streets. Helicopters flew overhead. We snuck out of the city.

On the New Jersey Turnpike, the traffic was stopped. Several protesters abandoned their cars in the middle of the roadway across the Turnpike and blocked traffic. The vehicles had to be towed.

We were caught in the jam. A few hippies exited their cars.

"What are they doing?" I asked.

"They're tossing Frisbees," David answered.

"C'mon. Let's join 'em."

Soon, the New Jersey Turnpike became a Frisbee playground between the cars involved in the tie-up.

Those that stayed in their cars refused to look. With their heads and eyes straight ahead, they didn't join in our fun, let alone create some.

The war continued. The government was like the people driving the cars on the Turnpike; they didn't want to see us either. But, we were there! Eleven thousand were arrested on May Day. Three thousand more were incarcerated in the days afterward. A revolution nearly happened! Good people tried to stop the war. It went on with a life of its own.

Who is responsible? Maybe all of us are. We pay the taxes and are the soldiers. Like Buffy Ste. Marie stated, "Without us, all this killing can't go on."

We were so poor that several times I paid for things with stamps. The unions supported us with paper and postage, not money. I bought gas or my meals with stamps. It violated the law, but who cared? Certainly not I! I was not above anything.

That winter, I wore a baggy, green coat with pockets. I cut holes in the bottoms of them. When I went shopping, I stuffed expensive things in the pockets and they slipped down through the holes. I rearranged the coat, so I could fit more food. I rationalized that I only stole from a big company. In the summer, I needed another ploy.

"Look at the bottom of the shopping cart," Ben-G began one day. "It has a runner. Put your meat bags on there and when we check out I'll distract the checkout girl. I'm good at that. You push the cart past the register while I talk, mix the unpaid bags in with the paid, then load them all on the upper part of the cart."

"What if we get caught?"

"Just say you forgot them. But, we're not gonna get caught. Believe me."

We never were. Today, the carts don't have the runners down below, probably because of people such as we.

Stealing. God commands us not to. But I wasn't sure of God then. I was wrong. I remember the story of Robin Hood—stealing from the rich to give to the poor. Regardless of the motives, it is wrong. The Ten Commandments forbid stealing. To identify Robin Hood as a hero is contradictory. Either thou shalt not steal or under certain circumstances it's okay.

I stole from supermarkets. I rationalized that I pilfered from a company with plenty of money. The reality is they simply pass the cost on to other consumers, working stiffs, like me. I stopped.

What about killing or stealing a life? To plot to slay another human being implies right is known and a boundary is crossed. The borders become clear between "Us" and "Them." The killers become criminals. Some kind of reward is offered, usually Heaven. But they must be taught that they will go to Hell if they commit murder. I hope if they know that, it will stop. That may not be politically correct but it is the truth.

Let's examine the relationship between fanaticism and religion. On the left, there are "true" believers that are secular like Communists, women's advocates, the gay liberationists and others. What about the right? It's mostly religious in nature. How many Jim Bakkers and Jimmy Swaggerts do we need before we realize what they are? Crooks. But, if anyone truly repents, we should forgive and let the judgment be God's.

We tolerate them as long as they don't threaten us. When fanatics kill people, they have gone beyond the Pale. But, it's up to God to sort it out. "Thou shall not kill." I reiterate; there is no asterisk. Besides, who am I to judge? (Please read Matthew 7:1-2.)

Most of our cars were registered in my name. They were given nicknames like "Oof" because that was printed on the license plate or "Hawk" because it was a Falcon. "Hawk," sported a hole in the floor, had no heat, and windshield wipers that didn't work. An unwound metal clothes hanger connected to each blade. Two people, one on either side, were required to move them. Rain was an adventure for the driver.

Our group went in the Chevy, "Oof," to a Sly and the Family Stone concert at Madison Square Garden. Its doors didn't open, but the windows did. Nine of us entered through them.

En route there the driver, Larry, stopped suddenly at a railroad crossing. "Get out!" he shouted.

"Why?" I asked.

Larry pointed to the smoking hood. All of us scurried out through the windows. If the car exploded we didn't want to be stuck inside.

""It's only the carburetor," Larry said after he lifted the hood and extinguished the fire.

We re-entered "Oof" and continued to Madison Square Garden. I wonder what witnesses thought.

Another one was named the "Mystery Car," because it wasn't registered. The "Mystery Car" could only be driven at night when the cops couldn't see that it wasn't. When the "Mystery Car" died; Ben-G and I stripped it at 3:00 in the morning. Even though the "Mystery Car" was mine, I couldn't prove it because I lacked the registration.

"I'm amazed you stripped it so fast," I noted.

"It's my ballpark now."

"That was a real work of art. You should try out for the Guiness Book of world records."

A fourth was named "The White Whale". Val's dad wanted to do his part, so he gave us an old, big, white, Lincoln. It served us well until the rear axle broke and the tires went askew in the middle of Bloomfield Avenue.

Larry Hawley was a refugee from Vista. Before moving in with us, he had worked to get blacks registered to vote in Alabama.

I met Marcos Merced, a friend of Cesar Chavez, and the head coordinator of the Boston boycott. Marcos was with the union since the beginning. He was a good organizer, but I don't think Marcos tried to understand us.

"I don't like what you're doing in Jersey, Gringo," he said to me.

"Why?"

"That's not the way we are."

I didn't defend our position. I should have. I guess he

thought we were too radical. Maybe Marcos was a little envious because the Jersey boycott was so free and crazy.

During the summer Edie transferred to Buffalo. I wrote to her, and we became closer.

At the time, there was a moratorium on the lettuce boycott, so, to keep the organization intact, we boycotted grapes instead. I went with the New York boycott to Hunt's Point in the Bronx (a big produce market several miles long and protected by a gate). At first, we used walkie-talkies. Some of us entered it about 5:00 A.M., while others stayed outside in cars. The people who went inside relayed information via radio to the waiting vehicles, about who bought what. License plate numbers were copied so the cars outside could follow the nonunion fruit. The boycotters in the pursuing vehicles picketed the store that sold the scab grapes. Sellers sent the grape lugs back to Hunt's Point to avoid the picket line, and the process began again.

After awhile, I went in alone, armed with a transistor radio pretending it was a walkie-talkie.

Speaking into the transistor radio, I'd whisper, "License plate, New York 123QWE, 8 lugs."

The lugs invariably were unloaded. Nobody wanted to be picketed; but they didn't know no cars were outside and that I was bluffing.

House meetings evolved into an art form. I always

scheduled them around dinnertime, so I could eat. I gave a motivational talk to increase the interest of whoever was there. I distributed leaflets or buttons and collected money. It worked because most people wanted to help. They didn't wish to see themselves as part of the problem.

Two people did the store checks now. It gave us an opportunity for guerrilla theater. First, I went in and spoke with the produce managers. Then, the other boycotter jumped in with a book hanging out of his pants. It read *How To Make Homemade Bombs*.

"I personally hate violence, but I'm not responsible for my supporters," I confided halfheartedly.

It was a variation of "Good Cop, Bad Cop." It wasn't nonviolent, but the grapes came down. Cesar would have a fit if he knew, but Cesar never learned of it.

Sometimes store checks used three people. The guerrilla theater tactics expanded. I went in first and struck up a conversation with a produce manager. The other two fetched a shopping cart, filled it and meandered over to where I talked with him. When we had a verbal altercation, they intruded.

"That's scab lettuce?" one asked loudly.

"Sure is," I answered.

"I ain't shoppin' here." The two abandoned the stuffed cart (called a shop-in) in the middle of the aisle, left the store and encouraged others to join them. Most times, a few people did.

All of us worked long hours, possibly eighty a week. Between giving talks, store checks, house meetings, picketing and leafleting; we were busy.

David Lawless left and nobody wanted to be head coordinator. I reluctantly took over the job because I had been there the longest.

We played the "Who and What" game. My companions and I sat in a circle, passed a fork in one direction and a spoon in the other. When the fork was passed, the person doing the transfer held it out, and said to the one receiving the fork, "This is a who."

The person receiving it, asked, "A who?"

The originator said "A who," and then the receiver responded, "A who."

Then he or she passed it on to the third person, saying, "This is a who." The third person asked "A who?" The second person turned back to the originator and asked "A who?" and the originator replied, "A who." The second person then turned to the third and said "A who." The third person then passed it on to the fourth and so on, all the way around the circle.

The same thing would be applicable to the spoon, except "What" was substituted for "Who."

The game was easy until the one in the middle held both utensils going in opposite directions. Then the central person became confused and did not know what to say or do. The fork and spoon would get mixed up. The middle one, would say, "A who," one way, and "A what," the other. It was laughable.

I liked the game because it required teamwork to win. Everyone was successful when the utensils went around the circle appropriately. All lost if the fork or the spoon didn't. Sometimes, the utensils made it, but most times, not. Failing was funny. What other errors make you laugh when you lose?

I fell in love again with Edie. We went to Maryknoll in Ossening, New York, for a conference with Cesar. The whole East Coast boycott was there, about eighty people.

Cesar watched us play the "Who and What" game at breakfast. "What are you doing?"

I explained the game.

Later, the boycotters met. "Form a circle," Cesar ordered.

Cesar started playing the game by passing the fork and spoon. At the mid-point, the person became confused. Cesar laughed.

"Will you marry me?" I asked Edie one evening while we lay in the grass of Maryknoll, losing ourselves in one another's eyes.

"Yes," she replied without blinking. I was in ecstasy.

We made wedding plans.

Then, I received a letter from Val. She had broken up with Jimmy and wanted to see me. I went to her house and took her out to dinner.

"Want to go to Hershung Park to talk?" she asked afterwards.

"Sure. Why not?" Like I said before, I am stupid.

She kissed me when we were alone. I nearly surrendered. But, I was engaged. I wouldn't break up a second time because of her. I had to be faithful, didn't I? This time, it wasn't with Val. I had Edie on my mind.

I pushed her away. "No, this is all wrong. I can't do it."

Edie went to see Brian about the same time. He wanted her to come back, but she didn't leave me. I thought we were meant for each other.

Edie and I couldn't be engaged and live in different boycott houses, so she transferred to Jersey.

At the time, we were in the process of moving from Montclair to Jersey City. They are in different counties; Edie and I couldn't get the marriage certificate in Montclair. The date of the wedding needed to be postponed until later for us to obtain the proper papers in Jersey City.

Postponed? Who postpones a wedding?

We didn't get one until *after* the marriage ceremony. By then, I had a birthday and, consequently, my age was wrong. None of the parents ever asked us to produce one. Who goes to a wedding and asks for ID?

Our ceremony was held outdoors. Lee and Tamara Kobel, supporters of the boycott, offered their farm in Freehold. The day was bright and clear.

Edie and I couldn't find a priest or rabbi to wed us. Finally, Jack Easley, a supporter priest who lived in

Jersey City near us, said, "I'll do it, but only if I don't sign the marriage certificate. It will be outside my diocese and I don't want any more trouble with the bishop. I'm in enough hot water now about the war. I don't need to get expelled from the priesthood over a wedding."

"No problem" I answered, thinking *I don't have one anyway.*

By the time Edie and I obtained a paper, another priest, Bill Gowlik, who wasn't even at the ceremony, signed the certificate. It didn't matter to him. Since our marriage, he had left the priesthood. The ceremony was for our parents, anyway. I wrote the words. Johnny was my best man and Audrey, Edie's sister, was the Maid of Honor. David Ruprecht took pictures. It was in early May with flowers blooming.

Her parents made a present of a car and mine gave us some money. What a glorious day!

Weddings are a big deal. Most times the bride has questions. That's what you read about. But, I say the groom wonders too. "Am I doing the right thing?" The finality of it is awesome. God hates divorce. (Please read Malachi 2:13-16.)

The wedding was a complete success. Our friends, the hippies, were on the right side of the house. Everybody else was in the front or on the left. The nieces, nephews and cousins, met each other. They frolicked in the fields near the house.

When we left for our honeymoon, I made the mistake of calling the boycott house to see how tings were going.

Marcos answered, "You lived together before the wedding! This honeymoon is a fake, Gringo!"

I should have told him to get lost, but I didn't. He knew how to make me feel guilty. So, we returned.

Sex and marriage is another one of those issues about which people feel very strongly about. Personally, I now think sex is only for marriage but then I saw it as a possible prelude. We shouldn't let our hormones do the thinking. That's a prescription for disaster.

Edie and I left for our second honeymoon in June with two other couples, Michael Ventra and Lea, and their friends, Phil and Monseratte. We were going out West to retrace part of the trip I had done in 1969. We traveled in two cars and used three tents. One of the vehicles was our wedding gift car, and the money came from my parents. They intended for us to spend it on setting up house. Wisely, not what my parents thought as frivolous. In retrospect, the money was well spent.

The first day, we didn't know but drove through Hurricane Agnes on Route 80 in Pennsylvania. Rain poured all day and trucks and cars were driven off of the highway. I was afraid to look at the side of the road because I might see damage.

It rained in Ohio too. The sun didn't appear until we reached Indiana where we made camp.

On the second day, my companions and I drove past Chicago and into Kansas, camping at a lake.

"Want to join us for dinner?" a long-haired hippie with a Volkswagen van asked.

"Sure, groovy," I answered.

People were friendly then as long as you were on their side.

The food was cooked on a campfire.

"Make sure you add salt," a female voice came from inside the van.

Some things never change.

Then, we were at the Rockies. After my first experience, I wanted to climb Pike's Peak correctly. First, all of us would get acclimatized at the base camp. Then, we'd hike up the mountain.

This time, we took the incline up to a little over nine thousand feet. Then, we backpacked into the camp at about ten thousand.

"We'll stay here for a day," I was the 'experienced' hiker. "Then we take on the mountain."

"Not with me you won't," Edie panted.

"Me either," Lea seconded. "This is good enough."

"What about the rest of you?" I asked.

"I'll go," said four-foot-ten Monsie who was from the mountains of Venezuela.

"Me too," said Phil and Michael nodded his head.

Two days later when Monsie reached the summit first, I said, "The oxygen level is higher closer to the ground."

"Really?" she asked.

I must have had a glint in my eye because Monsie continued, "Oh c'mon," and waved her hand.

Afterward, we drove through the Rockies and camped on the other side, visiting Mesa Verde, the Grand Canyon, Bryce and Zion; then on to Las Vegas.

Michael forgot he wore a Bowie knife for camping on his belt. When Michael and I went to the men's room, a guard with a gun conspicuous in a holster followed us.

"What's that on your belt?" he asked.

Michael turned red, and answered, "A Bowie knife."

"Registered?"

"N-no," Michael stammered.

"Then I have to ask you to leave."

"What!" I exclaimed.

"Right now," his beady eyes became beadier. We were evicted. Not just from the casino, but from the city! Here my companions and I were in the middle of the desert, and the casinos want to bring people in, not throw them out. I never visited Vegas, again. They don't need my business anyhow.

In California, Edie and I went south to visit Bobby and Vera in Los Angeles while the others continued north. Bobby wasn't home, so Vera took us to the LaBrea tar pits and a museum.

After L.A., it was on to Santa Barbara to visit Chris Shields. She took us to the beach in San Louis Obisbo, to see Spanish churches and a Marx Brothers film.

Edie and I spent a week at Big Sur where we played volleyball every day.

"Say, what's that smoke?" I asked from the courts as a cloud of it billowed into our campsite. We found out.

"Evacuate now!" a policeman bellowed through a bullhorn.

"What..."

"Now!"

So we left. There was a big fire and if you didn't want to get fried you had to leave quickly.

Edie and I visited with Kit Brira in Palo Alto. We needed to decide if we wanted to go back to the boycott. If "yes," we would return to the East. Where our parents and others were.

"I think I'm pregnant,' Edie announced. "I've missed a period."

"The union will pay for your delivery."

"Let's go back."

It was settled.

In Nevada, we needed to buy a new tire. After that, Edie and I didn't have enough money for motels, so we drove straight through and slept in the car, making it across the country in less than three days. The battery went dead and we didn't dare turn off the car because it would never start again.

Edie and I reached Philadelphia and her parents. I guess they were glad to see us. She was pregnant; I had no visible means of support; and we were both radicals. What more could anybody want?

Marcos was now head coordinator in New York. I quit being *El Jefe* of the Jersey boycott when I married. When I returned from the second honeymoon, Marcos put me to work organizing in Greenwich Village. We lived in Jersey City at the boycott house, and I rode the PATH train every morning under the Hudson River, past the World Trade Center into New York City.

There were many of us who did. The first person paid, and then shifted the turnstile halfway so those following got a free ride. Others passed through as if they paid, avoiding the arm, so it stayed midway and did not lock.

One morning, the last person was Jack Easley, the priest.

"And WHAT are you doing?" asked a cop from the shadows. "I can't believe my eyes," he continued as he emerged from the dark. "And you a man of the cloth."

"Let me explain."

The burly cop raised his hand for silence. It was obvious he had trouble deciding what to do. "I'm gonna let you off with a warning because of your collar," the cop finally blurted. "But don't let it happen again." He walked away, shaking his head and muttering, "Thought I'd seen everything. Guess not."

My companions and I were human billboards in the mornings, going to wherever there were crowds, usually the train stations.

Penn Station has a steep escalator, maybe three stories high. "Farm workers are dying in the fields to pick your vegetables!" we shouted from the top of the stairs.

At first, the commuters wanted to get off. But, where could they go? The escalator ascended toward us. By the end of the week, the commuters were smiling at us.

Cesar came to town in a caravan that traveled across the country. He gave a speech at Riverside Church and another one at St. John the Divine where Coretta Scott King was in attendance. Cesar's brother, Richard, traveled with him and was his bodyguard. There was a bomb scare. Richard appointed all the boycotters, including me, and some of the supporters, to be additional bodyguards for Cesar. I took the job seriously.

I'll get the bomber.

I could hear the themes of *The Man from U.N.C.L.E.* and *Mission Impossible* playing in my head. Without any tools or weapons, I was going to be a bodyguard.

I was assigned to follow a member of Cesar's entourage who carried a briefcase and couldn't be identified as the person he pretended to be. When the prospective bomber made a phone call, I positioned myself so I could read the numbers. He saw me.

"Listen, you know why I'm here," I began. "Why don't we get something to eat?"

"Okay," he replied.

We went to a local diner, away from the church where Cesar was speaking.

After the meal, I realized I didn't have any money.

"Can you pay for my meal?" I suggested as if it were his idea. What a bodyguard I was! After he disgustedly picked up the bill, "Now, can you open the briefcase?" There was no bomb in it. We parted ways.

Back at the church, Geraldo Rivera wanted to interview Cesar.

"You can't because there has been a bomb threat," I said.

"Don't you know who I am?" he asked. I should have replied, "No. Don't you?" That would have been a blow to his ego. Alas, I didn't, instead I was diplomatic.

"I can identify you, but not your video and audio men. Sorry, it's not going to happen. Not on my watch!"

Geraldo left probably wondering who the jerk was.

"Increase the number of boycotters!" Cesar pronounced into the microphone from the podium.

I interpreted that to mean to take people in off the streets. I invited a man in and Marcos made me sleep on the floor next to the couch where the homeless person slept.

In the morning, the man awakened early and made himself breakfast. One of the burners on the oven didn't work right. He turned it on; the burner wouldn't ignite, and the man forgot to turn it off. Then, he left.

When I arose, I lit a cigarette.

CABOOM!

The oven exploded! I was thrown heavily against the wall.

Marcos laughed at me.

"I could've been killed!" I exclaimed.

Marcos laughed harder.

That ended the experiment taking in people.

God certainly watched over me that morning. He must have been like Marcos.

On Election Day, 1972, I was arrested for the third time. Marcos and I went to Harlem to distribute leaflets about McGovern to the people going in to vote. There were signs about a hundred feet away from the booth. It was illegal to hand out literature within them. But, inside the poll was a picture of Nixon! That was definitely illegal!

"You can't have a picture in a voting booth," Marcos said to the policeman attendant.

The cop was angry with **us**! He responded by moving the signs further away to the middle of the block. That meant we would have to move. Who wanted to get arrested for McGovern, anyhow?

"Take down the picture," Marcos demanded.

Again the policeman moved the signs, this time to the corner.

I intended to move again, but Marcos insisted, "Take the picture down, now!"

"I don't have to listen to a wetback!" the policeman shouted.

Marcos saw red.

Now, I had a choice. I could move and abandon Marcos, or I could join him. I picked the latter.

We were arrested and spent the day in jail until the polls closed. Then, miraculously we were released.

All during that period, Edie carried our baby. We went to Planned Parenthood figuring the pregnancy should be planned.

"We need some help," I began.

"Here for an abortion?" the secretary asked without looking up.

"An abortion!" I exclaimed. "We want no such thing!"

Edie and I didn't want to wipe the baby from her lap, so we never returned to Planned Parenthood. Instead, Edie and I took La Maz classes at the La Leche League. They were new at the time. My mouth was drier than hers.

On the day she went into labor, the doorbell rang. I opened the door to two cops.

"What do you want?" I asked pleasantly.

"Does Joe Thek live here?" one of the policemen replied.

"That's me," I tried to be helpful.

"You're under arrest."

"What!" All I could think of was Edie in labor behind me. "Why are you here?" I asked brusquely.

"You've got unpaid parking tickets from June," one policeman informed me.

This was the end of January. "Wait a minute! I wasn't even in the state in June!"

"But your car was."

Then I remembered I loaned my car to Larry Hawley when I left on my second honeymoon. He ran up parking tickets on the car registered to me. I subsequently learned that Larry didn't believe in paying parking tickets. He parked next to hydrants or faced it the wrong way, anywhere to save a few steps. One thing wrong, however, Larry forgot to inform me of this belief. Now, I had Edie in labor with two cops on my doorstep trying to arrest me.

"Can I pay tomorrow?" I asked. After they learned about Edie, they replied, "Yes."

I drove Edie to the Margaret Hague Hospital. A nurse came out after examining her.

"She's in false labor and got a shot of Scopolamine. She has been discharged to home."

Everything was all right, for a while. Then, Edie asked, "Are there spiders on the wall?"

"No. Why?"

"'Cause I'm seeing some."

That did it. I took her back to the Hague where they wouldn't allow me in because I was a man. Edie was admitted, and I went home to sleep. It had been a long day for everybody.

The phone awakened me at five A.M.

"Hello?"

"Congratulations!" a female voice emanated from the receiver. "You're the father of a bouncing baby boy."

"What!" I exclaimed, but she had hung up.

It was not false labor after all. Edie delivered Joshua

during the night. She is completely Jewish. In her tradition, the parents cannot name a baby after someone living, but they can take his or her first initial. That's where the "J" comes from.

It was February 1st, the same birthday as Suellen's. Joshua had long fingernails and black hair. He had the cutest little smile. The war in Vietnam ended a couple of days before he was born. It was time to celebrate!

The hospital wouldn't let me stay, so I went to a scheduled shop-in at A&P headquarters after paying the parking tickets. Marcos dressed up like Santa Claus.

"Ho, ho, ho," Marcos said. "And here's a balloon for you."

He handed out helium-inflated balloons to the children at the doorway of an A&P grocery store adjacent to their headquarters. We had talcum powder ready for the new baby so we dropped some inside each balloon the day before. They read "Boycott A&P" on the outside.

When the children went into the store, eventually, they let go of the balloons, which floated to the store's ceiling. The manager couldn't very well leave balloons saying, "Boycott A&P," in an A&P store. He ascended a ladder with a needle to bust them.

"I'll get those picketers," he muttered from the ladder.

When the balloons burst, the talcum powder inside sprayed all over his face until he resembled a mime.

We conducted a shop-in. The destruction of food didn't bother us; after all, children were destroyed in the fields every day. It was a questionable tactic.

After a meeting with the bigwigs in A&P, they agreed to sell only union lettuce. We won and it was the right time to leave the boycott because I was burned out. And, now, we had a son.

My Child

Where will you be
When I am gone?
What will become of you?
Have I taught you
All that you need
To make your dreams come true?

I have tried
Going sightseeing,
Places you wanted to go.
To make you see
The universe,
To teach all you could know.

If I've failed
In the trying
To reveal what is true,
I'm just a fool
Who was blinded
By my own point of view.

JOSEPH C. THEK, MD

Wisdom and truth
Really do exist,
Although I've led astray.
I may not know
Where they are now
You'll find them your own way.

Of all the things
You have learned,
Of all you've understood.
It's certainly
Good to be wise,
But wiser to be good.

My child, you see,
I'll be leaving,
You can be on your own.
Please don't forget
All of our talks
Or the seeds we have sown,
They just need love
To be full-grown.

*Please remember when I am gone
There is Someone Who gave His Son.

*This verse added later.

Chapter Six
COLLEGE LIFE

I had a son. Everything changed. Before, I could be carefree, only answering for Edie and myself. Now, I had additional responsibilities. Another life dependent on you can do that. I should have felt the Hand of God in my life, but stubbornly, I didn't.

I lacked money and the future was questionable.

What potential do I have? Being a young Saul Alinsky can't support a family. I have to change.

While reading Somerset Maugham's *Of Human Bondage,* I was impressed.

Now Philip is a real hero. He realizes that his painting will never support him, so he becomes a doctor. Not a bad idea. That way, he can make a living **and** *help others.*

When I reflect upon it now, I'm sure God was looking over my shoulder the whole time. I wasn't reading the Bible, so God influenced me through Somerset Maugham.

My alternatives were medicine and law: both provided a career while I raised a family.

So what if I have no experience in either? I'll get in law or medical school some way. After all, I spent three years with the farm workers. Anything is possible! If I choose medicine, then I can use my science credits. I don't have a lot of time. Medicine it is!

Watergate was in the news. Nixon was getting his comeuppance. We were glued to the TV and the Senate hearings. I should not have been. God has everything in His powerful hands and there is no need to worry. That understanding came to me many years later. To show you how caught up with this world I was, on the night Nixon resigned I celebrated.

Now I think of life as a long lesson. The test follows on Judgment Day. I pray I pass or else I will join Nixon.

We are all called to repentance. It's throughout the Bible. In the Old Testament, please see Jonah 3:7-10. For the New Testament, please read Matthew 3:1-2 and Luke 13:1-5.

The message today is the same as it was then. Will we ever listen?

Edie and I quit the farm workers, and we moved in with my parents. She was twenty and I twenty-three. I enrolled on the final day in Paterson State College. Another day and I would've missed the whole semester. Coincidence? I think not.

Up until then, Paterson State was a teachers college. It

had a pre-med program and was cheap. It cost three hundred and seventy-five dollars for my third year because half of the tuition was paid for by scholarship.

Living with my parents lasted a couple of months. We lived upstairs in my old bedroom.

Jap, the dad of a good supporter of the union, Wayne Rutley, was a chef at a local catering place that did weddings and big parties. He offered me a job. Mostly, I cut tomatoes, stuffed capons, scooped ice cream, loaded the dishwasher, or scrubbed pots and pans.

Jap and I were the only kitchen staff who spoke English. The waiters were Iranian, and the kitchen helpers were from China and Poland. The Chinese went down to the Passaic River and stared into the water, then, with a quick motion, put a hand in the moving water to catch a fish.

They lived above the kitchen and were paid off the books. Leo, the owner, fought with them about overtime all the time. He made out like a bandit.

Orientals, Iranians, Poles, Americans—we are all people. I think we need God to point that out.

Leo became angry, and maced the Chinese.

"I get you!" one exclaimed and went after him with a kitchen knife.

Jap intervened. Throwing up his hands to halt the Chinaman, he courageously barked, "Whoa! Put that down before someone gets hurt!"

The boss didn't know how close he was to going to Hell.

I hated Leo. Any possible way, we would get revenge. I took home milk for Josh. Leo caught me because I was not a good thief. I remembered something Dad claimed. "If you steal a little, you're a worker. If you steal a lot, you're an owner."

I quit. Working in the steaming kitchen was grueling. It made the summer weather seem cool.

I needed money, so, I started caddying again. The greens' crew hired me to dig ditches. There is always a need for a strong back and a healthy constitution. Eventually, I became the water boy.

Being a caddy and a greens keeper had its advantages. If a golfer angered me, the next day I put the hole near the crest of a hill in the early morning while I cut the green. When I caddied afterward, I chuckled to myself as the golfer missed the hole and the ball rolled down the hill.

"Look where the greens keeper put the hole!" cursed the golfer. "If I get my hands of him I'll wring his neck! Now I'm gonna four putt! This isn't miniature golf!"

Don't mess with me.

I didn't act like a Christian then. Old habits like "an eye for an eye" are hard to overcome. It must have been difficult for the Jews who followed Christ. We all have to try daily.

When it was hot, I drove a sprinkler cart down the middle of the fairway. If a golfer had irked me the day before, I watered the hole ahead of him. If the golfer wanted a decent score he had to play in water. If he really riled me, I preceded him around the whole course. I'd sprinkle one hole at a time, so his whole day was spent playing in water. I was not one to get angry but looking back now it wasn't a Christian thing to do. We are all sinners, saved by grace.

Once, at about eight at night on my twenty-fifth birthday, I had to remove the sprinklers from the ninth hole before dark. It was on a slight upgrade, so I climbed out and let the cart roll to me to save time. The wheels turned and I was pinned between the sprinkler head and the cart. There I was at dusk, in the middle of the fairway, with the water still running.

At first, I laughed. Then I realized no one would find me until morning.

"Help!" I yelled repeatedly.

About nine **o'clock** (Time must be Irish), someone at a party in the clubhouse heard me screaming. It could have been much worse. I was trapped for about an hour. After I was released, I turned off the sprinklers and went home.

It **was** worse there. Dad trimmed the bushes in front of the house earlier in the day. This is his story in his words.

"'Say, do you wanna borrow my electric hedge-cutter?' Mr. Ross (a neighbor) asked when he saw I was struggling."

"'Sure,' I answered. *Now how does it work?* I wondered."

"When I started to cut, suddenly the power went out. *What happened?* I looked. I hadn't cut just the bushes but the cord too! Mr. Ross was not too pleased when I returned it."

"That's not all," Mom interjected. "I backed the car into the one across the street. Nobody got hurt."

Now you know from whom I get my expertise!

Edie and I knew a Margot Hummer in Weehawken. She was a supporter of the farm workers, ran a Peace Center and a boarding house too. We moved into it. From there, I could commute to school.

When I started at Paterson State (now it was called William Paterson College), the instructors didn't know what to make of me. I was an unknown: in pre-med and a transfer from NCE from three and a half years earlier.

I was unconventional. A bee flew into the organic chemistry lab. The other students yelled, "Kill it! Kill it!"

"Wait!" I interrupted.

I placed a Styrofoam cup over the bee. Then, I put a piece of cardboard over the mouth of the cup. Now that I had the insect captured, I went to the window, set the cup outside, and let it go.

Afterwards, I had a new lab partner, called Joe Robistelli. Through Joe, I met Dominic Ruffalo. He was taking Organic too, but more importantly, lived in West New York near Weehawken. We could drive together.

On the first day, Dominic and I were supposed to have an Organic quiz. He picked me up in his sister's Volkswagen beetle. It snowed. Dominic took the back roads. He lost control and the car slid down a hill.

"Are you hurt?" he asked after we hit another car and we stopped.

"Nope."

Dominic and I missed the Organic quiz.

Maybe I should commute with someone else. But the accident wasn't his fault. It could've happened to anybody.

The decision to stay led to a long relationship with him. He was in pre-med too. Dominic, born in Genoa, emigrated to the U.S. when he was nine, learned Spanish before English, and became my good friend.

Dominic was a year behind me in college. His girlfriend, Aracely Sanchez, was born in Cuba. Every date was chaperoned, mostly by her older sister, even after they were engaged. Theirs was a whole different world.

Through Dom, I met "Funny" George Castano.

George's uncle was serving time in a prison as a hit man for the Mafia. The Castano family still admired him, even in prison.

When George went to Europe, he bought a motorcycle and toured the countryside there.

"Where is Canada?" a traveler asked him.

"I'm not sure," George replied even though it is only one state away from Rutherford, New Jersey, where he lived. That ignorance inspired him to want to be pre-med.

I accompanied George, Tommy Thek, Michael Ventra, and Dave Triolo, to New Hampshire.

Oh great! Tommy and Dave again! What will it be this time?

We stopped at a lean-to near the timberline. A return to Mount Washington in November was a second chance for me, although we climbed the other side now, away from the wind. I remembered how the mountain beat us. Johnny thought he was smart staying home.

George put on his backpack at the lean-to near the base of Tuckerman's Ravine.

"What are you doing?" I asked nonchalantly.

"I'm going up," he replied pointing at the immense wall of rock.

"Up there? It's steep and dangerous."

"Want to practice hiking." He ascended like it was just a trip around the block.

Dave owned an Eddie Bauer sleeping bag, which could withstand the elements.

"I don't need an Eddie Bauer," Tommy began. "It's not that cold."

Here we go!

"And it isn't raining," Tommy continued. "Or snowing."

"All right, all right! We'll see who needs it when it is," Dave retorted.

"This is the Northeast, not the Rockies," Tommy smirked. "Besides, we're in a lean-to."

"Are you forgetting our last trip?" I asked.

"That was then. This is now," he answered like that somehow made sense.

Tommy continued to jibe him. I don't think Dave slept that night because of it, Eddie Bauer or not.

In the morning, we climbed the mountain, and then returned to the camp.

"Let's go into town," I remarked.

"And break camp?" George asked.

"Yeah. We could get a motel room for the night," I continued undaunted.

"Really communing with Nature," Dave scoffed. "No thanks. I'm tired. I'd rather stay right here."

"Besides, you have nothing to be afraid of with your Eddie Bauer," Tommy ridiculed.

"Laugh if you want," Dave replied. "At least I'm prepared."

"And I'm not?" Tommy shouted.

Better defuse this situation. Things could get ugly.

I rose and started to walk.

Turning toward me, Dave asked, "Where are you going?"

"Into Conway, you can stay here if you want."

George and Dave camped again under the stars. A bit romantic. They made me want to stick a finger down my throat.

Tommy, Michael and I, had enough of roughing it. We hiked to the bottom and stayed in a motel in Conway. The three of us visited several fast food restaurants because we couldn't decide what to eat; so, Tommy, Michael and I, chose everything. We were non-discriminating. (Speaking of eating, Dad was afraid to sit next to Johnny at the dinner table.

"Why won't you sit next to Johnny?" I asked one night.
"He might eat my arm.")

George and I became good friends in spite of the camping trip.

In the summer of 1971, while I was with the union, Tommy and I paddled down the Delaware River from Callicoon. Johnny and Dave were in the other canoe and we all camped in Narrowsburg.

"C'mon! We can beat them," Tommy urged.

For some reason, I agreed. We raced but who cared? Tommy and I should have enjoyed the river and the peaceful clear waters. Instead, we sped over them in the vain attempt to beat Johnny and Dave!

Life is like that too. We rush through it. Why? Shouldn't we slow down and observe all the things God created?

When it was over, Tommy drove me home in his sports car. He did ninety in the hills by High Point. Like I said, we were stupid. Who knew any better? Not us!

We also camped in the Adirondacks. One time, our group climbed Mt. Colden. We hiked a well-marked trail. There were seven of us including Johnny and Tommy.

We met campers on the path.

"There's a shortcut up," the leader stated.

Since the trail was boring, we were all ears. I should have known better.

"You can bushwhack up the Dike," he claimed.

I still don't know what "bushwhack" means, and I wish I didn't know about the "The Dike".

It's a dry waterfall that splits two cliffs rising about fifteen hundred feet out of Lake Colden. We went around the lake, on ladders and wooden planks extending from the rocks. After the water, the seven of us zigzagged through the underbrush until we arrived at the base of "The Dike."

We started climbing, without ropes, hand over hand. If someone fell, he would take along whoever was behind him. My friends and I looked for crevices in the rock for handgrips. After fifty feet of climbing, I asked, "How do we get down?"

"We don't," Johnny replied.

I looked down. That was a big mistake. I got dizzy.

"Cut the crap!" Johnny commanded. "Don't look down!"

I realized there was no returning and the only way left was to continue upward. Johnny laughed his maniacal laugh as if defying the gods. It echoed down the valley, bouncing off the cliffs. I was angry, but proceeded.

As we climbed, the incline became more recessed. To the left and right of us were walls of stone, with cliffs on their other side. I didn't look down again.

Finally, we made it back to the trail. I could see why the path avoids "The Dike." Only stupid people climb it.

We went on another trip in the spring of 1973. Johnny was a teacher by then, so, he took ten students from his school with him. We were supposed to meet Tommy and two of his friends at the campsite.

One of the kids had an accident driving to the Adirondacks. The car flipped and landed in a bog. No one was hurt, but the car couldn't be used. We were forced to decide: either cancel the trip or rent a Ryder truck and put all of the students with me, in the rear.

Since Tommy was waiting, and everyone wanted to go to the mountains anyway, we decided to rent the truck.

Johnny drove with his two friends sitting with him. I was in the back, in the dark, with the kids and gear. Once the door came down, those in the back were shut off from the outside world. I was happy that there were no claustrophobics in the group.

Johnny stopped for gas. He forgot how high the truck was and hit the overhead fluorescent light of the gas station. The light, an upright "T," was bent, so it formed a "J."

"Say, what are you doing, kid?" the irate gas station owner asked.

"Sorry," Johnny answered.

The owner was mollified, a little.

On the way out, Johnny hit a mailbox. In the back, all we heard was CHPLUNK. We didn't know what to expect. Perhaps it was better that all of us couldn't see.

We met Tommy, and his two friends, at the campsite near a raging river.

"You're late," Tommy said.

"Wait 'til I tell you how we got here," I replied. "It's lucky we made it at all."

Luck? Our angels were looking out for us.

The next day, the ascent began. Our path was supposed to take us on the long route, around Lakes Colden and Algonquin, up the Opalescent (the headwaters of the Hudson River), past Lake Tear of the Cloud, to Mount Marcy.

That was the plan. When we were on the wooden planks, around Lake Colden, The Dike came into view.

"Say! Why don't we go up it?" Johnny suggested.

"With the kids?" I asked.

"They have to grow up someday. Might as well be today."

"Are you crazy?"

"Come on, it would save time."

"Not if someone gets killed it won't. Let's go around it."

"Are you chicken?"

"Darn right I am. After yesterday I thought you'd be worried about safety."

There is a saying in Japan that all men climb Mt. Fuji once. Only fools climb it twice. I didn't want to be a dead fool. The hike to Mt. Marcy continued. It was a good thing because Johnny never bothered to send home permission slips, as I discovered later. Wasn't that nice? The kids were in our hands, and the Adirondacks will never be the same. Everything considered I don't know who was worse, the kids or we.

Near Lake Algonquin, one of the students noticed that I fastened my pants with string, not with a belt. I secured it that way because, at the time, I was a vegetarian and didn't use animal products. Tommy tied his with string because it was cheaper. Johnny wasn't wearing a belt.

One of the kids asked me, "Mr. Thek, why do you hold up your pants with string?"

This was a perfect opportunity to fool them. Without missing a beat, I turned to Johnny, "You mean, you didn't tell them?"

Without an eye blink, he struck his head with his hand, and replied, "No, I forgot."

It was my turn to concoct a story. "Because bears smell leather," I answered.

"Oh," the student replied apprehensively.

The trek continued. It was muddy and cold.

"There's a Carvel ice cream parlor at the top," Johnny told the kids and they kept climbing.

"Wonder why they keep falling behind," he said while scratching his beard.

The adults made it to the top. Then, we looked down at the kids climbing and noticed their pants were dirty. When they got to the top, I asked one boy, "Why are your pants caked with mud?"

"I didn't want the bears to smell it, so I threw my belt into the woods. My pants kept falling down."

"Hey, there's no Carvel up here," another student realized.

"They must have moved it," I retorted.

"Yeah, to Indian Falls," Johnny agreed. "It's on the way down." The students believed him, and I thought I was gullible!

That night, for some reason the ranger put on a bearskin. There must be some kind of ranger school where you learn to dress up like an animal. He was on all fours and scared the kids. Two of them were black, and so was the night. They ran into the camp. All you could see were the whites of their eyes rolling around.

The black students thought he was a bear smelling leather. Before I could stop them, they threw their wallets into the river! Be careful what you say; somebody might listen!

I stared into our fire, fell asleep and dreamed of something I read about the final attempt to rebuild the Temple in 361 A.D. Later, I went back to books to find this passage by Will Durant in *The Age of Faith* pp. 347-48. Julian is Julian the Apostate, a nephew of Constantine who was Roman emperor from 361-363 A.D. and an enemy of Christianity. There is no greater testimony than one of a foe (speaking of Durant, no matter how inadvertent it was).

From these afflictions the Jews were saved for a moment by the accession of Julian. He reduced their taxes, revoked discriminatory laws, lauded Hebrew charity, and acknowledged Yahweh as "a great god." He asked Jewish leaders why they had abandoned animal sacrifice; when they replied that their law did not permit this except in the Temple at Jerusalem, he ordered that the Temple should be rebuilt with state funds. Jerusalem was again opened to the Jews; they flocked in from every quarter of Palestine, from every province of the Empire; men, women, and children gave their labor to the rebuilding, their savings and jewelry to the furnishing, of the new Temple; we can imagine the happiness of a people who for three centuries had prayed for this day (361). But as the foundations was being dug, flames burst from the ground, and burnt several workmen to death. The work was patiently resumed, but a repetition of the phenomenon—probably due to the explosion of natural gas (according to the author)—interrupted and discouraged the enterprise. The Christians (Were they really Christ-like?) *rejoiced at what seemed a divine prohibition; the Jews marveled and mourned. Then came Julian's sudden death; state funds were withdrawn, the old restrictive laws were re-enacted and made more severe and the Jews, again excluded from Jerusalem, returned to their villages, their poverty and their prayers.*

I find it curious that Durant doesn't mention that the Temple was built twice before and no problem with natural gas was noted.

Contrast this secular account with what the Bible states happened to Nadab and Abihu (sons of Aaron who were offering unauthorized fire to the Lord). (Please read Leviticus 10:2.)

Interesting.

Dominic wanted me to major in biology. He joined its club, was even on the Biology basketball team. One time, the game was close with a couple seconds to play. The ball came to him. No one was around, and he shot.

Swish!

What a shot! Nothing but net!

The problem being it was the wrong basket! Dominic scored two points for the other team and they won!

I majored in chemistry with a minor in biology. Dominic eventually switched to it, too. I received all A's the first semester. I transferred from NCE with a cumulative average of 3.18. Now, it was over 3.3.

I began to study for the MCATs to be accepted into medical school. While I was in college, Edie made outlines of the books I read. I even took a course to improve my grades.

On the morning of the test, the other students were nervous, but I wasn't. I had a son and couldn't afford to be. I moved away from them. Their anxiety could be contagious. I know now that God was behind me.

The MCATs were like the SATs except there were four parts; English, History, Science, and Math.

The scores for each of the four were based on a perfect eight hundred. Anything above five hundred was good. When my scores came back, my low was five hundred sixty for Science (I hadn't taken all of the courses yet), and my high was seven hundred ten in Math.

Suddenly, I was a celebrity and everyone wanted to know me, even teachers who were aloof before. They *wanted* me in medical school. I would take a flagging pre-med program that never before placed anyone in medical school, and deliver it, by myself.

I applied, concentrating on schools in or near New Jersey, since the reciprocity with other states was poor.

We were still living at Margot's. One of her tenants, Hannah Manson, was on the third floor and she had several annoying habits, like leaving her alarm clock set. I was in the kitchen on the first floor when her radio blasted away at six in the evening. Hannah wasn't home yet from work to shut it off; so I climbed the stairs to the third floor. After several trips, I tired of hearing it.

Ill get her!

I threw the alarm clock out of the window: a factual case of seeing time fly.

I was eating my lunch at work one afternoon when I noticed something amiss in the Oreos.

What's this?

The creamy white centers were missing! Hannah ate them and then put the brown tops and bottoms together to hide it! When she left, there was no love lost.

The Kobels, (Lee, Tamara, and son, Daniel) replaced her. Before, they had rented the farm where Edie and I were married.

The Kobels were good people. When Lee came down with Job's syndrome (staph boils all over his body),

Tamara never complained. She kept on being Tamara and raised their son.

Margot drove an old Volkswagen beetle with bumper stickers covering it.

"They're holding up your car," I claimed.

One time, Margot stopped to pick up a hitchhiker in New Jersey on the way to her farmhouse in upstate New York. He was unusual, in his fifties, slightly older than she. The hitchhiker wore checkered pants that didn't match his checked shirt. He was going to tell jokes at Eddy's farm, not far from where she was going.

The conversation turned to the bumper stickers on her car. "I have a nephew who boycotts lettuce," the hitchhiker commented.

He was my Uncle Ray—younger brother of Dad's!

Uncle Ray was an athlete. He went to grammar school with Hugh Carey, future governor of New York. Uncle Ray received a basketball scholarship to Princeton where he met Brendan Byrne, who became governor of New Jersey. Uncle Ray was in both the New York City police and fire departments.

He was drafted into the army and was in the Battle of the Bulge. His squad was cut off from the other Americans. Bullets started to fly, so, they jumped into a foxhole. A potato masher, a grenade, landed in it. Uncle Ray dove on top of the sergeant to save his life. The potato masher rolled under the officer. It exploded killing the sergeant, but Uncle Ray was unscathed. In effect, he saved himself at the expense of another.

Uncle Ray was never the same. He drank. When we received phone calls from local jails, Dad retrieved him.

"I went to school with two governors and was in the New York Police and the New York Fire Department," Uncle Ray bragged after being booked one night.

They stuffed his head into a toilet and flushed it because the police didn't believe him. Every word was true. Well, almost, he could exaggerate a wee mite.

Our basement was the dumping ground for all his junk. "Someday it will sell," he tried to convince us. It never did.

Once, on Long Island, Dad was driving with Uncle John, his oldest brother, and Uncle Ray in the car. We were in the back going to see Uncle Pete, Aunt Henrietta and Tommy. *En route*, Uncle John had a coughing spell because he suffered from emphysema.

Dad stopped alongside the highway.

"Better get out and put your arms on top of the car," Dad suggested.

Uncle Ray, who got out of the car first to let Uncle John move past him, took his own wallet out to see how much money he had.

A passing cop stopped.

"Freeze!" he shouted while he pulled his gun from his holster and pointed it at Uncle Ray.

"What's going on?" Uncle Ray asked as he spread-eagled.

"You're not gonna rob this man!" the cop yelled.

"Rob him! I was doing no such thing! He's my brother!"

I envisioned bailing him out of some dark and dingy Long Island jail.

Finally, Uncle John stopped coughing long enough to verify the truth of Uncle Ray's statement.

Like I said, Uncle Ray was an athlete. One time, we were playing golf and Uncle Ray pulled out his driver on the fifth tee. There were trees to the right of it. When he hit, the ball struck one of the trunks squarely and bounced back toward him. Uncle Ray caught it in his bare hand and teed up the ball again. In one motion, like he expected it to happen, he teed up and hit the ball again. This time, it soared down the middle of the fairway. How can you penalize someone after that?

Uncle Ray didn't have any visible means of support—a real vagrant. Edie was sure Uncle Ray worked for the CIA. Pretty good cover if he did.

One of his friends died naming him executor of the will. How could someone expect him to settle anything? A pop-up tent on top of a small trailer was involved. It resided beside our garage. Uncle Ray certainly didn't have any place to store it.

Then, he died in a car crash near Suffern, N.Y. Dad was devastated; it's the second time I saw him cry. Dad became the executor of Uncle Ray's will. He had been driving drunk. They don't mix. No one else was hurt.

At the funeral, a woman named Betty appeared. We

discovered that Uncle Ray lived with her for a long time. He was driving her car the night of the accident. Dad conferred with my Uncle Pete. They decided to give her the money, what little there was, to compensate for his death. Uncle Ray would have liked that.

God has a special consideration for orphans, widows and foreigners. (Please read Deuteronomy 10:18-19 and John 19:26-27.)
In effect, Betty was Uncle Ray's widow. Dad just did what was right for her. I never forgot it.

I wanted to get my own place. Margot's was nice, but there was no telling when another Hannah could move in.
When Dominic's tenants moved out of the first story, Gilda, his older sister, moved from the basement apartment in his house, to the first floor with her children. That left the basement empty, and we moved into it. I was in my senior year at William Paterson, waiting for a response to my application to medical school.
I met Dominic's maternal grandfather, Mr. Macaluso. He was a crossing guard for the local school children. During World War II, Mr. Macaluso piloted his own boat. He was sunk in the Mediterranean three times; twice by the English, and once by the Germans, after they became enemies. I don't know how the grandfather survived with everybody shooting at him. I guess Mr. Macaluso could swim.

Dominic's dad was born here, in Carteret, New Jersey. Mr. Ruffalo ran from a card game where someone was killed. The cops nabbed him. He was deported as an undesirable to Italy, even though Mr. Ruffalo was a native of this country. Back then it didn't matter.

Mr. Ruffalo liked Mussolini. I couldn't say derogatory things about the dictator in his presence, even though the man died thirty years before.

Dominic told me the story of hunting with his dad. "My father, being small, insisted I cover him with leaves and leave him in a ditch. I did. He says he saw something brown go by so he shot at it thinking it was a deer. But it wasn't a deer. It was a cow! Dad had to pay the farmer for it. I think we'll be eating hamburger for awhile."

The basement apartment was small: three rooms, besides the kitchen and bathroom. In one of them, we put a foam rubber mattress on the floor. It wouldn't fit if the door were shut.

Josh stayed in another, which gave us a living room in the third. They were cozy. At least that's how Edie and I defined them.

The boiler room was adjacent to the apartment. I studied in there because it was quiet, once you grew accustomed to the furnace noise. Dominic and I brought a cat home from Comparative Anatomy lab to dissect and worked in the boiler room. Formaldehyde smell filled the air.

Mr. Ruffalo burst in very agitated. He yelled something in Italian.

Dominic yelled back also in Italian.

Mr. Ruffalo then screamed at his son.

I looked at Dominic quizzically. Then they talked in the foreign tongue for a while. Finally, Mr. Ruffalo left.

"What was that all about?" I asked as we went back to work.

"Dad thought we killed the neighbor's cat, and were dissecting it in his boiler room!"

We laughed, but that man was dangerous.

In my senior year, I mainly took chemistry and biology courses with Dominic. Once, in Inorganic lab, Dominic and I mixed the solutions for *aqua regia* backwards.

Dr. Ryerson, our Inorganic Chemistry professor, erupted into the room. "Get out, now!" he shouted.

Once outside, we asked, "Why?"

"Because you liberated chlorine gas, you dimwits! The whole building was evacuated!"

In the winter, I tutored. I also went to the unemployment office to see if I could collect partial benefits because greens keeping was a summer job.

"I'm a full-time student," I explained to the clerk "But I'll be rehired in the spring. Can I get partial unemployment benefits?"

"Let's see," the lady began pulling up my work record from her database. "You worked too many hours for partial unemployment."

"Well, it was worth a try," I answered dejectedly as I turned to go.

"I'm sorry," she continued without raising her head. "It will have to be full benefits instead."

"What!" I exclaimed turning back to her.

"Yup. Full unemployment. No doubt about it."

I didn't argue any more. It was more than I had expected. That winter, Edie, Josh and I lived like royalty.

In the spring, I went with Dominic on a canoe trip through the cranberry bogs of the Pine Barrens in South Jersey. It was truly a land time forgot. I lived in New Jersey most of my life and never heard of the Pine Barrens. I fell in love with the quiet, peaceful rivers that flowed through it.

Once in Comparative Anatomy class, I burped. It was loud enough for Dr. Rosenberry, the professor, to stop writing on the blackboard and turn around. The whole class, then, swiveled to stare. They gaped at me, but I turned around to stare at Dominic sitting quietly behind me, minding his own business. He didn't know why the other students were eyeing him. It was Kafkaesque! I was off the hook because they blamed Dominic. So much for minding your own business!

I thought my application to medical school would be improved if I volunteered for an ambulance. Dominic and I did and worked nights.

Sergio Sergovis from Cyprus joined us. We played *Risk* until the early hours of the morning, or until he attacked Dominic, whichever came first. Usually, they occurred jointly. Sergio loved to attack Dominic and I knew it.

"He's getting ready to attack you," I instigated.

"I am not," Dominic defended himself. "Just building up. Don't want to be attacked."

"Then move back a country," Sergio said.

"And let you come in. No way!"

"I dare you to invade him," I whispered to Sergio.

That was all that was needed. Sergio and Dominic rolled the dice for a half-hour. Armies collapsed. He couldn't resist. I sat back and watched. Sergio wasn't going to sit by and let another European, win. I, as an American, was okay. I just laughed, and won.

The papers arrived for an interview in Newark and a second one at Rutgers. I was excited, never having been to one before, but I was confident.

At Newark, a black doctor asked me, "Why do you want to be a doctor?"

With my eyes downcast, I replied, "I want to help people. I've been on the farms of America. It's a nightmare. Young mothers can't afford day care for their babies so they take them out in the fields and put them under the reeds to protect them from the sun. They are forced economically to leave them there unattended.

"Then, the thresher goes through, cutting the reeds. Eight babies were killed like that. I think there is a better way." For a moment I thought I was back on the boycott.

I looked up. He was crying. At the time, I knew I was in. God must have been listening too. I meant every word of it. Whether or not I got into medical school was not the point; the truth was.

At Rutgers, a student interviewed me.

"You might be one hundred-ten this year," she explained, "and only one hundred-eight will be accepted. If you reapply next year, the admission team would take that into consideration and you might be placed below the cut-off."

What I heard her saying was to try again.

Without anything to lose, I told her everything. The interview went well after that. The fact that a student interviewed me never crossed my mind.

I applied to seven out-of-state schools, but never received an interview. I guess the reciprocity between states came into play.

I received word in the mail that I was accepted to medical school; first at Newark, then at Rutgers. I was surprised I was approved there; I expected a rejection. Shows you how much I knew. God watched over me even then.

I needed to choose but the pick was easy.

I've had enough of city life. It's no place to raise a family.

So, I chose Rutgers. The college was in rural Piscataway. It was, to me, a country setting with grass, trees, and a golf course. I could attend school there and live nearby with my burgeoning family.

In the meantime, Edie was working in the office for the

farm workers again. She took Josh with her. I expected to work for them too, once I completed my residency. After all, I would be thirty-two someday anyway, right?

Chapter Seven
MEDICAL SCHOOL AND THE SHELTER

I wanted to resolve some issues with Val before I entered medical school. The summer of '75 provided the opportunity.

I went to her old house where her mother opened the door. "What are you doing here?"

"I've come to talk with Valerie."

"Let sleeping dogs lie."

Val was inside listening. "Let him in."

I entered and we talked. Val had errands to run so I tagged along. She married on the same day I had; our problem was to different people. Val had a child named Amy, around Josh's age. I wanted to straighten some things out and found they were more crooked when I left.

"I'll see you sometime," I reassured her.

"Sure."

I left with Edie and our son for New Brunswick (close to the school) in the summer of 1975. Edie worked for the farm workers again and someone was needed to occupy the two-story union house.

We planned that I bike to school, thereby staying in shape, while Edie use the car when she needed it.

It may have worked, too, except for thieves. One night, when I was on the first floor watching the Mets get no-hit, I heard a noise in the bathroom upstairs. The fire escape ran to its window. Edie was in the kitchen near me, but Josh was asleep in his second floor room.

I went to the steps and shouted, "Take anything, but leave my son alone! I will stay here!"

After a while, I climbed the stairs carrying a hammer as a weapon. I decided it was not a good time to discuss nonviolent tactics. Edie followed closely behind me. We saw two sets of footprints in the bathtub. It was a good thing that I stayed downstairs. God knew what He was doing.

Edie and I went to make sure Josh was safe. He slept without a care in the world. The thieves left him alone.

We continued to our room. Edie looked around and noted, "Everything they took was already broken. Maybe when they learn this they'll get angry and come back."

"They're certainly not pros. We were in the house! We could've run into them. Probably on drugs. There's no telling what they'll do."

The next day, I boarded the windows to the fire escape. No one was going to invade my house again!

This is no way to live!

Fear is crippling, worse than being beaten or even death.

Then, we invited Wayne Rutley and Lisa Noel for dinner.

"There's no room for us at either of our homes," Wayne complained. "What do you think if you shared a house with us?"

"That might work," I thought of getting my family away from the thieves. Besides, after my experience with the farm workers union, I was an expert in communal living. Wayne was studying law and couldn't afford his own house.

Edie and I moved again, this time to Bridgewater. The large two-storied country house had three bedrooms, one and a half baths and a basement suitable for my reading purposes.

Entering medical school was scary for me: I would be with students from Ivy League Schools. I was just somebody trying to get along. I wore a chip on my shoulder; out to prove to them I belonged.

I discovered an indoor basketball court there.

I don't know how, but I'm gonna get on it.

Over a hundred students packed the lectures. You screamed to ask a question. The yelling served two purposes: one, to be heard; and two, to get the instructor's attention.

This ain't for me.

Each lecture was taped. Different people were

responsible for typing each lesson so there were legible notes for all topics presented. The school owned a mimeograph machine, which I knew how to use from working with the farm workers union. The other students didn't.

"Look, you need a printer familiar with the mimeograph machine. Otherwise, it could get broken," I told the school administrators.

They eventually agreed and chose me as the printer. I collected the typewritten notes, mimeographed, and distributed them. Soon, I didn't attend lecture hall, but shot hoops in the gym instead.

Monday through Friday is not enough time to dissect the cadaver. I have to work on the weekends too to get some things done.

When a big dissection occurred, several students shared the body, combining two tables. When the skull needed to be opened, the others became queasy.

"Give me the drill," I said with bravado. *I'll show those Ivy Leaguers how it's done.* So, I took the drill and exposed the brain thinking I was striking a blow for the little guy. Shows you how stupid I was. God didn't let me get sick and for that I'm grateful.

In Physiology lab, I argued with the instructor about using mice. "Wouldn't a film be enough?"

"No!" she refuted my protests. "You must see it."

"Why? So the mice have to die a painful death?"

"I don't think it can be appreciated any other way."

"That's bull!" I stormed.

She slammed down her notebook on a counter top. "Listen! It's the way we do it and so will you!"

She was a professor; I was a student. The experiment went ahead as planned.

The papers from the note-taking service, of which I was now in charge, needed to be available before the tests. So, I hired a tempestuous apprentice, named Rick Hernandez. He was from Fifty-ninth Street, in the same block as Dominic, via Cuba. We became good friends.

We started a basketball league. I wanted Rick on my team. That started a minor brouhaha.

The blacks wanted their own team. One of them, John Fontana was excellent. Because the court was small, John could shoot as soon as the ball came in.

Six-feet-five Alan Kellen and Larry Sawyer, who was also over six feet, were on my team, which was good too.

The Bakke case was big in the news then. He was refused admission to medical school because Bakke was thirty-two years old. He sued, protesting that the rejection was because of his white color.

I had mixed feelings about it. On one hand, I saw what affirmative action and quotas could do. It was supposed to insure that the inner city would have doctors when the students returned. However, the blacks in our college were not from New Jersey. The students who were Afro-American with good grades were off at Harvard or Texas, not Rutgers. To fulfill the quota, other sources were tapped. They even had an African prince. I doubt he would set foot in the inner city let alone set up practice there.

However, affirmative action also increased class size. Rutgers was a small medical school with student numbers in the teens before state aid. With affirmative action, the number ballooned to around a hundred. That way, the state school could accommodate the twenty percent black students, and the whites too. In effect, the white student population went from the teens to eighty. I would not have been accepted into medical school if it weren't for affirmative action. I was left in the middle. I just want justice to be done.

We won the basketball title. White men can jump!

One night, I received a phone call from my brother Johnny. "I got the math teacher's job in New Mexico," he bragged.

"Great!"

Then Johnny related his story. "I wore my only suit on the way to the interview. On the way there, I became low on gas and stopped. In New Jersey there's always an attendant to pump gas. Not in New Mexico. There you pump it yourself. So, I did. At least, I tried.

"I got out and pumped the gas but I spilled a good amount on my suit.

"Driving to Los Alamos, it stunk. I opened all the windows, hoping the air would evaporate the gas smell.

"When I got to Los Alamos, the principal insisted on interviewing me.

"He sniffed. 'Do you smell gas?'

"'No,' I lied. Of course I smelt it!

"'Must be coming from construction workers outside.'

"He rose from his desk to close the windows. It got worse. Then, the principal took out a cigar and was about to light it when I jumped up.

"'Don't light that match!' I screamed. Well, now I had to tell him the whole story.

"'That's a good one!' the principal laughed. He told everyone in the school and I got the job."

Edie went to work because finances at home were tight. I thought it was temporary; everything turned out quite differently. Her job was at a youth shelter, placing disturbed kids. She met Vicki Gurki, a fellow worker, and Wayne and Sue Durban, the house parents who lived there all the time. Sue had a son, Jonathan, from a previous marriage, who was a year older than Josh. They became good buddies.

At the Christmas party, I met one of The Shelter kids, fifteen-year-old Jimmy.

I didn't want Edie to work because that meant I was not providing for her and Josh. I could either quit school and get a job, or do what I was doing. I thought she would follow my lead. How was I to know I would follow hers?

Vicki became director. The shelter moved, but it

needed a permanent place. Over the summer of 1976, I looked for work and took a job running recreation at the shelter. Now I would get paid for playing basketball! I thought I was in Heaven!

The Gnostics thought they knew things. Much publicity has been made recently about *The Gospel of Judas*. It was found in the '70's. My initial reaction is, "Why is it coming to light now?" (2007)

Further study indicates it was written in 300 AD and copied from an original Greek text 140 years **after** Jesus and Judas died (which means about 170 AD). So originally it was part of the Gnostic gospels.

Several thoughts: the Bible is God's Word. If He wanted *The Gospel of Judas* to be included in the Bible, He would have done so. Are we not casting doubt on His power?

It is claimed that early church leaders found *The Gospel of Judas* heretical "because of its disagreement with the conventionally accepted gospels of Matthew, Mark, Luke and John." (article in The Los Angeles Times by Thomas H. Maugh II in April of 2006) Those gospels were completed by 100 AD. Maybe they were believed because they were true. The Gnostics had their own axes to grind with plenty of time to do it. Why should anyone believe them? Judas, obviously, didn't write it. A Gnostic did—someone who didn't even acknowledge his real name on it. It is like comparing eyewitness accounts of Abraham Lincoln's assassination with a politically correct version written today. Which one would you believe?

Although, sometimes, an unbiased, far-removed opinion is what you need. (Gibbons and Toynbee come to mind) The Gnostics were definitely not that. The closest we can come to that is Luke. He is the only non-Jewish writer in the New Testament and an historian. He never knew Jesus and his accumulation of the facts is compelling.

Satan is a liar. (Please read John 8:44, then continue on in John 13:23-27 where Jesus tells the apostles that someone would betray Him.)

Early church fathers didn't decide the contents of the Bible, regardless of what they thought or what any article claims. God Himself did. To say we wrote It misses the mark completely.

Our local newspaper (The Daily Sun) claims that Judas "...turned him (sp.?) over to authorities only because Jesus asked him to,..." To be crucified? Why does Jesus ask the Father to take this cup away from Him three times in the Garden of Gethsemane? Why the Crucifixion where Jesus cries out to the Father (Please read Matthew 27:46 echoing Psalm 22:1.)

The crucifixion, the central point of Christianity, isn't even mentioned in *The Gospel of Judas*. It would be laughable except that many will be fooled by it.

My job was different from everyone's because I was funded from SETA, a government agency. I worked at the shelter under the new director, but the purse strings were controlled in Trenton.

We do a lot of strange things for money. I tithe, but not because the Old Testament says we should. Beginning with Abraham it's laced throughout the Old Testament. (Please read Genesis 14:18-20.)

Tithing is really an Old Testament law, but we are no longer under the law. (Please read Romans 6:14.)

No, I don't tithe because I have to. I tithe because I want to. It is pleasing to God. (Please read 2 Cor. 9:7.)

Plant seeds and God will water them. And, please notice that It says "giver" not "tither."

Just to confuse you, there is Matthew 5:17 which seems to indicate that Old Testament laws are to be obeyed.

So I tithe.

Vicki liked to play basketball and challenged me to games. She was around six feet tall and a starter on her college team. No offense to women who play, but Vicki couldn't keep up with me. Maybe she liked to lose.

I needed cash, so Vicki assigned me as an umpire in her women's softball league. I thought I knew the rules. In one game, they played the prison team and the other umpire called in sick. So, I worked behind the plate calling the game by myself. The prison team took the field first. When the first pitch was hurled, it was so fast that I thought it might hit me. I ducked.

"Stree-ike!" I called, again upright. I figured since the ball was thrown so hard, it must have gone over the plate.

Besides, it was against the prison team. I didn't want to argue with them.

"Ump, you need glasses," the batter hissed under her breath, not looking at me.

I acted like I hadn't heard and let the matter drop.

Living with Wayne Rutley and Lisa Noel didn't work. Nobody's fault, just two couples with different agendas. Edie and I relocated to Somerville.

The three-bedroom garage-less apartment was basically the second story of a house: not as big as the previous house, but the apartment was adequate. A stairway ran up the front, and a spiral one in the back. I studied in a small attic cubicle.

We lived around the corner from Somerset hospital. I volunteered in the family clinic that summer. I even wrote an article about patient satisfaction (or dissatisfaction depending upon your point of view). The apartment was closer to school and the shelter, with a Carvel ice cream stand nearby. But, I was still a commuter.

An office building stood next door. Whenever I locked myself out, which was often, I climbed the tree between it and our living quarters, jumped off the tree onto the roof of the second story. I opened the window, and *voila*, I was in the kitchen! Easy, wasn't it? Mountain climbing came in handy.

Edie was pregnant when we moved and in October, Jeremiah was born. Now, we had two boys.

When Jeremiah was a toddler, all of us went to the Red Shanty reunion—a yearly gathering of friends. We played volleyball and I enjoyed the game. My son's little ball accidentally went below the sandbox. He tried to retrieve it, but it rolled next to a beehive.

As a dad, I couldn't let him go near it, could I? My reaction was to lift him and the bees stung me before I had a chance to think. I demand the line of Hamlet be read, "To bee, or not to bee." I was stung thirteen times. Maybe it was bad luck, I don't know. I see the Devil's work in that conclusion. Please remember that thirteen people were at The Last Supper.

Jeremiah escaped injury, while my legs ballooned. Thank the Lord, I'm not allergic to bees. I wonder if any of them are allergic to us.

Dominic stayed in pre-med at William Paterson. He debated whether to go to osteopathic school, or to become an M.D. Dominic described to me the interview at the osteopathic school in Philadelphia.

"Do you speak Spanish?" The interviewer examined his credentials.

"Yes."

"You're in."

So much for being an M.D.

The second year, I no longer had a chip on my shoulder; I was just another student who wanted to pass.

I remained in charge of the note-taking service. That year, I didn't attend a single lecture. It was a waste of precious time but I read diligently. I took the school tests and passed with high grades, buttressing my habit of not attending lectures.

My parents gave us a Dodge Swinger. Edie drove to work in the Nova, and I went to school in the other car. Josh rode with me to the Day Care Center, while she took Jeremiah with her.

On our way there, I taught him the alphabet. "**F**' for **f**ence."

"**F**-**f**ence" he replied **f**rom his car seat.

It was **f**un to see Josh progress.

The government tested our medical knowledge three times. The first exam was following the second year and lasted two days. I prepared for it all year long. I passed, then, I entered the third year, which was practical experience in the hospitals.

We were called "Roads Scholars" because Rutgers didn't have a teaching hospital. The students commuted to a hospital where the instructor lectured us after we saw the patients. It influenced our second year when we had to choose where to go for each rotation (Medicine, Surgery, Pediatrics, Gynecology, and Psychiatry). Each hospital was noted for something different. I needed a partner and chose Rick.

I juggled being a husband and dad with medical school, trying to keep the two lives separate. If not one, then the other would rear its head. It wasn't easy for either Edie or me. We were always busy.

I kept my job and worked nights or weekends at "The Shelter," as it was called. The children became "Shelter kids." Mostly, they were teenagers from broken families, or in which one parent was sick. All of us tried to give them love. That's what they needed, not jail.

That summer, Edie and I took our boys (Jeremiah was less than a year old and still crawling) and went with Larry Hawley, his wife, Kathy, and their daughter, Jessica, to Bear Mountain. We rented two cabins by a lake. A mother, and her five-year-old, Byron, occupied the next cabin. I taped gumdrops to a tree deep in the forest, where it couldn't be seen from the cabins.

Cupping my hand next to my ear, I claimed, "I just heard a squirrel speak."

At first, Josh and Byron were suspicious. They had never seen or heard of a talking squirrel.

"Must be a leprechaun," I continued. "He told me there was a gumdrop tree to be found."

With that Josh and Byron ran into the forest to eat the candy. They saw the tape glistening and ran to the tree. They began to stuff their mouths with gumdrops.

"You have to plant one for next year!" I called.

They did quickly and then ate the remainder.

Larry took Josh and me with his daughter out in a rented boat on the lake. It was fun to watch him play with his beard when he wasn't rowing around the peaceful lake. What a beautiful place!

Larry had a temper. "I was driving once along a divided highway. It was winter, so I was wearing a ski mask. Kathy and I had a fight. I got so mad at her I pulled off the road onto the shoulder. When I did, I threw my ski mask at her, crossed over the highway divider, and hitchhiked the other way. Kathy didn't wait long but took off with the car.

"Soon someone stopped to pick me up. A while later, there was a police car in front telling us to pull over and another behind. I wondered what the driver did.

"'Get out of the car now! And put your hands up!' a cop yelled.

"So, we did. I thought this guy must be a real wise guy.

"'Why did you throw your ski mask away?' the cop asked.

"'What?'

"'A bank was just robbed. We thought you did it?'

"I started to laugh.

"'And what are you laughing at?'

"'What kind of a bank robber hitchhikes for a getaway?'

"'A stupid one. Maybe you.'

"'Oh brother.'

"I explained about the fight with Kathy. They let us get back in the car. After a few miles, I noticed that the driver was trembling. He pulled off the highway again and said, 'Get out! I never want to see you again!'"

I rocked the boat with laughter.

I arranged to see Val at her apartment. Who knows why I kept going back. Perhaps I liked misery.

"I almost died from a burst appendix," she confessed after we exchanged a few pleasantries. Flabbergasted, I didn't know what to say.

"I have another child, Matt. He's in the playpen, now." It was difficult to realize I was not the dad.

She and I went together to the basement for something. We were alone. Val was beautiful in her cut-off jeans. I felt like kissing her, but struggled to stop myself. Oh, Satan was having a field day that day!

"George is working late," she said. "Why don't you stay for dinner?"

"Okay, but then I have to go."

She smiled and cooked some spaghetti.

I didn't know then I would not see her again for fourteen years.

The Shelter moved again: this time to a house in the middle of the community: perfect for us. Four bedrooms were upstairs with a TV room at the end of a long hallway between them. We could watch the kids from there. Next to it was a bathroom. The fire escape was outside one of the female's bedroom windows.

I was responsible for teaching birth control to the kids.

"You take Birth Control Pills each day for one month," I began.

A hand in the back shot up, "Ya' mean ya' don't put 'em in?"

"Put them in? Where?"

"Ya' know, down below on the night you have sex."

I could see this was not going to be easy.

The neighbors didn't want us and I don't blame them. Who wants a bunch of teenagers living next to them? But, where were they to go? They weren't juvenile delinquents.

I was responsible for taking them on hikes. On one, I concocted a story. "It was right here," I stood at the top of a cliff. "I had the kids out hiking, like today. One of them fell over the cliff and lost his arm. It was replaced by a claw. We called him 'Jack the Claw'."

"Oh come on," someone snorted.

"Really! I swear."

The seed was sown. When a stranger stopped by the mailbox for a moment one day, I exclaimed, "It's him! It's 'Jack the Claw'!"

It didn't matter who he was. Wayne and I couldn't let an opportunity slip by to insist it was 'Jack the Claw'. Whenever something was missing, it was blamed on him.

Wayne and I rigged up a hanger near the girls' window, a string tied to the bottom. We attached the free end of the string to the bathroom window. By pulling on it a certain way, the hanger clattered against the window of the girls' bedroom without our being seen.

One night as the females were going to bed, I went into the bathroom, tugged the string, and it rattled the hanger against their window.

"What was that?" they screamed.

"It's 'Jack the Claw' on the fire escape!" I shouted.

More screams.

Wayne, on the first floor, clanged noisily up the fire escape, and ripped off the hanger.

"I just saw a man running away. I think it was 'Jack the Claw'."

There was no sleep that night.

We had a big, blue van for the teens. On a clear, wintry night with the moon shining on the snow, I took them for a ride through the nearby Duke Estate.

That's odd. The bushes moved.

I stopped. So did they. I started again, and the bushes did also.

What's going on?

My curiosity piqued, I parked and emerged from the vehicle. There were hundreds of hoof prints in the snow.

Deer? Where?

I was amazed, but crossed the road to learn why the branches moved. As I neared, I realized they weren't bushes at all, but antlers! I stumbled upon a herd of deer, maybe a hundred. If they spooked in any way or ran at me, I was a goner. I respectfully retraced my steps silently in the snow.

Another time, I wanted to remove my desk from my parents' house. I needed the van and some boys to get it, but if I informed my mother too early she would cook a meal for all of us. I didn't want that, so I waited until we were ready to leave, giving her about a half hour notice.

"Mom, this is Joseph. I'm coming with six kids for my desk. Don't cook."

When I walked through the door, Mom sat at the dining room table across from Dad. Between them, was a plate of twenty-one hamburgers!

"We were just sitting down for lunch," she smiled. "Do you want to join us?"

I don't know how Mom did it. I threw up my hands in surrender.

I should have looked for The First Principle, for the meaning of life. Sometimes we get so caught up in minutia that we miss The Big Picture. Whatever we chase will not make us happy. Solomon was correct in Ecc. 1:9.

Without God in our lives, we struggle to accumulate as much as we can. Frank Capra was right too; "You can't take it with you."

Jimmy was placed in a group home. He hated it and ran away. I discovered him asleep on my front stairs.

"Where are you going?" I was half-asleep, too.

Awakening, he yawned, "Greenwich Village."

"Why don't you come in here?"

He did and gladly never left.

Now, we had three boys

My third year, I drove to the hospitals. The first rotation was Internal Medicine. I spent six weeks at Raritan Hospital and then at Hunterdon Hospital for another six.

The first six at Raritan were awful. An upper level resident there exploited my ignorance. He made himself look good at my expense. Some residents even made fun of my accent.

Petty! If this is what it's like, I should quit.

Rick convinced me to stay.

Then, I went to Hunterdon.

If it's the same, I'll quit.

But Hunterdon was more laid back and more my style.

Hospitals are not constructed like houses. Parts were built at different times. To go from one tower to the other, we took a shortcut across the intervening roof. It was like a deck on a ship, flat, easy to walk on, but high above the ground.

Edie and I put Jimmy in a special high school for his senior year. Sometimes, he would lock himself out and climb the tree, also.

Jimmy often sat on the County Courthouse steps whenever it was sunny. One time, the police brought him home for smoking marijuana. Another time, he held up placards from one to ten whenever women passed. Jimmy was not too bright.

"What are you doing?" I stormed.

"It was meant as a joke."

"This is not some Olympics!" I slammed his door.

I took him and his friend to see the waterfalls at Child's State Park in Pennsylvania. On the way home, a state trooper stopped our car because it looked suspicious to him.

The policeman asked Jimmy, who was not driving, "Do you have any ID?" A normal person would answer, "No, I don't." Not he. Jimmy removed a picture from his wallet with no printing on it, and pointed to it, "That's me." The next thing I knew, I was spread eagled with my arms on the roof of the car while the Statey frisked me. I never took Jimmy to the park again.

Then the winter of '77–'78 came with its three big snowstorms. For the second and third, I was stranded and slept at the hospital for a few days. Residents skied to work. On the highways, the entrance ramps were plowed, but not the exits. You could enter, but not exit. Entire cities were closed.

We built an igloo in our backyard and used it as a slide. I poured water on the igloo, to convert the snow into ice that lasted all winter.

Edie had to go to work one morning. I shoveled the driveway, but the plow came by and blocked her in with new snow. She gunned the engine of the Nova and went through anyway. It was like going through a ring of fire at a circus. White powder went everywhere. The starter came off, but Edie drove on.

That winter was a turning point for me. Hunterdon was like an oasis in the desert. The residents and doctors were friendly. I did my rotations for six weeks of medicine and surgery (the other six were at Raritan) there, as well as eight weeks both of gynecology and psychiatry. The twelve weeks of Pediatrics at Muhlenberg with Dr. Palore completed my third year.

During the gynecological rotation, I lost my wedding ring when I was scrubbing for surgery. I lathered my arms, removed the ring, and put it in the greens I wore, and then forgot about it.

After the surgery, I changed to my work clothes. The laundry took the greens. It was too late. By the time I remembered; the ring was gone. Maybe it was an omen.

Today, I think a marriage is between a man and a woman and should last for life. I am not the best example, as you will see, but God intended it that way. (Please read Matthew 5:32; 19:6 and 19:9.)

According to God, there are no such things as "irreconcilable differences." I should have listened.

Rick met a nurse at Hunterdon. She lived on a farm where we often ate lunch. Even the cows seemed to be friendlier there.

In the spring, Larry Hawley had a car accident and was paralyzed from the nipples down. His thoracic spine broke at the fourth vertebrae. His ankles were fractured too. Larry would never use them again anyway, right? The doctors decided to repair the ankles on the morning after the accident anyway. I read his chart.

During the night, he exclaimed, "I can't breathe!"

"It's nothing," the nurse said and ignored him.

Larry died. Alone, I examined the initial chest x-ray in the basement. "He had a hemothorax!" I shouted to no one. How many other errors were covered up both in his case and others? "If they hadn't been so preoccupied with his broken ankles they would have seen it!" I agonized.

Even as a third-year medical student, I saw his chest was filling with blood. It turned out that the Azygous Vein was clipped when the thoracic spine broke. His death could have been avoided, and I knew it!

Thinking of Jessica, I urged Kathy, "You should sue them."

"Perhaps it's a blessing."

"But Larry was a cerebral person anyway. Even if he never walked again, he was still valuable."

"It's a blessing," she repeated and never sued. Larry was a classic case of missing the forest for the trees.

The ER should have picked it up.

Jimmy graduated from high school. I don't know how he did it: maybe with smoke and mirrors. After graduation, Jimmy moved to California but couldn't keep a job out there.

In my last year in medical school, my rotations were in doctors' offices. One of them was ENT, in the office building next to my apartment.

"Say you look familiar," the secretary commented while I waited. Later, she exclaimed, "I've got it! You live next door don't you?"

"As a matter of fact, I do. But how did you know?"

"Because I see you climbing the tree to get into the house."

So be good! A secretary may be watching! God always is. What a profound realization that is. Omnipresent. It boggles the mind. We are never alone. Everything we do is known. But then, I was just climbing trees, ignorant of any secretary, or Anyone, watching me.

The match, where you did your residency, occurred in the fourth year. It was similar to applying to medical school all over again. The student rated the hospitals he or she wanted to go to and the hospitals did the same. The match chose where you went. It was a lottery: one never knew where one was going. Interviews were conducted.

There weren't any ER residency programs in New Jersey at the time; I chose to interview in Pennsylvania and Ohio. Edie is from Philadelphia, so, that state looked good.

On one trip, I picked up two teens hitchhiking.

"Where are you going?" I asked as they climbed in.

"To the mall," one answered.

"It's cold," I noted. "Look, I don't need that coat back there and you will. Please take it."

They did as they emerged. Then they vanished. When I glanced to see where they had gone, I didn't see them.

Where did they go? Maybe down a side road I can't see from here.

Perhaps they weren't boys. I foolishly thought they were then, but now I think they were angels. Anyway, be careful to whom you offer rides. You never know who it might be.

Through the match, I was assigned a residency at Geisinger Medical Center, in Danville, Pennsylvania. It was the one I wanted. Geisinger was like Hunterdon, laid back, friendly. My ignorance would not be a joke there.

Lacking money, Jimmy hitchhiked across America in March, 1979. I received a call from him one night.

"I'm stuck," he told me.

"Where are you?"

"I'm in this awful rain on Route 81 on the Virginia-Pennsylvania border. The guy I'm with is from France. Can you come and pick us up?"

"I'll be there as soon as I can, but it will be at least a couple hours." As I hung up, I realized I didn't have a car that could make the trip.

I called Rick.

"Can you pick me up?" I explained what I had done.

"Sure."

One problem was traveling through Harrisburg. Three Mile Island had occurred then, and the area was evacuated.

Rick and I went anyway, stopping for gas near Three Mile Island. There was no one at the pumps and the station was closed.

"What do we do now?" he asked.

"Go until we find one open."

"We're almost on 'E' now. What happens if we run out of gas?"

"We turn into pumpkins. I don't know."

We were about to run out of gas when we found an open station and pulled in. If we stuck our hands out the window, the radio probably would have played.

Rick continued south on Route 81. When we saw the sign for Hagerstown, he exclaimed, "Wait a minute! There is no Pennsylvania-Virginia line!"

I examined the map. The two states don't border each other anywhere.

"Where is Jimmy? On the Virginia-West Virginia border, or the Pennsylvania-Maryland line?" Rick questioned.

"I don't know. Keep driving: maybe we'll find him."

"That's just great!" he replied angrily.

Rick and I passed the Maryland border: no Jimmy. We crossed the Maryland-West Virginia line; still no one. I visualized the smoke escaping from Rick's ears. He was like a firecracker. It started to rain.

Good! It will douse him when he explodes.

The rain grew heavier. On the Virginia border, I saw a guy standing and Rick stopped. "Do you speak French?" I asked.

"*Oui.*"

"Get in."

We found Jimmy trying to keep warm in a dry, donut shop.

"Well it's about time you showed up," Jimmy complained. "You're very late. I was just about to give up on you."

I thought Rick would punch him.

After that adventure, he rented an apartment with Chuck. Jimmy moved his things out of our house to his new place. He stayed in New Jersey when Edie and I moved to Pennsylvania. We were separated, for a few months.

I graduated in May. Edie had to leave the Shelter. Three and a half years is a long time. She had Jeremiah in that time, and we rented the apartment. Edie wanted to stay. I would have liked to, but it was time to move on to Geisinger and residency. Every new beginning is also an ending.

Chapter Eight
Residency

We went to Geisinger. Johnny, on his way to teach Air Force kids in Japan, helped us with the move.

Edie and I lived in a house on the grounds at Geisinger where I could take calls from home. There were eight houses in our unit. In the front was a big, shared, grassy area with trees along the side for the boys.

Bob Bagley, also an emergency medicine resident, lived behind us. He ate off his murdercycle, I mean motorcycle, in his kitchen.

"What are you doing?" I asked Bob the first day in the ER when he walked in on his hands.

"I want to show how flexible I am. My brother can do it and he's an astronaut. I just want to be like him."

"There has to be another way."

Bob left after the first year, leaving a spot open.

My second patient had a rhythm disturbance of his heart. He was okay when I saw him: no extra beats on his EKG and monitor. I ordered a digoxin level, and discharged him.

Later that day, I asked Mike Little, one of the attending physicians, "Say how long does it take for a digitalis level to come back?"

"Digitalis or digoxin?" was his response.

Oops! I'd made a mistake. This wasn't medical school where a mistake could be easily corrected.

"He's not on digoxin but on digitalis!" I exclaimed.

"Don't worry," Mike said trying to calm me. "Digitalis breaks down to digoxin and a level will work."

So, I waited until the next day when it was back.

The digoxin level returned high, so I called the patient. The daughter picked up the receiver.

"We would like to bring your father back," I began.

"So would I. He went to Bingo last night and died."

I felt like dying too.

"Thanks for calling."

She thinks I'm expressing my condolences. Maybe I should find a different line of work.

To whom could I admit my mistake? Not the family; they might sue (which is a condemnation of our society. The people to whom the doctors need to talk; they can't). One has to admit mistakes to be a good physician. A doctor is only human.

Should I stay or go?

Yes, I made errors, but I honestly tried to make the situation better. So, I stayed. I didn't realize God was in control. I probably gave Him a good laugh.

In my first year, I did rotations in medicine, surgery, pediatrics, orthopedics, and the ER.

There was a derogatory term, "Gomer," for abusers of the hospital. It stood for "Get Out of My Emergency Room."

I didn't like the term and thought it dehumanizing. Whenever somebody applied it, I took offense. I was an ombudsman, not an enemy.

When call was due, it was for the whole hospital, including the units. I was nicknamed "Black Cloud" because whenever I was on, disaster seemed to hit. It was better than "007", or "License to kill".

One night, all the surgical residents were tired and sleeping. The attending surgeon walked me through an appendectomy. It was experience. I did all right. The patient lived.

Dr. Ross, the head of the ER, saw many patients at a time. In medical school, I cared for of one case before I moved on to another. I was stuck in a linear mode. Simultaneous was new to me.

Dr. Ross loved to tell jokes and stories. One of them went back to when he was a resident. His wife had prepared a good meal and placed it on the table. "How is it?"

"I'm so tired, I could eat dog crap."

The next time he was on call, Dr. Ross came home to what he thought was a hamburger on a bun on his plate. When Dr. Ross ate it something about the hamburger wasn't quite right. "What was that anyway?"

"Dog crap," his wife answered calmly.

He never claimed to be tired again.

One of Dr. Ross' ideas was to have a departmental meeting every three months where all could air their complaints. It established the basis of a satisfied and happy ER. Taking care of the patients and their complaints was enough. We didn't need other problems too.

One of the attending doctors was John Skinsiewski, which we shortened to just plain "Skins."

Skins took me aside one day and whispered, "When I was a resident here I went out with Bob Norton from ophthalmology. We peed on some guy's lawn, and got arrested."

"What!"

"Just don't let it happen to you," he continued softly.

"What? Peeing on someone's lawn or getting arrested?"

Skins loved to bowl. Our team from the ER included most of the attending physicians, and some of the residents. It was a handicapped league from the hospital and included fifteen teams.

Geisinger is in the middle of nowhere. We provided our own entertainment and took bowling seriously.

The alley was halfway between Danville, where Geisinger was, and Bloomsburg. Across the highway, was Brady's bar, where we watered after the games.

One night, I was on call for surgery, which should have prevented me from going. Skins phoned and asked my upper level resident, Dr. Whiteman, "Do you like bowling?"

"I love it."

"The ER has a match tonight, but we're short one."

I saw the excitement in Dr. Whiteman's eyes. "I'm ready to go."

"No, not you. Joe Thek."

"I don't understand."

"Will you take his call, so he can bowl?"

There were priorities.

Priorities. I still thought death was the enemy, the number one priority. Early in my first year a lady was admitted for an ascending paralysis as a result of Guillain-Barre syndrome. She lost control of her ability to breath and we put her on a respirator. I was on call every third night and saw her struggling.

All during that fall and winter we attempted to wean her from the blower but met with little success. We gave the woman a small blackboard to hold in her lap for communication. Every morning, while being attached to the respirator, the lady wrote, "Let me die." We couldn't let her die so we carefully weaned her from the blower. At first, it was during the daytime for a few hours. Finally, the lady could go through the entire day without a respirator. On the first night after she was totally weaned, she died.

All that work for everybody, especially her, down the drain. Or was it? I learned that some things are worse than death and that not every death is premature. At least, I thought this. I realize now that it is never up to me or us but to Him.

That first year, the ER bowling team placed second. It became my job to recruit residents who were good bowlers. When I interviewed students for the upcoming residency, one of my questions was, "What's your bowling average?"

Invariably, the interviewees thought I was kidding. They put in all that time, survived medical school and now some jerk wanted to know their bowling averages.

I wasn't kidding.

If it's over 175, they're in automatically. If they can bowl that high they must be able to stitch.

Isn't it good to know your doctor can roll a strike?

On day shift, I earned my initiation with twenty-four-year old Elwood Digby. I went in to see him by myself. A transistor radio hung under his neck. "Why do you have that tied on?"

"It's my pacemaker. I'm here to have it checked."

I looked at his chart. Elwood claimed to be allergic to psychedelic eggs, soap operas, and Pennsylvania.

I was in the room alone with him. His pupils were like saucers. I didn't know what to do, so, I took the transistor radio off from around his neck. Then I dropped it, the transistor radio came apart in pieces. Elwood choked and turned blue.

This is not a good time to convince him it's not a pacemaker.

Dr. Ross entered the room. He picked up the pieces of the transistor radio, put them back together and placed the radio around Elwood's neck. The patient started to breath normally again and his color returned. Without saying a word, Dr. Ross left the room.

The night shift included nurses Mary "Ma" Washington and Linda Lutz. We had a large skeleton on wheels for instruction.

One night, I switched off the light in the bathroom. I made eyes out of little paper cups, and put them on the skeleton. Then, I put a cigarette in its mouth. I wheeled the skeleton into the unlit bathroom and waited for Linda to go. At about six, I heard her scream.

Dr. Ross became the vice president of the hospital and left the ER. Nobody could fill his shoes.

He cured Elwood's dad of impotence. Mr. Digby named his three sons after him.

"Curing him was my biggest mistake," Dr. Ross said.

When Edie and I went to Danville, Jimmy stayed in Somerville. He was nineteen now. Jobs in New Jersey (including one where Jimmy dressed up as a bee) didn't pay enough, so, he moved to Danville to his own apartment. Jimmy worked in the hospital as an orderly.

That first year of residency, that internship, was difficult especially when I was on call for surgery and internal medicine. When I was on rotations, I took it. That way, I knew the patients and why they were admitted.

I learned the human body, both models (thank God, there are only two). I saw many patients and became a good resident. The ER saw everything except penetrating trauma. It lacked a knife and gun club. There is only so much you can learn from books. I needed hands on experience as a teacher too. More on that later.

There were students under us. That's how I met Tom Major. He was two years behind me. Tom came over to my house during lunch many times. Both of us played guitars and sang songs we wrote.

The ER docs took melodies from the radio and gave them new words. They unveiled these songs at parties. Pretty soon, I acquired the knack also.

Love me, love me, love me I'm an administrator I wrote to the tune of Phil Ochs *Love me I'm a Liberal.* Somehow, the words got posted on the bulletin board. I thought I was going to get fired, but I was never discovered as the author.

There was a residents' union encompassing about one hundred and fifty doctors at Geisinger, in most disciplines. I went to the meetings every month. It was responsible for the moonlighting schedule. The residents did a lot of extra time because they didn't get paid much. With my background, I was a natural.

I started IVs because there was no IV team. All of us were called "scut boys". When I was on call, they beeped me on the pager if an IV infiltrated. I became good at beginning them. You had to be to eat.

There was a brouhaha about helicopters.

"We need one," Dr. Snow, the new director, demanded.

"Are you joking?"

Dr. Snow didn't laugh. "The residents will fly."

A new building was needed with a landing pad and an elevator to take the patient directly to the units. So, we moved out of the old ER too and built a new one.

Everything was going up: the helicopter, the new ER, the census. Geisinger modernized and lost something in the transition.

The new ER sported inside windows. The doctors now viewed the waiting room. Elwood's dad came with the other two of his sons beside him like bookends. He was about five feet eleven; they were big boys, about six feet five. The dad carried a jar filled with spiders. He plunked it on top of the counter.

"I want to know what kind of spiders these are."

I was sitting there reading. I lifted my head. "Are you talking to me?"

Mr. Digby nodded his head.

I looked at them. They were neither Brown Recluses nor Black Widows—the only two poisonous American spiders.

"I don't know what kind they are. Why do you want to know?"

"Because they're all over my house."

That doesn't surprise me.

"Don't worry, they're not poisonous."

"How do you know, if you don't know what kind they are?"

I was getting angry. Then, he lifted the jar off the counter, "Being the poison center I know you have books and you could look up the names of these spiders. Since you ain't, I'm gonna phone your boss, and get you fired."

"Be my guest."

With that, the dad turned around and went into the waiting room. The sons followed him like puppies. I could see him through the windows. He placed a call. His face went from anger to happiness. Then, the dad hung up the phone and returned to the ER.

"Dr. Ross knew what kind of spiders these were!" Mr. Digby lifted up the jar.

How did he know? Dr. Ross hasn't even seen them.

"What did he say?"

"Dr. Ross asked me one simple question. One, which you could've asked."

"What's that?"

"'Do they have wings?' I looked. I told him they didn't. He said, 'Then, they must be land spiders.'"

With that, he held the jar aloft and ran out the door yelling, "They're land spiders!"

The Miracle of Lake Placid occurred while I was at Geisinger. I was on call but managed to see some of the game on the TV in the residents' lounge.

When the U.S. beat the Russians, it was like the Mets of '69 all over again. Nobody expected it. An amateur team beat the pros. An analogy is Notre Dame beating the Super Bowl champ.

Miracle? Maybe. We make a lot of miracles and predictions. How about this one? The entire Bible, both New and Old Testament are filled with predictions, called prophecies, of the future. I am again amazed that God could mention Cyrus by name both in Isaiah 44:28 and again in Isaiah 45:1. Look it up! The Babylonians obviously did not or else they would have slaughtered all boys by the name of Cyrus. There it is in black and white. If that's not a miracle, then I don't know what the word means.

After my first year of residency, Edie and I moved from Geisinger's property to a house around the corner from the hospital.

It had two stories with eight rooms, but needed work. I painted the inside of the house with the help of a security guard named Joe Saint.

He gave us two big wooden tables. We kept the orange one downstairs in the dining area where we ate. The brown table stayed upstairs serving as a nice desk. I started writing again, something I hadn't done since my days with the farm workers.

The question of the existence of God arose again. My writing meant to answer it. I pray it does. He exists. We are not on our own amid what appeared to me a crazy universe. Then I didn't realize it. I thought we must muddle through on our own. Thank God, I was wrong.

The house was not weatherproofed. The owner and I blew in insulation one weekend. When the furnace broke in the middle of winter, I took hot showers at the ER every day. We borrowed a kerosene heater that was supposed to run clean, but didn't.

Edie converted part of the backyard into a garden. When the grass left behind grew too long, a neighbor told me, "There might be snakes in there!"

"Snakes? Where?"

"You'd better cut it."

That was enough. The next day, I bought a lawn mower.

There was a side porch and another in front with a fence along the street. The sidewalk was perfect for riding bicycles.

Jimmy rented an apartment near us.

After we moved, I entered my second year and directed interns to do the work. In the ER, Paul Lewis was one of the new residents. In the spring, I taught him how to hit a golf ball. I played chess with him too.

Paul could bowl. He taught me how to use a fingertip ball. As previously said, I stacked the team. Since it was a handicapped league, it didn't pay to win by a lot. You wanted a small winning margin. Early in the season low averages were established, also called sandbagging. That's how I started whirl-a-bowl.

"Watch this," I whispered to Paul.

We had already won.

"What are you doing?"

I started toward the alley normally, spun around once, and then rolled. The ball went in the gutter. The next time, it stayed on the alley, knocking down a few pins.

Not to be outdone, Paul rolled lefty.

Afterward, all of us visited Brady's. Paul liked to buy the drinks and watch others make fools of themselves. Naturally, I drank.

"Bet you can't drink a whole bottle of Tequila," he said to me.

"You're on."

A few hours later, I slurred from under the table, "Done!"

One of my second year rotations was in psychiatry. I went to the prison to interview some women who were purportedly on a fast.

The guard took me aside. "I think they're faking it.

Probably getting candy from the other prisoners. We need you to say they're crazy so we can give them water intravenously."

I saw two women.

"Why are you here?" I asked of two cachexic women, one white and one black with dreadlocks.

No answer.

"The sky is green today."

No answer.

I closed my notebook saying, "I'm wasting my time," and left the cell.

"They're whores of John Africa," the guard informed me. "They took over a building in Philadelphia. There was a shootout. Then the mayor ordered a bomb be dropped on the house. A fire resulted. The entire block went up in flames.

"On coming to prison, they refused to be tested for syphilis and TB. Hence, the so-called fast."

"They're not crazy, sociopathic maybe, but not nuts."

"You mean, we can't stick an IV in them?"

"No, you can't."

She, denied starting her IVs, was angry. Honestly, I didn't know who was crazier, the inmates or the guards.

Dominic came to Geisinger as a resident in Internal Medicine, a year behind me. He and I played poker at Dave (a resident in Pediatrics) Bain's house in the woods.

Brendon Nickel, another player, had some magic mushrooms. "Let's smoke these."

"What?" I replied. "Are you crazy? I might get a fungus in my lungs! Beer is enough."

Brendon gave a mushroom to Jim Reims, another player, and a resident in orthopedics. Jim got lost in the woods at four in the morning.

I don't know when public drunkenness became an ideal. It's an escape for anyone who believes that eat, drink and be merry is all there is to life. You want to flee from the suffering, the death, the seeming meaninglessness of it all. Why not go out and party for tomorrow who knows what will happen?

If you have no hope, as we didn't, then you take pleasure while you can and where you can. But that's a hollow philosophy, as I would find out. (Please read Luke 12:15-21.)

When on call, the food was free. You could eat whatever was there. It was pretty good for hospital food.

At the start of my second year, they placed me in the units with John Starsky as my intern. He was a big guy who ate everything. I mean EVERYTHING; even the crab shells that were stuffed. And fast! If you turned your head, he cleaned his plate. I swear Big John inhaled the food. The hospital passed a measure stating the residents could only eat a certain amount.

"It's the Starsky rule." I felt it was directed toward him.

Big John suffered a nervous breakdown. He was a patient in the psychiatric ward before coming to the units. Can you imagine, coming out of the hospital and being stuck with me as an upper level resident?

John lived in his car and flew an airplane. Despite that, he was all right. A little crazy, but hey, aren't we all? Big John fit right in, becoming one of the boys.

In the units, I became responsible for a young woman in her thirties, transferred from another hospital. We had no idea what was wrong with her but she was unconscious, on a respirator and her blood pressure was low (about 40). Everything shut down: her kidneys, her liver, her lungs. In other words, Anna was a train wreck.

She had a rash. Dr. Ayab, another resident, brought in an article about a new disease, Toxic Shock Syndrome (TSS). "This might be interesting. It fits her to a 'T'."

I read it. That was Anna all right. She had her period and was using tampons. Anna's hands peeled and her eyes suffered conjunctivitis. I learned then that the skin is an organ too. We often forget that and neglect our skin. Amid all the machines it was difficult to care for her.

I determined that she was not going to die on my shift. Every night I watched the monitors as Anna slowly improved. Finally, she was able to go home. Anna and I thought it was my work. Actually, Someone else was taking care of her all the time.

There is an adage in research medicine: "Publish or perish." So I wrote and published an article about my experience with Anna and TSS.

The residency increased to six people to accommodate the helicopter program. Flying became part of it. Because I was there before the chopper, it was my choice. I flew anyway.

The Susquehanna River was followed especially if it was foggy. The helicopter traveled so low it stopped at red lights.

When I was in the air at night, I couldn't tell up from down. The stars were above and below were the flickering lights of the countryside. They were sparse and looked like stars. The difference escaped me.

We were on call for the helicopter, and it was dispatched through us. I was working on New Year's Eve, a bad night for any ER. I got a frantic call from a paramedic to dispatch the whirlybird because someone fell down the basement stairs. Now, he was paralyzed.

There is something about a helicopter that makes a paramedic want to dispatch it. But the chopper is a two-way flight. First, the patient waits for its arrival; then he or she goes back to the hospital. If there is entrapment, or if the patient has to travel over fifty miles, the helicopter makes sense. Whirlybirds were designed for rural areas, not urban. If he or she can't be reached by car, then the patient should go by helicopter. Otherwise, an ambulance is quicker because it picks up and takes the patient to get definitive care. It's a one-way trip.

Try telling that to a Geisinger. The cost of having the whirlybird is enormous. There is the housing, the mechanic, the pilot, the flight nurses, the doctors, the special equipment etc. The hospital has a vested interest in hoping all patients can be flown.

I thought I recognized the address. "The man who fell down the stairs, is that Elwood Digby?"

A flabbergasted paramedic answered, "Yes."

"Then bring him in by ambulance."

When they arrived, he looked paralyzed. The paramedics put him on a litter. I stuck needles in his feet, but Elwood didn't move.

I was convinced he was faking it. So, I started an IV, ran it wide open, and waited.

Pretty soon, Elwood arose to urinate. Upon returning, he was paralyzed again. I kept him with four or five drunks overnight then he went home.

We recruited Dominic and Sal Amani from within Geisinger. Sal was an orthopedic resident and was well liked. Another recruit was Tim Bernard. He had a chicken that laid green eggs.

"Those would be good for St. Patrick's Day," I told him. Funny the things we remember.

When Tim went to Dartmouth, his wife stayed in California. I guess she didn't like him improving himself and desired a grease monkey. All of us have to make sacrifices to get where and what we want.

Sacrifice. (Please read John 3:16)

That the Son gave His life for **us** is truly amazing!

Edie and I took Dom and his wife, Aracely, bowling. Dom retrieved his ball at the return, swiveled, and rolled.

"Dom, get closer to the foul line and bowl off your left leg," I advised.

Dom still fired from the return.

"Closer to the foul line!"

Dom rolled from the ball return again. The ball went into the gutter. That wasn't bad enough. It was in the wrong alley!

"Hey, **YOUR** ball registered as a gutter ball on **MY** score!" the man on the next lane roared.

Oh boy! Better go before he hits Dom!

I never took them to the alley again.

I missed one meeting of the residents' union. While I was absent, they elected me president with Dominic as vice president. He was in charge of moonlighting and was called "The Don". He decided who went where and when.

Moonlighting was especially hard driving through snow and ice. All of us were tired, so we wanted twenty-four-hour shifts to make it worth our while.

Once, I was in St. Joe's ER in Hazelton atop a mountain, the highest city in Pennsylvania. It snowed all day, some nine inches. I gave up on relief arriving, knowing he had to drive up a big hill.

Phil Bocco not only made it; he was on time.

I became responsible for the residents' salaries, who flew on the helicopter, and for taking care of the nuns at St. Cyril's, a nearby Czech nunnery.

I negotiated for a raise at a time when money was tight. Skins was part of the group. "Shh! You've won."

I kept quiet (which was very, very hard).

Holding the tongue is very difficult. (Please read James 3:8.)

Yes, it is.

Deciding who flew on the helicopter was much more difficult than the salaries. Everybody wanted to fly. The obstetrical residents thought they should be with the babies; the pediatric residents thought they should be with the kids, etc. The room was in an uproar.

"Wait a minute!" Paul Lewis stood. We all turned to listen. "What about insurance if the helicopter goes down?"

The room became quiet. Now, no one wanted to fly.

There was an air crash involving a nearby helicopter. All five people, including the broken-hip patient, were killed. They should not have dispatched the chopper.

I was on one call where a boy severed his arm in a thresher. Our helicopter transported him to Johns Hopkins in Maryland where they could do the microsurgery needed to re-attach his arm. After dropping off him and his arm, the chopper re-fueled. My ears hurt badly. The helicopter doesn't have a pressurized cabin.

After the trip, I took the easy way out and quit flying. By the end of the summer, the boy was throwing a baseball again.

There were still the poor, old nuns. They paid far less than what a resident earned moonlighting in an ER, five dollars an hour compared to between twenty-five and thirty. Nobody wanted to care for them. I tried to convince Family Practice that it would be good experience, but they weren't interested. So, the responsibility fell to me. There I was, this agnostic doctor, taking care of Czech nuns.

God placed a nurse named Sister Leona there. She did everything. Sister Leona even waited until the morning before calling me to sign a death certificate.

In 1980, our daughter, Shannon, was born. Edie wouldn't let anyone but me start an IV. When she was in false labor, I took her home with a heparin lock to flush it. A few days later, Edie went into real labor and delivered. We finally had a girl!

My wife had her tubes tied. I nearly had a vasectomy instead, but God gave me a haunting dream about my Aunt Angie instead.

What about Eddie? What if I want another child?

I couldn't do it. We're not really in control anyway.

God is in the pilot seat and we are His co-pilots. I sometimes think that we would like Him to be **our** co-pilot. It doesn't work that way. He's the Boss. The Bible puts it this way. (Please read Isaiah 45:9 and Jeremiah 18:6.)

Edie and I agonized about Shannon's name. If she were a boy, we were set on the name 'Jordan'. He could join the 'J' club and it was Jewish. Edie and I figured if a boy could be named after a river, why not a girl? We considered 'Merced,' the name of the river at the base of Half Dome. But, neither of us is Spanish. After reading about how the Shannon River started (A teen-aged girl was told by both her parents to stay away from a certain well. She went anyway, fell in and died. The well gushed forth a river of water named 'Shannon'. At least, that's how I remember it.), we decided that was a good name. Her middle name is Kelly.

There wasn't any penetrating trauma in Danville. So, I went to Pittsburgh and the Center for Emergency Medicine. I met Bill Ranetsky there. He was a paramedic, a couple of years older than I, and liked to play chess. We became good friends.

Bill married twice, with two sons from his first marriage, Jason and David. They were about Josh and Jeremiah's age. His parents raised them.

I stayed at the University of Pittsburgh dormitory. Every night, I listened to Kool and the Gang's *Celebrate* overhead. I just wanted to sleep.

Penetrating trauma came through Mercy's and Presby's ERs. I discovered that Presby and Allegheny were at war over a helicopter. It sounded familiar. To get a whirlybird into the city, it landed at the Pitt football field, so, both hospitals wanted to build a heliport. Allegheny eventually got a chopper. When Presby acquired theirs, Allegheny got a second. I didn't want to get involved, especially after a helicopter crashed into the river.

Bill wanted me to teach a dog lab at the Center.

"This is how you intubate," I showed the paramedics. "To start a central line you do this," and I poked the dog with a needle and catheter. The adage was, "Watch one, do one, teach one."

I met Bill's parents. His grandfather was thrown out of the Communist Party for being too radical. Bill was unfortunately raised an atheist. He looked at it as fortunate.

Ronald Reagan, our new president, gave a speech on television. I didn't care for him as Governor of California and I certainly didn't like him as president. That's okay though, he probably didn't like me either.

I went on ambulance runs and met other paramedics. They invited me to bars where Bill hustled chess with the Pennsylvania state champ.

After the rotation in Pittsburgh, I went back to Geisinger and Edie. We were accustomed to taking separate vacations, so, my absence was not a hardship for her. At least, that was my rationalization.

I enjoyed my last year at Geisinger. Dominic served his second year with Sal Amani in Emergency Medicine. On March 15th, I called him. Ara answered. I stated, "Beware the Ides of March." She hung up. I didn't know they were having trouble with a peeping Tom. Ara thought he called.

On April 15th, I called again. The babysitter answered, "Mr. and Mrs. Ruffalo are out to dinner."

"This is Mr. Hochstetter with the IRS," I pretended. "Mr. Ruffalo is in a lot of trouble for cheating on his income tax. He'd better call me back."

And I left my number figuring Dominic would return the call and we'd have a good laugh.

What I didn't know was that the babysitter's dad was the accountant who did Dominic's taxes. She went home and reportedly cried, "Daddy, the IRS is after Mr Ruffalo!"

"What!"

When Dom came to work the next day, he looked worried. "The IRS is after me."

I kept quiet. I think Dom is still waiting for them to audit him.

On a helicopter flight, Tim Barnard did a particularly good job. The patient went to Williamsport Hospital where a neurosurgeon operated on him. Dom called Tim and pretended to be that brain surgeon. "You did velly bad job."

"What!" Tim exploded angrily. He ran into Dr. Ross in the hall who happened to be passing through.

"I just got off the phone with the neurosurgeron in Williamsport," Tim began. You could see the red face, hear the pressure of speech. "This guy is a real nut! He said I did a very bad job!" And Tim was off. He gave Dr. Ross an earful.

Dom and I approached them and Dom tugged on Tim's sleeve.

"Not now. I'm busy!" he said with some annoyance. "Now where was I? This hick surgeon..."

Again Dom tugged on Tim's sleeve. He pulled his arm away and said, "Get away, will you? Can't you see I'm talking?"

"But it was me," Dom whispered so only Tim and I heard.

He didn't understand and continued to berate the neurosurgeon. "He's a real jerk. If I could get my hands..." Suddenly in mid-sentence, the idea popped into his head that it wasn't the brain surgeon calling, but Dominic. Who knows what Dr. Ross thought? Maybe that Tim was maturing before his eyes and had the confidence to take jibes thrown at him. I wish that were true of all of us and we could listen to Christ and turn the other cheek.

Greg Cooney, another resident and I went to California ostensibly for a conference. Each year, the hospital sent the resident to a conference. It was an added perk. The real reason we went was for a vacation.

We signed in and Greg said, "I have a friend out here. Want to see him?

"Sure."

We rendezvoused with Greg's friend, Al, who showed us Oakland and Berkeley, where he lived. Al was a doctor who lived with roommates. "Want some grass?"

"Why not?" Greg answered.

And we smoked a joint.

"Say, want to go to the ballgame?"

Now any mention of baseball was an instant hit with me. "Sure."

He took us to the Oakland A's game against the White Sox.

The pitcher got hit with a batted baseball. Which team? I'm not sure. Who was winning? I didn't care. I had become both ignorant and apathetic.

"Should we run down on the field?" I asked. "After all, we are doctors."

While we hesitated the pitcher got up and wasn't hurt, eliminating the need.

After dropping Al off, Greg drove the rental car through Berkeley. *A Rocky Horror Picture Show* played at the cinema that night. The movie was just over and the audience was spilling into the street. In the crowd were boots, chains, and other paraphernalia. The pedestrians were dressed up to mirror the people on the screen.

"What's that?" Greg pointed to a man dressed totally in leather with a whip.

"Just ignore him and keep driving."

"This is plain crazy!"

"It's normal for California."

The next day we were off to Napa Valley for a wine tasting tour. Some of the wineries I banned were now serving free wine. Greg and I couldn't resist. The boycott was over anyway. I don't know how wine connoisseurs do it without getting drunk. By the end of the day, we certainly were a little tipsy.

"Want to go to Yosemite while we're in the neighborhood?" Greg asked.

I remembered the spectacular beauty of El Capitan and Half Dome from thirteen years before.

"It's better than any conference."

And we left for Yosemite. Greg and I climbed Half Dome again, taking the same route I took in 1969 to go up. Nothing was changed.

Greg and I climbed up and down Jacob's Ladder. After we came down, there were wavy lines through my vision. It only lasted a few minutes.

"Look over there," Greg pointed.

Two bare-breasted women were hiking. The wavy lines disappeared.

Everything in California is different.

San Francisco reminds me that homosexuality is a sin according to the Bible. The very word "sodomy" comes from Sodom. (Please read Genesis 19:24; Leviticus 18:22 and 20:13. In the New Testament Romans 1:26-27 and 1 Cor. 6:9-11.)

I don't advocate "gay bashing." It is very un-Christian. But, homosexuality is still a sin. Why else would God, through Paul, list it with other sins? I really don't understand how there can be gay churches. What Bible is being read?

We should love the sinner and hate the sin. Can the Bible be any clearer?

When the transgressor is punished, we feel sorry for

him or her because we can see them. What I am saying is that they are putting us all at risk because of their lifestyle. Do we matter to them?

I agree with Morton Downey, Jr., who said, "A__holes are exits, not entrances."

But, I'm getting way ahead of myself again.

After our return, one night my abdomen started to hurt. I called the hospital. "Who's on for surgery?"

"Dr. Price," the nurse answered.

Oh darn! I don't like the way he operates even if he is the Chief of Surgery. I'll just wait until morning when the shift changes.

My abdomen hurt worse. I couldn't sit quietly any longer. So, I walked to the hospital around the corner. With each step, I guarded my right side.

Must be appendicitis.

Larry Sherwood, the ER Doc who took Bob Bagley's place, evaluated me. I forgot it was a Friday night and the Chief of Surgery was on all weekend and would not be off in the morning. I figured the residents would do the surgery anyway.

"I'll do the surgery," Dr. Price insisted after evaluating me.

What can I do? I'm done for. But it's only an appendectomy. Even I can do that.

Dr. Sherwood looked at my monitor. "You went into bigeminy." (every other beat was abnormal and could lead to ventricular fibrillation and death). "You're flipping a lot of PVCs (**P**remature **V**entricular **C**ontractions). Don't worry about the surgery. It's a piece of cake."

*I know it is. Even I did one. No, I'm not worried about the surgery at all. I'm worried about **who** is doing it!*

Jimmy was the orderly on duty. He prepped me and placed a Foley catheter in to eliminate my urine, hooking it up to a bag. It is unusual to have your son shave your belly.

The wait was forever. When I was finally taken, I thought everything went well.

During my recuperation, I was supposed to urinate without the catheter in place. When I tried, something unusual to me blocked me up. *What's in there?* Then I peed some air. *How did that get there? Dr. Price hooked up my bowel to my bladder somehow. He fouled up my insides!*

So I went back to the ER. But, it was only air from the Foley insertion. It's not easy being a patient, but I was learning. Why do you think they're called "patients?"

I assistant coached soccer with Jeremiah's team when he was around five. The American football field where they played was next to a stream. Keeping the kids away from it during practice was difficult. They just wanted to skim stones.

"Play your positions!" I ordered at the beginning.

It was a lost cause. When the ball was kicked, they all

ran to it. Soon, there was a cloud of dust, like Pig Pen, around the soccer ball with all the kids kicking at it. It's a wonder no one got hurt.

"What are you doing?" I yelled to the goalie.

He swung on the horizontal part of the end zone post whenever the ball wasn't near him.

"Get your head in the game!"

Winning soccer for them was not a priority.

I had to decide where to go once residency was over. Edie and the kids would be moving too. I had to plan for all of us. Where was the best place to raise my family?

I took a protractor and drew a circle with a sixty-mile radius on a map. The center was Port Jervis, New York. I could live anywhere in it. The circle was close enough to my parents, sister, and New York City for a day trip by car. Scranton was on the edge. Wilkes-Barre was too far.

I wrote all the hospitals in that circle to see if they needed anybody. I was fishing for work. The only response I got was from Peter Lynch in Scranton, who coordinated the ER, or dispensary as it was called, at Mercy there. He was the brother of the nun who ran the hospital.

"Being of Irish descent, we think the poor should be cared for," Peter said. "You'll be the medical director of the ER someday."

That was what I wanted to hear. I thought money was important. So, it was Scranton.

Money. God is very clear on the subject.

(Please read Matthew 6:24; 19:23-24 and 1 Timothy 6:10.)

Yet, after all these years, we still go after money. Why? (Please read Luke 12:27-29.)

So why worry about money? We were instructed not to. 60% of marital problems are financial. It's time to get our priorities straight. Being concerned primarily about money is the Devil's work. NOTHING is more of this world. Yet 2 Corinthians 4:18 tells us this world is temporary.

Chapter Nine
MARRIED LIFE AND OLD FRIENDS

I went to Scranton Mercy for an interview and met Sister Robert John, who ran the hospital. I was impressed that it reached out to the poor.

"I promise you that you will be director some day," the "good" sister said.

My Catholic upbringing resurfaced. It never crossed my mind that a nun would mislead me. The fact she was Irish-American also helped to convince me.

I'm finally out on my own in the real world.

I didn't feel God's directing hand. I was like a fish in a milk bottle, too stupid to turn around.

After the interview, Peter Lynch showed me the town of Clarks Summit outside Scranton. "Here's where all the doctors live," Peter informed me as he drove on. "They have good schools here."

That's music to my ears. I can live here.

Edie and I needed a house and bought a split-level in Clarks Summit. It is said that, "behind every good man, there is a good woman." That was true in my case. Yes, we had our problems, but we worked them out. It was generally a good marriage. Maybe Edie was a tad much into woman's lib, but I lived with it. The fact is that women **are** oppressed. Not all feminists are female. It wasn't my fault the world is that way. Then Valerie re-entered the picture and…but I am getting ahead of myself.

The house we purchased was near the bottom of a hill. Upon our arrival, we still had our rusty old Nova. I thought Rust-o-leum came in one color. I learned too late that it could be bought in many shades. As a result, assorted colors covered the gold Nova from where I applied it in various years. Eight-year-old Louis Krueger, the oldest kid of the neighbors' across the street, screamed while holding his mother's hand, "Look, Mommy, they're in the army!"

"Shh!"

"But the car is camouflaged. Are we supposed to see it?"

"They're not in the army. Let's go inside." Our arrival was misinterpreted by many. So much for first impressions.

Edie was dissatisfied being a doctor's wife, whatever that is. She returned to school, enrolling in a college nearby named Marywood. At first, Edie took arts and crafts courses. I thought she would use some of my money earned as a doctor, to open a store in Clarks Summit; so, I supported the idea. However, school diminished her time with the kids and me.

Then, Edie selected business courses without consulting me. I should have objected, but I didn't.

A woman needs to have her own life, and not be defined by the man. The market for morality is open to all. Aren't we all equal?

I thought that was the way it was because we made it that way. Now, I realize we're equal because of God. (Please read Gal 3:28.)

When entering our new house, you could go upstairs to the living room, or downstairs to the children's play room and the garage.

Jimmy had trouble with drunk driving and lost his license after we left Danville. I split the two-car garage and made a room for him.

There was a railing on the landing over the foyer where you came in the house.

"I don't like it." Edie pointed to where it extended in the living room.

"Why not?"

"Because you can see into the living room when you come in."

So, I built a wall where the railing was, to separate the living room from the downstairs. I painted it, but the seam showed. I papered the wall and the seam was still visible. Finally, I decided on fancy plywood.

"The carpet doesn't match the wall," Edie complained.

"Why not?"

"Too light."

So, I bought a gray rug that was the same color. Shannon christened it by vomiting on it.

"The new carpet doesn't match the other walls!" Edie exclaimed.

"Why not?

"Too dark."

So, the entire upstairs was altered, taking the wallpaper off with a rented steamer. What started as one wall became the whole house!

"It would be so-o much easier to keep clean if you used oil-based paint," Edie advised.

What did I know as a novice? I applied oil-based paint. It was fine, until I tried to clean the brushes.

"The paint won't come off with water!" I exclaimed in the bathroom. "It's making a mess! Guess I'll have to use turpentine!"

We had a big back yard, with pines on either side and an open middle area. I remember because I mowed it. Who invented lawns anyway?

When I used a rake and shovel to clear the rear garden, about forty by fifty feet, black liquid oozed through the ground.

Oil! I thought and entertained visions of Jed Clampett's bonanza.

It wasn't anything so valuable. Our back yard was a big drainage field for the cesspool. The yard abutted a ditch just off my property.

Beyond it was the high school track. On one side was a hill, where I took the kids sledding. At the opposite end was the north campus of the high school, where the juniors and seniors went.

The house was a split-level and Edie couldn't cope when I worked nights.

"Shh! Daddy's sleeping," she repeated many times.

Kids make noise. Their function is to disrupt their parents' lives.

While I was there, I maintained my friendships with both Pat McCarthy and Ian O'Grady.

"What's Pat doing in the backyard?" Josh asked.

I looked and Pat's arms and legs appeared to cut the air in slow motion.

"Practicing karate," I answered as if everybody did.

Pat dated Bev Barr. She came to my house and read some of my writing. Bev was an artist, who had a daughter, Janine. I was amazed how much Bev resembled Edie. They could pass for sisters. Pat moved in with her and shared expenses.

She planned a surprise fortieth birthday party for Pat and invited Edie and me. I invented a tape of the basketball game with, "Shoot, McCarthy, Shoot," on it. Our children were the crowd in the background. I played the tape at his party.

"He shot before getting to mid-court," I announced in the middle of the tape. "Time stood still as the ball left his hands. For a moment, the crowd was hushed. The ball flew through the air and went toward the basket. But it kept going past it and above the backboard. It ricocheted off the stanchions and went out the open window! The ball bounced down the walkway and tripped the mailman!" I gave the tape, along with a book he had loaned me, to Pat as a birthday present. He vowed revenge.

Pat produced a video for my fortieth birthday in which he interviewed different people about me, including my parents.

"He was the reason the Dodgers left Brooklyn," Dad claimed. "He would yell profanity at the players from the stands."

Pat interviewed a man in combat fatigues, who allegedly was General Maury Chavez.

"Thek hated doctors at the M*A*S*H unit in Vietnam," he avowed. "But he loved this Nubian queen and always came back."

I supposedly fathered a black girl while there and had a lover, named Jan, with another daughter.

"When is Dad coming in?" Janine asked Jan on tape.

I was lampooned as a doctor. Finally, Edie was videoed.

"While Joe's been running around having all these affairs, I've had a lover of my own," she averred. "Want to see him?"

Edie held a picture up to the camera. It was of me in a clown mask. We had a good laugh. I guess "turnabout is fair play."

Once I finished my residency, Ian O'Grady took me up to the camp to winterize it as he did every November around Veteran's Day. The camp lacked heat and a bathroom. It boasted an outhouse and was cold. We roughed it for three or four days.

Across the lake was the cliff from which Ian and I jumped in our teen years. Nothing had changed. The pines were still bent from the constant northwest wind.

Ian fixed it up inside. There were two bedrooms on the porch and two small ones inside. I slept on the lower bunk bed in one. The kitchen was small, but long. If one wanted to wash dishes, you filled a pot with water from the lake, heated it on the gas stove, then poured the hot water in a plastic basin in the sink. Nothing was easy.

A pot-bellied stove stood in the main room of the camp. We made a fire in it with wood that Ian chopped the previous summer. Paper came from the local news. The stove made the camp livable. Getting up in the frigid morning to start it was quite a chore.

A hutch held dishes; shelves with books (I remember reading Taylor Caldwell's *A Pillar Of Iron* there when I was sixteen. To be young again!) occupied the walls. Ian and I used to eat and play chess at a table that was still there. A couple of couches and chairs invited lounging. Ian loved to fix old radios at a desk covered with them.

There was no phone. That's an instant priority. If you wanted contact with the outside world, you called from Hubert's house in Plessis.

Ian and I went drinking and driving (don't tell anyone) on dirt, back roads. His car had four-wheel drive and went nearly anywhere. He had a CB radio in the vehicle in case we were lost.

Everybody had satellite TV: it didn't matter if you lived in a shack; you had a dish in front of the house. In the middle of nowhere, we saw these big, white, monstrosities as status symbols.

Symbols. There is only one that is important—the cross. Everything else is an idol. Money, titles, games, balls, clubs etc. can't be taken with you when you pass on. Pictures on a wall can't come to life. (Please read Acts 17:29.)

I remember Ian's scaly hands. The cold must have affected them badly.

Every time we went to the North Country, something went wrong: the pump froze; the car ran out of gas, or was stuck in the mud.

"I want to see some local color," I said one evening.

"Come on."

He took me to a bar in nearby Teresa. We entered as a man toted out a woman on his shoulder. I should've turned around, but I was curious.

A woman hit another in the face then a man carried her out by her hair.

"I went to a bar where there was a fight," Ian began, "bottles and chairs flew everywhere. After I left, the bar caught on fire. The police arrived. Arrests were made. The bar never reopened."

We visited the First Rate bar in Plessis. They had a pool table and a one-armed bouncer. I liked to play, so, I asked a young man at the bar, "Do you want to play?"

"Me?" he asked and pointed to his chest.

God must have been with me because I lost and left the table. He challenged another fellow to a game.

Ian poked me on the shoulder, "Move to the end of the bar."

"Why?"

"Just do it."

After I did, I asked, "Why does the bouncer only have one arm?"

"You'll see."

The young man I'd been playing hit his opponent over the head with his cue stick. I thought all heck would break loose. I had visions of broken mirrors, flying chairs. But the bouncer controlled the situation like it was an every day occurrence. He drew a gun out of his coat calmly with his one arm and pointed it at the instigator who left without saying a word.

Hmm! Glad I lost!

Adjoining the bar was a dance hall. A blonde asked Ian, "Would you like to dance?"

"Sure." They left deserting me in this dangerous place.

Soon, a young lady, with two brothers flanking her, sidled up to me. "Wanna dance?"

I wanted to reply, "What is it about this place? Aren't the men supposed to ask the women to dance?" but seeing her brothers I replied, "Okay."

She had "summer teeth:" (some were there and some weren't). While dancing, I wondered, *Where is Ian?*

The lady, I use the term loosely, asked, "Why don't you come home with me?"

Looking at her two big brothers, I thought, *They will beat me to a pulp. Where is Ian anyway?*

I got them drunk and avoided a fight.

Ian returned from somewhere outside. Everybody was tipsy, except for us. I was too scared to drink, and Ian was busy watching everybody. When the bar closed, they all piled into their pick-up trucks. We waited and watched the vehicles plow over front lawns, garbage cans, and bushes like bumper cars. It's a wonder no one was hurt.

"I've seen enough local color," I said.

Ian drove back to the camp.

I still pursued that elusive First Principle, the bedrock from which everything else is derived. It's there as long as one doesn't give up looking. We stumble like drunks in pick-ups playing bumper cars running over garbage cans. There are those who will deny that He exists. As I age and gain more experience, He becomes obvious. Why didn't I see Him sooner? God had His reasons for His apparent disguise. I'm just glad I finally did see.

Bill and I kept in contact. I visited him in Pittsburgh several times. His parents lived nearby and raised Bill's sons for unknown reasons.

"What about your two wives?" I asked repeatedly.

"We need some rain," he'd say or change the subject with another innocent comment.

Finally, I gave up and accepted things as they were.

"Why are we stopping?" I asked one afternoon on the way to his parents to visit his boys.

"We can play *Asteroid* here."

"But Jason (Bill's oldest boy) has a cello performance tonight!"

"We have time."

"You're addicted to computer games."

Bill bought a dog, Chauncey. He was a Springer Spaniel who loved to jump, mostly on me.

Bill met Mary and they eventually purchased a house in East McKeesport, outside of Pittsburgh.

"Chauncey has fleas," Bill said.

"No wonder my ankles itch."

"I have to fumigate the house with a flea bomb."

"Don't let me stop you."

Mary loved flowers. She was always growing something in the garden.

"What kind of flowers are these?" Mary asked pointing to her latest bumper crop.

"Red and blue ones."

She laughed, then said, "They're Impatiens and Morning Glory. Come on. We'll go to the Botanical Gardens and teach you some names."

But I never learned.

Bill was offered a position at Reading Hospital. It was a promotion where he would be in charge of a pre-hospital program for several counties. I liked the idea because it brought my friends closer to me; but they had to leave their parents and Bill's boys in Pittsburgh. Sometimes one has to go, and he accepted the job.

Edie and I visited them during the winter.

"Look at the snow!" she exclaimed on our way there. "It's higher than our car!"

"That's just the piles. We can make it."

After we arrived in our Chevette, Edie started to sneeze.

"It's the dogs," she said. "I'm allergic to them."

Edie never visited them again.

"Why don't you come down and lecture?" Bill asked me. "If we have time, we can play golf or poker and watch some movies."

Pretty soon, I was going there twice a year for mini-vacations by myself in the spring and fall.

Once, Bill invited me to a nearby golf course. We played a par three over water. Bill hit his first shot directly into the lake. Determined, he teed up another ball. Right in. Finally, Bill hit a beautiful shot that headed straight for the pin.

From the other end of the lake, a duck took wing. The bird flew towards the middle of the lake. The ball hit the duck in flight. The bird continued, but the ball plunked into the water below. Bill didn't try to hit a fourth ball.

"You win the hole," he told me, then walked off the tee. Did you ever try to swing while you're laughing?

"Want to go to a Risk Management meeting on Saturday evening?" Bill asked.

"Okay," I answered all the time thinking, *Who meets on Saturday evening?*

It was a poker game! In a way it was 'Risk Management' because the executives of the hospital played, as well as the minister. Where else could we get them all together?

Saturday meetings, or in the Old Testament, the Sabbath. Christians worship on Sunday for several reasons.

Christ rose on that day. (Please read Luke 24:1 and John 20:1.)

The apostles worshipped on Sunday. (Please read Acts 20:7.)

Pentecost occurred on Sunday, not Saturday. (Please read Acts 1:8.)

The matter of the Lord's Day is broached. (Please read Revelation 1:10.) To John, the Lord's Day was Sunday.

Then there is the law. But we are no longer under the law (Romans 6:14). If we were we would have to follow everything, not just the Sabbath. We would never shave (Leviticus 19:27). Why try to re-establish the law? (Acts 15:10) We are free now. (John 8:31-32)

This is not to say that we are ungrateful to those who came before. (Please read Romans 9:1-5.)

Mary and Bill were married in 1985. They were unable to have any children, so, they adopted two brothers, Jason and James. Odd, the older boy was called Jason. Now, Bill had two sons with that name. It was confusing.

The new boys were about seven and six.

"All our names begin with 'J'," I said. "We should form a club."

"What will we call it?" James asked.

"That's easy, stupid," Jason snorted. "We'll call it the 'J' club."

"And Jason will be president and you, James, will be vice president."

"What will you be?" James asked.

"That's easy. You need someone to record the meetings so I'll be the secretary."

"Isn't that a girl?" James asked.

"Sometimes it's a boy."

"We need a greeting," I said. "Something to start the meetings."

"How about an awesome handshake like this?" and Jason did a little dance, tickled the palm of my hand before grasping my wrist.

"Everybody has a handshake. Ours has to be special." I thought for a moment then said, "I know. Get on the floor and form a circle."

"What are you doing?" James wondered as he got down.

"Now, remove your shoes and shake the foot of the person next to you with your foot."

The boys did it with each other then with me. That's the way the footshake was born.

I passed a Carvel ice cream store on the way to their house. "I saw a sign in the window on the way down. It said, 'We made too much ice cream. Help us eat it.'"

"Can we go, Dad?" James asked.

"Not only can we go, we have to help."

Bill and I went hiking to prepare for our mountain climbs (more on them later). Once, when we took the boys, I went ahead and made a lollipop tree.

"Why are you taking us on this stupid hike?" Jason complained.

"Are we near the top? Can we turn around yet?" James asked. Whining takes a lot of energy and air. It's a wonder they could breathe.

On the way down, Bill whispered to me, "Maybe they want some cheese with that whine."

I stopped abruptly. "Shh! Did you hear that squirrel?"

Both boys shook their heads.

"He says there's a lollipop tree up ahead."

The youngsters must have sprouted wings as they flew down the mountain looking every way for a lollipop tree. We sat on a rock and watched as they searched. Suddenly, Jason and James stopped. The cellophane covering the candy glistened in the sunlight.

"I see it! I see it!" they shouted as they jumped up and down.

They headed for what looked like to the untrained eye an ordinary maple tree. Jason and James started to tear the pieces of candy off the tree in delight.

"We have to bury one," I said catching up to them.

No questions were asked. In the ground it went.

That childlike humility and faith is magnificent. (Please read Matt. 18:3-4.)

Bill and Mary started raising dogs. Chauncey sired Simon, but they needed a female, so, they bought Pearl. Now they had three Springers in the house. Yes, they sprang all over me!

"*Do The Right Thing.* What a name for a movie! Does it mean that rioting is the right thing?" Bill asked after we watched the flick.

"I hope not. At least it's a better movie than *Eraserhead.*"

"My home video is better than *Eraserhead.*"

Bill and I often debated the state of the world. We argued from every viewpoint, both of us as changeable as the ocean.

In retrospect now, I should have looked for the First Principle more. I could have discussed it with Bill. We were both lost and didn't know it. Bill and I were looking for lollipop trees and talking squirrels. It's far better to stick to God.

Josh and Jeremiah played soccer. Jimmy was hired as a cook. Shannon eventually played softball. Edie and I were always driving someone somewhere. Time was valuable.

I took the children bowling every week. When it was warm, I played golf with Jimmy, Josh, and Jeremiah. Louis Kreuger usually came too. Shannon was too young.

"Computers are fun," Josh said. "Why don't we get one?"

"Just what you need, another toy."

"They can improve your mind."

Kids know how to manipulate their parents. That was all I needed to hear. I was sold.

"Tonight we will start reading Aristotle's *Ethics*," I said one night to Josh. He rolled his eyes.

But you can't remove the legs from a table and expect it to stand.

"I hate this stuff," he said.

If I continued, Josh would start hating me. Actually, Christian-Judaic morality is the best. What was I thinking?

Neither Edie nor I knew what we were doing, but between us were responsible for four children. Try explaining that to a nine-year-old. We thought they needed something secure while growing up. An identity. Maybe the truth is more important.

Edie and I attended a meeting of mixed marriages endeavoring to get guidance. A marriage between a Catholic and a Jew was considered mixed. But, marriages are made in Heaven. Even though we were never legally wed and didn't have a piece of paper, we were still married.

Edie and I attended several meetings and discussed many problems. We discovered the other couples were looking to us for answers. At the time, I wasn't aware of any and we raised the kids that way. I thought you tried to respond to situations by doing what was right. I should've asked "Why?"

After three years, I finally completed the work on the rugs and walls.

"We should move," Edie said.

"But I just finished."

"That's the point. The house looks good"

So, we moved. The new house was still in Clarks Summit but on a steep hill in another area of town. The kids could stay at their same schools.

The big home had two stories and five bedrooms. A pool, with two redwood sheds for changing and storage, was in back. Inside the fence was a flat lawn. I tried to grow a garden, but it was useless and the children converted it to a Wiffleball field.

Outside the redwood fence was a hill that I had to mow. I rued the day lawns were invented.

"I don't like the plywood walls in the living room beside the brick wall," Edie said.

Here we go. Against my better judgment, I asked, "Why?"

"Too dark."

So, I asked Bob Eckert, a friend of mine, about it. "No problem. I can wallpaper them."

The dining area was connected and would need to be done too.

After three layers of under paper, I said, "I can still see the seam," by now an expert at seeing them.

"I don't understand why it's showing."

"But it is."

We gave up, and hung the good gray marble paper atop it. The border was mauve and distracted one from the seam.

"What about the carpet?" Edie asked.

I know what that means.

"What do you suggest?"

"We should go shopping for a new carpet. The living room should be carpeted but the dining room should be slate."

"You should be an interior decorator."

Edie didn't seem to notice the remark.

The next day, we bought blue carpet with a divider for the living room. For the dining room Edie and I purchased black slate.

"How do we clean it?" I asked.

"The salesman said to add vinegar to the water."

The wood holder for the corner fireplace that divided the two rooms was on the slate.

"This is perfect for our rock collection," Edie pointed to the other side of the fireplace in the huge foyer where the chimney went through the middle of the house. So we put a rock that came from the Great Wall of China, according to Johnny, alongside one from the Berlin Wall. Dad said, "Johnny probably got it in our backyard."

When the tub upstairs broke, "I think we should get a new one," Edie said.

I ordered a modular one-piece tub, with a shower and fiberglass walls.

"How do we get it upstairs?" I wondered.

"We carry it."

"What do you mean 'we'?"

"I don't like this counter," Edie said of the kitchen.

"Why?"

"Because it has these whorls in it that trap dirt."

"We can't replace it."

She pouted.

"Well, we can't. It's custom made."

Edie finally relented.

My library was being transformed as I collected leather books to replace my paperbacks. Everywhere you looked, volumes were found.

One night, Shannon, who was four or five at the time, couldn't sleep. She arose from bed and stood on the stairs leading to the family room where I watched T.V. I could see her legs, but not her face. Shannon hadn't descended the stairs far enough and was dancing. When our eyes met, she stopped. I saw by her face she was searching for an excuse for being out of bed.

"And what are you doing up, young lady?"

"I had a nightmare."

"Do you want to tell me about it?"

"No."

"Why not?"

"Because it's PG13."

The very next night, Shannon's legs danced on the stairs again. She met my stare and halted.

"What are you doing now, young lady?"

"I had another nightmare."

Against my better judgment, I proceeded, "Do you want to tell me about it?"

"I'm pregnant."

"What!"

"And I'm gonna name him Freddie."

I was paid back with interest. Now, I ask you, how can anyone stay angry at answers like those? I surrendered and laughed.

Shannon was fond of talking (Does that sound familiar?). She was around six when one day the phone rang in our kitchen. I was in the dining room speaking with Dad, who was visiting, so Shannon answered it. After a long twenty minutes, she hung up and joined us.

"Who was it?" I asked.

"Don't worry about it."

"Why?"

"It was a wrong number."

Another time, eight-year-old Shannon, who was having trouble with her homework, faced me. She put out her right hand and commented, "This is west, right?"

I nodded my head.

Shannon turned around. She stuck out her right hand again. "This is west, right?" Shannon had a problem with directions.

I never knew what to expect from my children. It was like living in a three-ring circus. The first day Josh had his license he came to me. "Dad, I've got something to tell you."

Uh-oh. This can't be good.

I put down the newspaper and said, "Go ahead. I'm listening"

"I hit a car today."

Ouch!

"Was anybody hurt?"

"No."

At least I'm glad for that.

We received a phone call one afternoon. "This is the principal at Josh's school."

"What happened?" I exclaimed.

"Josh had a fistfight in the parking lot after school. He and the other boy are okay but I will have to give them both detention."

I never did discover the reason he fought.

Jeremiah became the detention king of Clarks Summit. It began in eighth grade. One afternoon the phone rang again.

"This is the principal at Jeremiah's school."

By now, I was used to the calls.

"What did he do?"

"It seems his friend put a lit cigarette in the wastebasket and left. Jeremiah did too. The garbage caught fire and the sprinklers were activated. Fire engines arrived and the school was evacuated. Jeremiah won't say who did it."

"What's the penalty if he doesn't tell?

"Suspension and Community Service."

Jeremiah didn't squeal.

I was afraid to go to the mailbox because a letter from the school was sure to be inside.

One Sunday we were eating out with my parents when Dad turned to Jeremiah and asked, "Do you know the German for A-bomb?"

Jeremiah shook his head.

"Loudenboomen."

After a few minutes, Dad again turned to Jeremiah, "Do you know the German for H bomb?"

Again Jeremiah shook his head.

"Loudenboomen mitt blows hole in grounden."

The next day, Jeremiah asked his German teacher, "What is the German word for A-bomb?"

"There isn't one."

"Yes there is."

"Well, I don't know it."

"It's 'loudenboomen.'"

He received detention. It was a good thing that Jeremiah didn't ask for a definition of H-bomb.

Once, after I worked evening shift, I came home around midnight to find several young men sleeping on the living room floor. I woke them up. "Who are you?"

They didn't understand, so, I repeated, "Who are you?"

"*No habla Ainglish.*"

After my years with UFW, I could read a little Spanish, but not understand what is spoken. Edie came into the living room from upstairs.

"They escaped from El Salvador where all of them dodged the draft. If they get caught, a firing squad waits for them."

"What about my license? If I get caught, I will lose it and go to jail! And they're sleeping on my floor!"

What could I do? In effect, we were part of an Underground Railroad. The dodgers were *en route* to Canada. With my background, I had to let them stay. The next day, they disappeared never to be seen again. I didn't even know how many there were. Perhaps it's better that way.

So what if we are inconvenienced for doing the right thing? (Please read Luke 9:26 and Matt. 10:42.)

Edie and I celebrated everything. You name it; we celebrated it. Because she is totally Jewish, Edie didn't know how to make merry on Christmas. "I gave gifts to the bank teller and gas station attendant."

"What!"

"Wasn't I supposed to?"

"Actually, that's a good idea," I laughed.

I remembered why I had fallen in love with her. Beneath her worldly exterior, I think Edie might be a closet Christian.

One winter holiday, Edie and I were sitting in our dining room. Chanukah usually comes at about the same time as Christmas; so, we had put up the tree and placed a menorah on the table. On the wall, facing the table, was a picture of a woman celebrating the Festival of Lights. Johnny came from Japan with Yoko, his wife, and they spoke Japanese. Lena, married to Nick from Crete, conversed with him in Greek. To complete our scene, Dominic, visiting with Aracely from Cuba, and they chatted in Spanish.

The doorbell rang.

"Who's there?" I asked.

"The exterminator."

To get to the basement, we had to go through the dining room where all the different languages spoken and the lit Christmas tree and menorah provided an unusual background.

As we descended to the basement, the exterminator nudged me, "What kind of a house is this, anyway?" Good question. I lived there ten years and I never knew.

Nick was a short-order cook. Lena and he wanted their own business. I offered them the money, had the location chosen, and the owner signed the papers. Then, Nick reneged: the deal, and Lena's marriage, disintegrated. He departed, or so I thought. Now my cousin and her two children were homeless.

"What am I gonna do?" Lena wondered.

"Simple. You and the kids will move in with us."

"That's good of you, but how? I know this house is big but not that big."

"We'll have to make it bigger," Edie said. "We'll add on."

"Yeah. Mike and Josh can share a room," I said. "They'll be like brothers. You and Katherine will have your own rooms. What is family for?"

I couldn't expand the house laterally without increasing the tax assessment. Nobody said anything about raising the roof; I had a crane remove it. The roof hovered in the air while the walls went up and a new floor was added. My office, a studio, a full bath and a master bedroom replaced the attic. There were skylight windows and a pole. It was like a private apartment.

Lena and Edie became good friends. My cousin had her own bedroom on the first floor. Everything—the paneling, the carpet, the phone—was blue. We christened it the "Blue Room." Jeremiah's was next to hers.

Mike shared the big bedroom on the second floor with Josh. Shannon slept in the one next to them. Kathryn had her own near the top of the stairs and the laundry cubicle. She had some type of congenital defect that would approach blindness as Kathryn grew and went through puberty. Everyone was protective of her.

The kids were enrolled in school. I was busy taking the boys to sporting activities. Josh and Mike loved baseball and collected cards.

"Want to go to the flea market again this weekend to get some cards?" I asked.

"Sure," they said.

Then, Nick returned.

"I'll divorce him," a determined Lena claimed.

Then, he stalked the house. I never knew when Nick was going to appear.

"This is not fair to you guys," a frightened Lena protested.

"Come on," the sneakered Edie said, "We'll get a restraining order on him. Nobody's gonna scare me in my own house!"

But, Nick won the battle. In the end, Lena and the children moved back with him. They eventually moved to New Jersey leaving me with a much bigger house.

I took my family to Disney World twice. The first time we stayed in a hotel room.

"I want to watch the Super Bowl," the pubescent Josh whined.

I reacted angrily. "We come all the way to Florida and you want to watch a stupid football game!"

"It's not just any game, Dad."

I left the room, slamming the door. I was miserable thereafter, despite visiting the amusement parks.

The second time was great! I had learned how not to do things the first time. Richard and Regina had a time-share in a two-storied condo, which they loaned us. I pretended to be him to use it.

Jen Bryant, Josh's girl friend at the time, came along, so he was happy and out of our hair. I didn't see them while we were there. Chaperoning? What's that? Who chaperones the chaperones?

I studied Disney World and concluded; "We can see it all in three days."

"This isn't a contest." Edie tried to restore a little reason.

"For fifty dollars a day, it sure is!"

"Oh brother!"

We spent one day each, at EPCOT, MGM and Fantasyland. I went with Edie, Jeremiah and Shannon.

"Hurry up," I urged continually.

"Rome wasn't built in a day," Edie complained.

Everything was seen. We hurried here, ran there. For MGM and Fantasyland, we finished in the afternoon, for EPCOT, in the evening. The four of us saw Illuminations after eating dinner at the German pavilion. It had been a top-ten trip!

Josh graduated from high school and moved to Philadelphia. Now the house was really too big. Jeremiah moved into the old master bedroom on the second floor and Shannon kept hers.

Robert, an orderly from work who took Bob's job, had some trouble with his wife, Sheryl. He moved in for a couple weeks, taking Kathryn's old room. How was I to know Robert would return? Or that the second time he would stay for six months?

"We're brothers," Robert explained although he is dark and I am light.

Robert loved baseball. At games, he was a heckler. "Hey ump! Your momma wears combat boots!"

I tried not to pay attention.

"Hey ump! Your sister does tricks in New York!"

The umpire turned around and stared at me. I would rather sit on hot coals than go to another ballgame with Robert. One time, he won something there and was put on the field. Robert had to run to first base and beat a throw.

"You're out!" the umpire yelled.

"I was safe!"

"No, you were out!"

Robert poked him in his chest protector and was escorted off the field.

"That stupid ump! I was definitely safe."

Robert returned to his seat, and then yelled, "Your wife goes out with your best buddy while you ump the game!" It was a long night.

I took him golfing.

"Name the ten greatest bands," he said while we played.

"Now name the ten greatest solo artists," when we were done.

"Male or female?"

"Both."

"How about the ten greatest baseball players?" I asked.

"Or the ten greatest basketball players?"

Robert and I discussed marriage and family often.

"Parents should stick together for the sake of the children," he'd say.

"What if they fight? Should the children be subjected to that?"

At the time, I thought divorce was an option. The truth is God hates divorce. I would refer the reader again to Malachi 2:13-16 and Matthew 19:3-9.

We thought at the time that love was an emotion. It's not. Love is a virtue and can be worked on. It took years and a brain bleed to realize that, but I changed.

Robert taught me how to make real enchiladas and tacos. They are still a part of my diet. His mother is from

Mexico and he's from Albuquerque. Homemade tamales came in the mail.

Robert eventually returned to his wife. I think it was because of their daughter, Kendall. They went on to have a son. We are supposed to work things out.

"What if you die?" Edie asked. "I have nothing. Zip."
"Better get your diploma to play it safe."
"That's right. I have to go on."

There is a problem with Women's Lib. It doesn't take into account God's plan, only its own. Women, especially American women, don't want to hear that, but it's true. Submission is a dirty word to them. I can't think of a word more misunderstood. Often, 1 Peter 3:1-6 is used to show that the Bible is chauvinistic.

Lifting verses by themselves, of which I am guilty, can be dangerous. Sometimes it makes a point; sometimes it misses the point. As a wise preacher once told me, "Taking a text out of context is the beginning of a pretext." (So, please continue on to 1 Peter 3:7-9 which is usually not reported.)

God through Peter is saying that husbands have responsibilities too. This passage does not endorse man's mastery of woman. On the contrary, both are to be servants of God. (Please read Ephesians 5:21-25.)

Husbands and wives are commanded to submit mutually. How many men know this? Are we living up to our part of the bargain? (Please read Matthew 7:3.)

We can see that usually men fail. If men do not fulfill their responsibilities, all of them, women are not obligated to live up to theirs. I find it hypocritical of men to expect women to submit to them and they do not submit to women.

Jesus was, undeniably, the first feminist. After He had risen, Jesus chose to reveal Himself first to a woman. Not to his apostles, but to Mary Magdalene. (Please read John 20:10-16.)

That's incredible! After three years teaching the apostles and telling them about His resurrection, He appears to Mary Magdalene, a woman from whom He had driven seven demons (Luke 8:2)! (Please read Galatians 3:28 again.) No other ancient text gives women any standing and yet, the Bible says we are equal! To say the Bible is chauvinistic is very wrong.

Edie completed her business courses. But, what about the children and me? What about God? Isn't this a case of the tail wagging the dog? American women cannot be happy until they submit. American men cannot be happy until they submit. As long as they try to control or manipulate each other, marriage is doomed to failure. True submission is not another word for chauvinism. At the time, I thought erroneously that it was, with dire consequences.

Chapter Ten
WORK

The first year at Mercy Hospital, four doctors were assigned to the ER. I was in charge of the schedule. Peter Lynch, whose job was to oversee me, took care of everything else.

The ER was changing: it no longer was just for emergencies; it was a clinic too. Poor people who couldn't get appointments with doctors came to the ER. This translated into our being busy. At one time you could get some sleep while working the night shift, or trade war stories during the day or evening. That was no longer true.

"ER is a specialty now," I said to Peter.

"Aren't all ER docs temporary?" he asked voicing the opinion of the administration.

"I hope not."

"Aren't they just waiting to open offices of their own? Why would anyone want the ER as a career?"

No matter what I said, I couldn't get him to understand or change his attitude.

But, the regular ER schedule helps you lead a more normal life as well as functioning as a physician. I saw enough of devoting your life to your work, failed marriages, troubled children. For a stiff like me, it was perfect.

One hundred sixty-eight hours in a week, split four ways, equals forty-two. It was too much so we tried twelve-hour shifts. Then Jim Harley, one of the doctors, left.

"Say, we need a fifth doctor," I recommended to Peter Lynch one day.

"I'll see what I can do."

As a result, I recruited Dominic and Phil Bocci. They were finishing their residencies at Geisinger: Dom in Emergency Medicine and Phil in Internal Medicine. Now, we had two docs specifically trained in and for the ER.

I became the Director as promised, but, the hospital's ideas of a department were different from mine. I was in charge of the doctors, but not the nurses.

I should tell them to "Get Lost." But I have a mortgage and a family with bills. Besides, there's no guarantee that any other place is better. You can train a dog you know better than one you don't. Things could be a lot worse.

I can't uproot my family again. It's not just me.

So, I decided to stay.

"You will eventually get your own department," Sister assured me many times. I never did.

The schedule included vacation time, personal days and holidays. Every five weeks rotation included one week off. It worked; time to rest and putter about the house was needed. Or, you could take a mini-vacation.

Then, Jerry Carter, another of the original four, moved to Florida. I replaced him for twelve months with Scott Bagration, who was a year behind Dom in Emergency Medicine. Now, we had three ER schooled physicians.

Mercy had a quarrel with Community Medical Center (CMC), another hospital in Scranton.

"We don't trust Mercy," Tim, one of the seasoned paramedics, said.

I don't blame him. I don't trust them either.

The gist was that they had a Mobile Intensive Care Unit (MICU) and Mercy wanted its own. I brought in a doctor from Pittsburgh to critique our facilities.

"We need someplace for the helicopter to land," Sister said after he had left.

"A heliport won't work," I advised but I might as well advise a fish not to swim. "The buildings surrounding Mercy are too high."

She had visions of grandeur and I switched to a different movie that Sister didn't like.

"Don't want to die on the vine," she said.

Are you listening?

A compromise was eventually reached: we'd become the Regional Resource Center, and they'd be the Regional Trauma Center with the heliport. Mercy owned its MICU, but now CMC had two. I think it was like a toy to Sister. Whoever had the most, would win. Life shouldn't be that way at all. (Please read 2 Corinthians 4:18 again.)

Our MICU had a nurse on board. She/he replaced one of the two paramedics.

"We're losing jobs when nurses ride and security drives," Tim complained.

"Any solutions?"

"Yeah, get them off the MICUs."

"Ain't gonna happen. Sister wants them there."

"We've got an elderly man who went down…" and then only static because of interference from the mountains. Because it was a one-way radio I had to wait until the paramedic finished. "…Can I give him a bolus of Epinephrine? Over."

"I didn't copy. Repeat. Over."

"An elderly man went down…" nothing but static again. I waited until the static stopped.

"Where are you? Over."

Finally I heard a voice say, "The Notch. Over."

"This is not working," I commented to the nurse beside me. "The paramedics must be trained so they can act on their own."

Criteria were developed. Rather than let patients die, protocols were initiated through the local EMS.

All during that time I wrestled with the idea of God or no God. I didn't see Him in my work. Scales must have occluded my eyes. I asked; if He didn't exist, where did we come from? Evolution answered some of my questions in the negative. I tried to reconcile evolution and Deism. The only way was to say that the Bible is relative. God's day may be a billion years and not literally twenty-four hours. That was a satisfactory answer to me, then. But, that still meant a Creator. I tried not to think about it but the question gnawed away. It irritated like a grain of sand with an oyster. My pearl was yet to evolve.

I was fascinated with Socrates' question. "Is something good because God ordains it, or does God ordain it because it is good?"

If it is the latter, then morally we don't need God.

I was still in search of a First Principle.

I held a meeting concerning retirement at my house. I wanted to be sure everyone was covered. To do that, all of us would have to join forces.

"I have to act independently on this," Charley Sheer, the lone original left, informed us.

"That will destroy the group," I countered.

"That's unfortunate."

That night, I tossed and turned in bed. Finally, I realized I must fire him to allow the department to move forward.

But he's been here longer than me. I respect him. But it has to be done. Oh, why can't someone else be in charge? I just want to care for people.

A couple of days later, when we were alone in a car, I thought this the right opportunity. "Charley, you're holding us back," I began.

"How?"

Just be honest, a little voice inside me prompted.

"You know we can't form a group without your agreement so I have to let you go."

"WHAT!"

"I tried to explain the other night."

Charley started to hyperventilate.

"Just calm down," I soothed.

"That's easy for you to say! I have bills!"

I wanted to say, *you should have thought of them the other night*. After a pregnant pause, he continued more calmly, "When is my last day?"

"Two weeks."

"To tell you the truth, I knew I had to get out. I'm getting older. I need to start my own practice. This provides the impetus."

"We can help."

"Thanks."

With that we parted friends.

I hope I never have to fire anyone again. But, I did.

Stability. A lot is made of it. The Catholic Church especially builds on it. One verse in particular out of the whole Bible quotes Matthew 16:18.

We memorized that verse to the neglect of the rest of the Bible. But God in His mercy forgave us.

The Catholic Church claims that Peter was the first pope. Really?

This is important to me so I will spend some time with it.

In 1 Peter 5:1, Peter describes himself a4s an elder He sees himself as their equal, not as their pope.

I am indebted to Dave Hunt in *A Woman Rides the Beast* for the following observation. Paul sent the Romans a letter. In 16:1-16 there are a lot of personal greetings. Yet the letter was not addressed to Peter. In fact, there is no mention of Peter. A very curious omission if indeed he were the first pope.

I think we demean both Jesus and Peter in saying Peter was the first pope. Demean? Why?

Jesus, because we are saying His death wasn't quite enough. We, through the Church, had to subsidize it. I refer the reader to Hebrews 10:10 again. (See Chapter One)

Peter, because we miss the point that he was an ordinary man. (Please read Acts 4:13.)

Rock? Who is the Rock? There are many references in the Old Testament to God being the Rock. (e.g.; Deuteronomy 32:4, 15, 18, 30, especially 31; 1 Samuel 2:2; 2 Samuel 22:32,47; 23:3; Psalms 28:1; 94:22; 95:1 Isaiah 17:10; 26:4 to name a few.) Perhaps the most famous is Psalms 18:2.

Peter himself described Christ as "...the capstone." (Please read Acts 4:11.)

Yet the Catholic Church claims that Peter is "the rock."

Let's see how Peter acted if he were the first pope.

Immediately after Christ said "upon this rock" we see Him castigating Peter after Peter counseled Christ not to talk about His death. (Please read Matthew 16:23.) Not enough has been said about this verse. We concentrate on Matthew 16:18 instead.

In the Garden of Gethsemane, we are told in John 18:10-11 that Peter cut off the ear of the high priest's servant. Showing that even then Peter did not understand Christ's mission.

Peter denied Christ three times (Please read Luke 22:54-62).

Peter explains what happened to the crowd after Christ through him healed the lame man and the people ran to Peter (Please read Acts 3:12-16.)

The Jewish court recognized Peter and John as "...unschooled, ordinary men..." (Acts 4:13)

And Peter was unfit to be the first pope anyway because he was definitely married. (Please read Matthew 8:14; Mark 1:30; Luke 4:38 and 1 Corinthians 9:5 (Cephas is Peter))

Isn't it obvious Who "the Rock" is?

What was Jesus saying to us about "the rock?"

The answer lies in what happened immediately before. Let's set the scene. Jesus asked His disciples who they think He is. Peter replies in Matthew 16:16.

To which Jesus responded in Matthew 16:17-18:

He is talking here of Peter's faith. That's the rock. Not Peter the person.

Dom and Phil opened up their own practice together. Each doctor went part-time in the ER, sharing one full-time position. Where there were two before, now there was one. Scott Bagration moved to Florida, so he and Charley had to be replaced.

"We need double coverage," I informed Peter Lynch. "The census keeps increasing."

"I'll see what I can do."

Mercy was on the rising part of the bell curve. So, I recruited Scott Slade, Lisa Dillon, Rich O'Donnell and Tom Major. All of them were trained in Emergency Medicine. I knew Tom from Geisinger. Scott and Lisa were in his class, and Rich was a year behind them. Now, we were seven doctors, six ER trained, probably the only place in the country with that many.

We worked three shifts: days, evenings, and nights. Each had its own personality: days were mostly career nurses, evenings single caregivers, and nights not as busy. I knew everyone there. At first, the obstetrician wasn't in the hospital, so, I delivered babies. Maybe one hundred.

I ran to cardiac arrests, or codes as they were termed. When a patient was declared dead, the nursing supervisor opened a window.

"Why are you doing that?" I asked naively.

"To let the spirit out."

It was fun to work nights with the nurse Jean Marie Ziforski. I was sitting at the table in our conference room, when she came in and plopped down in a chair across from me. "I'm so tired. It reminds me of the time when I was eight months pregnant and ate a whole watermelon."

I looked up. To understand what I told her, you have to know about Pitocin. It's a medicine which we called "Pit" given by IV to induce labor. Also, everybody knows watermelons have little bugger pits waiting for a good chomp to ruin teeth. So, I began, "Didn't your doctor tell you not to eat watermelons?"

"No. Why?"

"Because that's where 'Pit' comes from."

She was gullible. That night Jean Marie looked up Pitocin. It isn't extracted from watermelons. We had a good laugh and thought the matter closed.

A year and a half went by. At three A.M., I was sitting across from Jean Marie in the conference room. Judy Penny, another R.N., seven and a half months pregnant, came in and sat next to her. "I'm so tired, I could eat a whole watermelon," Judy commented.

That caught my attention and I looked up. Jean Marie said, "I swear, I never told anyone about our conversation about 'Pit.'"

Another year and a half went by. Dr. Sleck, from Ob-Gyn, came to the ER one night to visit. He claimed angrily, "All the nurses on the floor are telling the patients to eat watermelons. If I ever catch the person who started that rumor, I'll—I'll kill him."

I didn't say a word.

Another year and a half passed. As often the case, I had to deliver a baby. I didn't recognize the mother. After the birth, I was informed she was a nurse on the Ob floor.

"I ate a whole watermelon last night," she told me. "I know it caused my labor."

I couldn't argue with a new mother so I threw up my hands and left the room. I gave up. Pitocin does come from watermelon pits.

As an addendum, years later Danielle (more on her later) was having her first baby. Because the father was MIA I went to Nesbitt Hospital, about twenty miles from Mercy. On the wall of Labor and Delivery was a picture. It was of watermelons.

One time, I was behind a patient asking him to take a deep breath. Jean Marie was stationed at his front. He didn't inhale. I had the stethoscope on the back of his chest listening.

"Breathe in and out," I ordered.

Still no sound. Jean Marie laughed.

"Breathe in and out!"

She became hysterical. I had to see what was so funny, so, I went around to the front of the patient. He was taking his **TEETH** in and out! The expression on the patient's face showed that he thought I was crazy, while she continued laughing.

Urine samples were put in little, clear, plastic cups. One night, Jean Marie was busy in another room. I ushered a groaning man into a room. By the tint of his urine, the patient appeared to have a kidney stone. He continued to moan.

Iced tea happens to look like bloody urine, so I put some in a container. Finally, Jean Marie came out to where I had the filled cup. The man moaned on cue.

"What's his problem?" she asked.

"I think he has a kidney stone."

I took his urine sample container, removed the lid, and sniffed.

"I don't think he's diabetic."

Then, I drank it.

Her color was as white or whiter than the sheet on the gurney. Jean Marie passed out, hitting the floor. She wasn't hurt or else I'd be in deep "doo-doo." She was gullible.

There's a huge difference between gullibility and faith. Gullibility is believing in things without evidence. Faith is believing in things with evidence. Abraham is a good example. He believed in God because of previous promises come true. Abraham didn't know how God would do it but he trusted Him to do it because of what He had done already. "Blind faith" is really an oxymoron. He believed God and was ready to sacrifice his son, Isaac. But He could raise him up again if necessary. Please read Genesis 22:9-12.)

We often hear it from Abraham's point of view, his

complete faith in God. What about Isaac? Seeing that knife must have been a real eye opener for him. It reminds me of Christ's sacrifice. Isn't it a foreshadowing of what was to come?

Somebody on nights was stealing our food. You can take other things, but don't mess with our lunches.

One night, a patient brought in a dead snake.

"Why did you bring that here?"

"To see if it's poisonous."

"It doesn't have pits so it's not poisonous."

We finished eating a pizza and I put the dead snake in the box and promptly forgot about it.

A couple of hours later, I called in the cardiologist. I was busy suturing when I heard him scream. Nobody touched our food again.

I met Bob Eckert, the orderly on night shift. Nancy, a night nurse, was carrying his child. Bob and I drove to climb Mt. Marcy in October, 1984. My car was small, a Chevette, with a stick shift.

When I caught a glimpse of the mountain from the Northway, I asked, "Is that snow at the top?"

"Sure is."

"I don't have snowshoes."

"We'll make it, somehow."

After the drive, we hiked in. Bob and I set up camp by a river where years before the student threw in his wallet. I knew the spot. We pitched a two-man pup tent.

"Do you have a permit?" the ranger asked.

"I've been camping out here for years and never needed a permit!"

"No permit, then you'll have to go tomorrow."

We retired early and tried to sleep. I kicked down the pole accidentally. The tent collapsed. I couldn't get up, so, Bob turned on the lantern to see.

"What happened?" he asked.

"My leg went into spasm. I guess it was the long ride."

He erected the pole again and yelled, "It's like an ice cube out here!"

Bob left the lantern burning for its heat.

"That lantern will use up all the oxygen in the tent and we'll suffocate," I insisted.

"Would you rather freeze?" he asked as he left the light on.

As soon as Bob dozed off, I extinguished it and tried to sleep.

Light awakened me.

"What ARE you doing?" I asked.

"I'm relighting the lantern. Somehow it went out."

As soon as he dozed off again, I put the lamp out and tried to sleep myself. When I dozed off, Bob would light the lantern. Neither of us slept at all.

In the morning, Bob and I discovered that it snowed sixteen inches on the top of Mt. Marcy. A French woman from Montreal on the trail looked at my sneakers.

"You'll never make it in those," she said in a thick French accent while pointing at my feet.

She was right; we should've turned back. But, I perceived it as a challenge; now come what may, I was going to make it, regardless of my footwear.

Who is she to tell me that I won't make it?

On the trail, Bob and I were huffing and puffing. Two men passed us.

It's bad enough they can talk but they're speaking French! This is America!

Then, I realized that Canada is America too. The Adirondacks are closer to Montreal than they are to New York City, even though Mt. Marcy is the highest mountain in New York State. Anger doesn't know reason, remaining foreign to it.

We reached the top. The snow came over the sides of my sneakers. I took them off to rest.

I should've worn boots.

On the descent, both of us traversed a small wooden bridge over a running stream. Bob, in his boots, had no problem. He crossed, but I, now back in my sneakers, slipped on the bridge and fell into the stream!

I jumped out and ran down the trail, where an astonished Bob caught me.

"Why are you running?" he asked.

"I fell crossing the stream."

"I didn't see. I was looking ahead."

I checked and nothing was broken. Only my pants were wet as the creek wasn't too deep. They soon dried while we hiked.

"We should break camp," I said upon our return. "Don't want that ranger to pay us another visit. Besides, it's cold."

"But it's three miles down and I'm tired."

"Just put one foot in front of the other and go."

"Let's go to a motel," he suggested warming to the idea. "We could each take a hot bath."

"Sounds good."

By the time I was done with my bath I heard him snoring.

The following year, Bob and I went with Tom Major, two security guards, and three paramedics for a climb up Mt. Washington.

Upon reaching the top, Tom stated, "I want to see the lake on the map."

"I don't think it's a good idea," I replied. "You don't know this mountain. I do. It's very fickle at this time of year and it's getting late. We should go back."

"I tell you what. Let's put it to a vote."

Against my better judgment, we did. Five wanted to see the lake while two others and I thought it a good idea to return.

"Why don't we compromise?" Tom asked. "You go down this trail and we'll see the lake," he pointed at the map. "You wait for us where the paths intersect."

"Okay," I agreed.

Two paramedics and myself started down the

mountain. The other five, took off for the lake. Upon reaching the point where the paths crossed, we stopped and waited. Then, the clouds came, rolling over rocks like waves. It became windy and cold.

"I think we should go or else we'll get caught in a fog bank," one of the paramedics claimed.

"That's not a good idea." I countered. "The others will wait and get caught in the dark."

"So what? They wanted to see that stupid lake."

"But someone could get injured. We would never know it and he would die. I don't think we should split up."

"We already have."

"We gave our word to wait and that's what I'll do," I stated resolutely.

"Even if it means dying."

"Yes," I answered firmly, but I was torn apart inside.

"For another five minutes I'll wait then I'm outta' here," the paramedic said.

I settled for that. God had the five arrive in less than five minutes. I don't know what I would have done if it was longer.

"How was the lake?" I asked as we started the descent.

"You mean the puddle," Tom tried to laugh.

God must look down on us and shake His head. We go off on tangents when we should not. If we stick to the path He has laid out everything will be fine. If we stray, anything could happen. If we depend on our own wits then we are in a lot of trouble. At that time, I didn't know

God. Therefore, we got into trouble. Thankfully, He's merciful and will intervene.

It grew dark while we went down the mountain.

"Where are we?" I asked.

"Lost," replied one of the paramedics.

"We are not," a security guard insisted. "I know perfectly well where I am."

"And where is that?" the paramedic asked.

"Right here."

"Very funny. But how are we gonna get out of these woods?

"Beats me."

Just then we saw a flashlight of some other late hikers bobbing along the path.

"C'mon," I said. "Let's follow it."

We kept the light ahead of us, tripping and falling a few times but getting out eventually. God taught me that I should always follow that inner voice even if it is whispered or other people disagree. It can be viewed as stubbornness. I prefer to think of it as tenacity. There are times to compromise and other times to hold your ground. I was learning.

That trip became important because that's when I invented the AHA (Alphabet Hikers of America). We climbed high peaks that were above timberline. The mountains had to begin with different letters of the alphabet.

"Does 'Half Dome' count as an 'H' or 'D?'" I asked Bob.

"Oh, I don't know! You started the stupid club. You can make its rules."

"Then I'll make it an 'H' and a 'D' because I've climbed it twice."

"Oh brother!"

Bob was right. Because I created the club, I could make any rules I pleased. God has the same right as the Creator. That's what 'sovereign' means. (Please read Psalm 135:6.)

We often overlook that. We want things OUR way and use Him like a puppet to get what we want. But, it doesn't work that way. God will bless America if He wants to not because we want Him to. When does He do it? Simple, when we obey Him.

"We have to make some allowance for mountains that begin with the same letter like Mt. Marcy and Mt. Mitchell," I said.

"Shut up already about the AHA!" Bob replied.

"Maybe we can substitute one letter for another if we've climbed two beginning with the same letter."

Bob stuffed cotton in his ears.

We find it difficult to create a simple club. God has created the whole universe. (Please read Collosians 1:16.)

Bob Eckert advanced to surgical technician. That's when Robert Confortini replaced him as a night orderly. He went to the University of Scranton trying to get into medical school.

Because his mother is Mexican, I advised, "Tell them, your name is Roberto. Maybe you'll get in as a minority student." Robert, or Roberto, never did.

Chris Cowper waxed the floors at 6 A.M. He loved sports and I played golf with him many times. He was with me when a man, who had been wandering the links, stopped and asked, "What time is it?"

I wasn't about to let this opportunity slip. Never wearing a watch before I became disabled, I lifted my arms instead. I knew roughly the time from when we started and pretended to read the shadows. I replied, "One-twenty." He accepted that without a complaint. After the eighteenth hole, I checked and was correct. Wonder what that man thinks.

I couldn't wait for the baseball season to begin.

"Take me out to the ball game..." I sang every night at twelve.

I erased a number in the right upper corner of the blackboard and replaced it with one less.

"What are you doing?" a paramedic asked.

"That's the number of days 'til O.D."

"O.D.? Overdose?"

"Nope. Opening Day."

Robert, Chris, and I, started a rotisserie league in baseball. It worked this way. Each person participating was given a certain amount of theoretical money to buy players. The member nominated someone to offer a price upon in turn. They went to the highest bidder. Once a player was bought, you subtracted the amount from your total.

I followed stats like runs produced, wins and losses. Every team wound up with a number called "The Thek Factor." There were enough baseball players for eight complete teams, so the league needed to expand its base. Through the grapevine, a pharmacist, Dane Crane, two paramedics, George Zeller and Eric Gerstner, Gordon Tracy, a night nurse, and the husband, Jim Lofton, of another night nurse, Karen Lofton, and Gordon's brother-in-law were included.

The bidding, done in March a few weeks before the season began, took about eight hours. It was usually at my house. The teams were pasted on the window in the dining room. Everyone wore a funny hat like poker.

"One dollar for Roger Clemens for a pitcher," Dane began beneath his hat.

"A dollar and one cent," Gordon continued.

When the bidding came to Robert, he said, "I can't bid on a player who gets thrown out of a playoff game. He can't control his temper. They should change his name from "The Rocket" to "The Firecracker.""

"You're a fine one to object about being thrown out of a game!" I laughed.

"A dollar and two cents," Chris countered.

"That's too steep for me," Eric folded. "I'm out."

"A dollar and three cents," George said. "After all, he is on Boston."

"I'm out too," Jim said.

It went around again until Roger Clemens was on someone's team. Then, we moved on to the next player. Beer flowed, pretzels and potato chips were eaten, sodas drunk, music blared. What a day! Another of those top ten.

Karen Lofton made me laugh.
"It never rains at night," she stated.
"What!" I exclaimed.
"No, clouds only come out during the day."
Another night, Karen asked, "Why do we rotate tires? Don't they rotate themselves?"
And she was a nurse!

Fran Preston was another nurse on nights.
"Why are you so upset and crying?" I asked.
"Grace Kelly was killed in a car wreck. I just loved her."
The next night, the first page of the Scranton newspaper said, "Grace Kelly dead. Should she be a saint?"

I'm sick of all this talk of Grace Kelly. We fought several wars to get rid of monarchy and she marries a prince.
Being of Kelly blood, it boggled my wee mind. I didn't need anyone with the Kelly name to intercede for me. I didn't know it yet but there is Someone much better, Jesus.

"Look, Grace Kelly is on the front page of the paper!"

Fran said upon entering the conference room where the paper lay on the table.

"I'll try to make her a saint."

"How?"

"I've got the coronation ceremony all set," I answered seriously. "Maybe we could get the San Diego Padres or the St. Louis Cardinals to attend."

"Oh come on."

"Really. The Catholic Church needs three miracles for sainthood. Personally, I think one good one should be enough. First, she was born in Philadelphia and married a prince. That's a miracle. Second, Grace received an Oscar for her acting. That's even a bigger miracle as anyone who has sat through *High Noon* or *To Catch A Thief* will swear. But, I can't come up with a third.

"Think for a minute. If the Church makes her a saint, the tree Grace crashed into would be chopped up and sold as amulets. Very Catholic! I am willing to split the proceeds with the Pope seventy-thirty. I'm not greedy. I even know the Pope's home phone number."

"You do not!"

"I do to. It's *Et cum spiritu tuo.*"

We had a good laugh.

God must be laughing. We are comical. We are stiff-necked, unruly, fight each other, etc. but for some reason He loves us. (Please read John 3:16 again and Romans 5:8.)

But I am getting ahead of my story again.

I liked working nights at Mercy. Fewer bosses around, there's less of a patient load and I did what I wanted. That's also the time when the crazies come in. People like me.

We saw many social problems. Once a lady was found sitting on a park bench at 11:30 P.M. She had disembarked from a Wilkes-Barre bus. I don't know how the woman boarded because she couldn't talk. The lady was brought—where else?—to the ER.

The woman communicated by pointing to different letters of the alphabet on a card she carried with her. I didn't have time to put the letters together, so, I rifled through her handbag to get information. I found her daughter's phone number inside and called it.

"Who is this?" a woman answered gruffly.

"It's Dr. Thek from Mercy, Scranton and your mother..."

"How did you get my number?"

"Well, from..."

Slam went the receiver! For a moment, I was as speechless as the mother.

This must be very odd for her. First, she's in a strange city at night and then the daughter hangs up. Very peculiar!

About a half-hour went by. A policeman called Officer Radly phoned and asked, "How did you get that number?"

What is it about this number?

"It was easy. I just went through the mother's pocket book."

Silence. Finally, Officer Radly admitted, "We've been after the daughter for seven years. When your nurse called us a few minutes ago, our detectives put two and two together. We need that number."

"I'll give it to you but I doubt she'll answer. Been scared off."

"We'll try anyway."

I was flabbergasted. I was with the mother for a couple minutes and I spoke with her daughter, who was wanted for a crime. I was part detective too!

I should receive a salary from the police.

The lady was sent to stay at her sister's.

I often felt sorry for patients. One night, a redheaded drunk came in. I discovered he was a veteran, so, I let him sleep on the gurney.

(I'm a softie for veterans. My Aunt Tess and Uncle John were the only US Marine brother-sister tandem to serve in both WWI and WWII.

Uncle John was a salty old coot who peppered his speech with expletives. He was not above inventing a few. His language could make a longshoreman blush.

And my Aunt Tess had a marvelous sense of humor. She once wrote a book called *I Slept With a Thousand Marines* and neglected to mention that they were all women. And no, she was not a lesbian; they were in a barracks.

Aunt Tess became a Lieutenant Colonel, the highest ranking woman in the Marine Corps in WWII.)

In the morning, I ordered a taxi to take him home. The drunk promptly took it and robbed a bank.

Will I get arrested? Am I an accomplice?

All day I avoided the telephone.

Evenings were very different from nights. Some shifts that I worked were busy. Our fun counteracted the exposure to others' pain. Most of the nurses were single and could stay up late.

I replaced Phil Bocci one weekend shift change for the doctors, when all the docs worked twelve hours.

"Check the chest x-ray on Trauma One when they do it," he signed out to me and left.

A little later, Betty Anne Liberto, the charge nurse that night who knew what was going on for once, buttonholed me and said, "Dr. Thek, you have to check the chest x-ray for the patient in Trauma One."

"I know."

Then, the radio blared.

"Got a cardiac arrest..." then static.

"Oh. ****!" I exclaimed. "I can't hear what they're doing!"

"Dr. Thek," Betty Anne tugged at my sleeve. "We don't have a room."

Exasperated, I shouted, "Make one!"

She moved the patient from Trauma Room One into the

hallway. The cardiac arrest patient went in there when he arrived. He didn't make it and died.

However, the x-ray request was never changed due to the bustle. The suite where the films were taken was right behind the nurses' station. The technician came down, took the dead body, and snapped a chest. I don't know how you can take a picture of a stiff, but she did. Then, the tech noticed he wasn't breathing and panicked. "Code! Code! He's not breathing!"

I ran into the room not recognizing the cardiac arrest patient. The paramedics, who brought him, thought I had started a trend. First you pump on the chest for a half-hour, stop, expose them to radiation, and start again.

I called a code.

"Dr. Thek, this is the man from Trauma One," Betty Anne informed me.

"I don't care where he's from!" It had yet to register with me. I kept on pumping. Then, it dawned on me that I was coding the same man twice!

I called it off, but the patient developed a heart rhythm on the monitor when we stopped! Now, what was I going to do? If the beat kept up, I would have to code him a third time. The paramedics supposed I was a genius. Betty Anne thought I was a dunce. The rhythm stopped, and I didn't have to cross that bridge. The man was pronounced dead for a second time. To God, it's only once. But to man, it's twice. We have to learn the difference. (Please read Hebrews 9:27-28.)

Betty Anne was a friend with Marilyn Carroll, another nurse. Marilyn was very funny. One night, some of us decided to play a practical joke on her. Ben Bowden, a paramedic, had us save Styrofoam popcorn for six months. His accomplice, Steve Finn, later married Marilyn. They wanted to fill up her car was with the small pieces.

"How do we get her keys for the car?" Steve wondered.

"We'll borrow them from her locker," Ben answered.

In the parking lot, Steve asked, "Now how do we get the Styrofoam inside the car?"

"Make a funnel out of cardboard. We'll pour it in through a crack in the back window."

It reached to just above the dash.

"But she'll see it!" Steve said.

"No she won't if we circle the car with industrial strength Satan Wrap first!"

When Marilyn entered the lot, we hid behind other parked cars. She saw the Saran wrap around her vehicle and hastily removed it with scissors. When Marilyn opened the front door, the popcorn pieces poured out.

She drove me home a few times. "Every time I put on the heat, Styrofoam comes flying out. I'll get those guys."

Months later, Marilyn did. Ben and Steve went to a conference in Allentown, about sixty miles away and Ben told me about the adventure.

"Marilyn and Betty Anne followed us. I didn't see them. When we parked, they water-painted the car."

I almost heard Marilyn saying, "I'll get those guys."

"It would've come out," he continued, "but I parked in the sun. The watercolors baked into the finish. When we returned, the car needed a new paint job."

That finished the practical jokes. They can be funny until someone loses an eye.

I remember other nurses.

"My brother needs a riding mower to cut his grass," Sheila McCabe said one evening.

"I could use a weed whacker on mine for the hard to get at areas," I responded.

"I have one of those."

"Part of my yard is on the side of a hill and I'm afraid to use a riding mower. But I have one that came with the house. The push mower is good for me. Keeps me in shape. Why don't we switch?"

It seemed like a good exchange.

Joe Silvia was another nurse on evenings. Once, we went to Hilton Head for a vacation with Jerry Donegal (husband of one of the day nurses and owner of an ambulance) and Terry Maris. To get on the golf courses, the four of us posed as pros from Scranton. Driving off the first tee, we hit one slice into the second fairway and three hooks into the woods. Jerry Donegal had a seventy-two on the front nine. The eighteenth came off the course with the ninth.

"Not bad," I said loud enough for the starter to hear,

"Seventy-two," as we neared him. The starter looked at us askance then we proceeded on to the tenth hole.

Jerry actually hit a ball into someone's basement. "What do I do now?"

"Play it where it lies," Joe answered.

Jerry went into the basement and we saw a ball come flying out the open doorway.

"What did you do?" I asked.

"The ball was sitting in the middle of the room so I just whacked it. That was probably the best shot I had all day."

"Lucky the owner didn't show with a shotgun," Terry said.

"Where did my drive go?"

"In the lake," Joe answered.

"We should call your driver 'The Divining Rod' because you're always finding water," Jerry laughed.

Afterward we wevt grocery shopping. Jerry took the wheel. Several young women in a red convertible pulled out from a side street and almost hit us. The driver flipped us the bird. Jerry sidled up to the other car at an intersection and rolled down the window. "Is that the number of your legal parents?"

The other vehicle peeled out, while I looked for a place to hide.

One evening, there was a patient in Room 8. As I walked back, I looked at the chart. Her chief complaint was she had an ant stuck on her uvula.

Now, how did it get there?

"I was drinking some soda, you know," the teen-aged girl sitting in the examining chair said nonchalantly. She wore pierced earrings everywhere: her nose, lips, eyelids, tongue. Getting them must have hurt. (I guess she never read 1 Cor. 3:16.)

"I took a big gulp. As I did, I saw this big old ant on top of the soda, swimming fast, you know, fighting to stay alive. It was too late to stop swallowing. So, I swallowed, you know. When I did, he hung on to this thing in my throat that hangs down, you know." And with that she opened her mouth and pointed to her uvula. I looked inside, and here, stuck to her uvula, was the dead ant. I was reminded of *The Pink Panther* theme, "Dead ant. Dead ant. Dead ant, dead ant, dead ant..." I removed it.

Poor ant! He must've seen the soda gush down the esophagus and held on for dear life. What way to go!

The very next patient was a teenager with an orange rash on her face.

"I swear; it's real!" the mother exclaimed as I came in the room.

I never saw an orange rash. I took an alcohol wipe and rubbed on it. The rash disappeared. A flabbergasted mother shouted to the daughter, "But you said you didn't use the markers!" I never uttered a word and left.

Occasionally, I worked days; after all, I was the director. The shift was usually busy. Once, in the newspaper, atheists were complaining about school prayer and Christmas songs.

"How can anyone not believe?" Michelle Abington, one of the nurses, wondered out loud.

How could anyone believe? I wondered at the time. I had yet to undergo my metamorphosis. I was still in the larval stage cocoon.

"We'll stay put, under nursing," Joan Kraft, the head nurse, said. "They're dependable."

The nurses were pulled from the ER to work on the floors when it wasn't busy. Everybody suffered.

Joan left for a teaching job in the hospital and Jackie Splawn became the new head nurse.

Good things come to those who wait.

I thought things would change, but they didn't. The ER was still a part of Family Practice and not a separate entity. The RNs were still part of the Nursing Department. I think the supervisors should have their brain waves checked to be sure they weren't flat line.

We became the dumping ground for everybody—the police, the doctors, the hospital. The ER was fully staffed and couldn't refuse anybody. When the hospital filled up (which was nearly every day) the overflow was held in the ER. RNs took orders from the doctors on the floors. They were not used to giving baths or medicines.

Dr. Rose was the director of the Family Practice Department. Technically, he was medical head of the ER. Jackie and I met with him, Sister, and other hospital bigwigs monthly. We never accomplished anything.

Once, a road crew was paving in a nearby town. On the street where they were, lived a patient of Dr. Rose's. A road-crew member wore the same shirt as he did. The patient left the house, but his wife stayed at home.

The crewman with the same shirt went into cardiac arrest. He fell into the tar and was unrecognizable. The wife thought it was her husband coming home. CPR was started and the man was brought to our hospital.

Dr. Rose worked feverishly through the tar to resuscitate the man. "That's funny," he noted as he pumped on the patient's chest. "He's lost some weight."

Finally, the man was declared dead. Dr. Rose went to the wife, "I'm sorry," he began, sitting down and taking her hand. "We did everything we could but your husband died."

After a while, she went home. Imagine her puzzlement when the woman saw through the glass in the front door a man waiting at the dining room table. He turned toward her as she opened the door. It was her husband! She fainted.

The day RNs were too serious for me, so, I tried to lighten up the atmosphere. When Jean Nick was pregnant, I put possible names on the board in the conference room. (Like Pick Nick, Saint Nick etc.) They were meant to be funny. Soon, I was using it to post many humorous lists. The supervisors didn't like them and erased the lists. It became a game. The nurses feared their superiors and walked around like they were stepping on red-hot coals. A union was needed.

A patient came in walking backwards.

"Why are you walking that way?" I asked.

"If I knew, I wouldn't be here would I? I thought you could give me an answer."

"Who do you think I am, for goodness sake? I don't read a crystal ball! I have no idea why you walk backwards!"

With that, he walked out of the room and ER, backwards. I guess he thought me stupid.

A man brought in a brown paper bag. He removed a dead, white muskrat from it.

"What do you want me to do with it?" I asked.

"Does it have rabies?"

"Now, how do I know?"

"No need to get nasty."

The man turned and left, leaving me holding the bag in one hand and the dead muskrat in the other.

We had a Xerox machine. I copied nearly everyone's picture. When Tom Major passed his EM boards, I put his photo everywhere. When the doctors looked in ears, they found it in the otoscope. Cathy Welch, a nurse, and I put the photo in the plastic sponges. Opening them, placing it inside, and then closing. We put the sponges on the bottom, to remind us several months later. Even the tubes where charts were transported had Tom's photo.

"Say, why is Tom's picture in the toilet paper?" asked Peter Lynch.

One morning, as I came in, a frantic nurse greeted me. She took me to Trauma Room One. A boy of nine was on the litter barely breathing. I intubated him and ordered a CAT Scan of the head. The boy was the lone son of a nursing supervisor, Anne Marie Rowlette. A couple of days later, he died. She, nor I, ever recovered.

A baby died from a BB gun. The entrance wound in the head was raised, meaning the gun was close.

"I swear the air rifle fell off the top shelf!" the mother insisted. "It was loaded and went off when it struck the floor. The BB hit my little boy."

I think not. The closet was clear across the room. I believe she shot him.

I went to the courthouse to plead his case. The witness before me was an expert in air rifles.

"The rifle could keep its pressure for up to six months," he testified.

In other words, the shot could have happened the way the mother described. I wasn't called and she walked free.

I thought about that event. We are not judges. Only God is and He will give everyone their due, either good or bad. We are commanded not to seek revenge both in the Old Testament and in the New. (Please read Lev. 19:18 and Romans 12:19.)

I must remember sometimes that there is no fooling Him, no matter how many so-called "experts" are brought in.

The media people were a trip! They wanted me to appear on television and tell asthmatics about the dangers of air conditioning. What dangers? If you know of any, please explain them to me.

Another time, TV wanted me to say a word about toothpick injuries. Someone had swallowed one and it perforated his bowel.

"Aren't seat belts a bigger issue?" I asked.

"No one will watch," the newsman replied.

"I'll be laughed out of Scranton if I talk about toothpicks!"

I was instructed to be friendly with the media people, so it was necessary that I speak about toothpicks somehow.

I thought for a moment, then, continued, "The driver of an auto was chewing on a toothpick. He didn't have his seat belt on. He hit another car and was flung up against the windshield. The driver swallowed the toothpick and busted his gut."

It never aired. The truth is boring.

We had six ER trained docs and one internist, as I said, probably the only hospital in the country with that many. The administration didn't know how good they had it. Each of us was excellent, but all good things must end.

First, Dom and Phil opened up a successful practice. They shared one full-time position between them. That corroborated what Sister thought of the ER being a steppingstone. Then, I lost Lisa and Scott. The edifice I built was crumbling. I wanted to evacuate before I became part of the rubble.

"Why don't you come in with Phil and me?" Dom asked. "We could use you."

"I like the idea of having a practice that no one can mess with," I said.

"Then it's settled."

"Whoa! I didn't say that. Your practice is established. Mine's not. In effect, I'd be working for you. Although your offer is generous I have to decline. I'm not ready."

A couple months went by. I was ready now.

"Want to go in practice with me?" Tom Major asked one afternoon at my house on the patio. "I need a partner."

"Sounds good," I said realizing that he and I were equals.

I stopped being the director of the ER, but still worked.

We established our office three towns over in Olyphant. Tom and I painted it, hired an interior decorator for the curtains and furniture, and rented the office from the Russian church through one of the security guards.

We hired a secretary and when we learned she lied on her application, Tom and I decided to fire her.

"Will you do it?" Tom asked.

Thinking of Dennis and Charlie I replied, "I guess I have the experience. I wish someone else did."

The real world is not so funny.

My cousin, Lena, took her place. Then Nancy Eckert's sister, Donna, became available, so we hired her.

We bought a computer for billing and record keeping, everything. All I wanted to do was care for people. There's more to it than that, but having your own shingle outside with your name on it makes it worthwhile. Almost.

"Do EKGs, spirometry and sigmoidoscopy on everyone," Tom advised. "They all need them and Medicare will pay. They take less time than a full exam and pay more."

"But I can't do procedures for procedures' sake," I flashed back.

"Think of it as overhead. If we don't put the right code numbers down, we don't get paid. We go under. Then everybody suffers."

I never had to worry about money in the ER. It's looking better all the time. If only I can find a little hole and crawl in so no one finds me.

The year was 1989. The Berlin Wall came down and I was still working in Mercy's ER in Scranton, Pennsylvania, with a family practice on the side. I smoked and tried many times to quit. It didn't help when a family practitioner asked his patients to quit for their health, smoked himself.

What an example I am!

One weekend, Bob and I put a stereo in my Chevette. The speakers were in the doors. Without telling me, he ran the wires to the passenger door over the ashtray and through the glove compartment.

On Monday, after working the day shift, I drove toward the office in nearby Olyphant. I was caught in a traffic jam, so I lit up a cigarette. The driver's window was broken, so I rolled down the passenger's to let the smoke escape.

When I went to snuff out the cancer stick, the ashtray was typically full. I put the cigarette in anyway and it started to smolder.

If I just shut the ashtray no oxygen will fuel the flame.

The ashtray was near the opened window. The wires from the stereo caught fire. In a moment, flames shot out of the glove compartment.

What's going on?

I kicked the dashboard, but the combustion wouldn't go out. Then, I realized how dangerous it was. I was stuck in traffic, with a driver's window that would not open, and a car on fire!

Have to get off this road.

I pulled onto an empty side street where there was new development construction and, I thought, no people. At the end of the road was a bucket. I parked the Chevette in the middle of the empty street and scrambled for the bucket. One of the new houses had an outside faucet, so I filled the bucket with water.

A man's head poked out of the house above me. "What are you doing?"

I pointed to the car.

"Go ahead!"

I ran back with the sloshing water to find a bunch of kids around the auto.

Are they playing ring-around-the-Rosie? Where did they come from? This is just great! The tires will explode and the valves will kill the kids! What a headline! Smoking Doctor Kills Kids!

I herded them away from the car.

When I returned, the inside of the Chevette was all smoke. Everything burned: x-rays, bowling ball, the driver's seat. I don't think Chevrolet installs anything unless it is flammable. There must be some kind of test. My personal mess added fuel to the flames.

The fire engine arrived, after it too, was caught in the traffic jam.

"Thanks for stopping," the firemen said.

"Stopping! It's my car!"

I guess they cannot believe that doctors drive other vehicles besides Mercedes. The conflagration was finally extinguished.

The Chevette was totaled, so I rode to work on the back of the fire truck. Who knows what the patients thought when I dismounted?

When I was safely in the office, Donna called Edie. Later I learned from Donna, the conversation went something like this.

"Hello. Dr. Thek is normal," Donna began.

There was a brief pause, and then Edie responded. "He's never been normal. What happened?"

Lena loaned me her car. It was also a Chevette. They must run in the family. The day after the fire, I drove home from the office. A cop pulled me over two towns away from where it happened.

"License and registration," he commanded after I rolled down the window. The policeman looked at me through his reflective sunglasses.

"What was I pulled over for?"

"Speeding."

Uh-oh. I thought he was gonna warn me about the studded snow tires she has on the car. I'm in for it now.

"You're not gonna believe this," I started.

He lowered his sunglasses. I could see from his beady eyes this cop was no one to fool with. "Try me."

"My license was destroyed yesterday in a car fire."

After a brief pause, he asked, "Are you Dr. Thek?"

I purposely avoided giving my name. "Why, yes, as a matter of fact I am. How did you know?"

The policeman started to laugh. I can take a lot of things, but ridiculed by a cop is not one of them.

"Please, give me a ticket or something," I literally begged.

He roared.

"Give me a ticket!"

The policeman laughed hysterically.

"'All I wanted was a Bud Light,' Torch," he replied.

I couldn't understand what was happening. *Why won't he ticket me?*

It turned out the cop was the husband of the fire engine dispatcher.

I went to the ER the next night.

"Hello, 'Torch'," Jean Marie said.

That does it! If the Berlin Wall can come down, I can quit smoking.

Soon after that, I decided an office was not for me either. I was happy in the ER where nobody paid me for the services rendered. I cared for people without worrying about overhead. The cost never concerned me. It was made for me, but I couldn't be in Scranton anymore. It had to be someplace else, where I wasn't the boss.

Speaking of the Boss (and I'm not talking about Bruce Springsteen), I didn't know that there was only One. I thought I had many. But what did I know? I was like an eighth grader, controlled in my thinking by hormones. But, I was learning. The elusive First Principle was almost attainable, but I kept falling back into the abyss.

Also available from PublishAmerica

SHINE AND INSPIRATIONS
by Tiffiney Rochelle Bradley

Shine and Inspirations is a text designed to teach humanity the purpose and role of prayer in everyday life. This book seeks to deepen believers' insights and understanding of how a continual prayer life will serve to strengthen the soul of believers and equip them in remaining encouraged while in the midst of life's stormiest situations.

Another book, entitled *Inspirations*, a collection of Christian testimonies, is included. Many of these touching testimonies explain how prayer served to stabilize and/or uplift those who testified out of situations such as HIV, severe physical illnesses, single parenthood, and hunger. Read, enjoy, and forever be inspired as you connect with the Spirit of Christ, which will enable you to Shine.

Paperback, 198 pages
6" x 9"
ISBN 1-4241-8489-4

About the author:

Shine and Inspirations came to life out of my call to serve the Lord, and my passion to help people. Prayer is having an intimate conversation with God. Having a Master's degree in Communications and having served in the field of education has been quite fulfilling, but publishing *Shine and Inspirations* has also been fulfilling, if not more so. What could be more exciting for a communicator and a servant of the Lord than helping others experience a dimension in Christ that I have already experienced.

Available to all bookstores nationwide.
www.publishamerica.com

Also available from PublishAmerica

THE GIRL IN THE PICTURE

by Charles E. Merkel II

Everything is going great for 18-year-old Brian Kitzmiller, who is assigned to a non-combat unit in 1967 Vietnam. His responsibilities include being the outfit's mail clerk, and he soon becomes a welcome face to everyone.

He carries a picture, which he has enlarged then placed above his bunk, of a girl from his hometown whom he really does not know but passes off as his girlfriend. As time goes on, the gorgeous girl becomes the most famous lady in the whole unit and the juicy stories abound. Brian does nothing to stifle this ever-growing myth. In fact, he enjoys his "legendary" status as he has never known anything but loneliness and obscurity back home.

Paperback, 266 pages
6" x 9"
ISBN 1-4241-3047-6

The lid blows off when a cruel skeptic from the same town arrives and Brian's life unravels. Wracked by relentless humiliation and scorn, his decisions from that point become reckless.

About the author:

Charles E. Merkel II grew up in Louisville and Indianapolis, the son of a state engineer inspector and an elementary school teacher. A graduate of the Indiana University School of Journalism and a Vietnam veteran, he has been published in various literary magazines nine times. He has worked as a regional sales manager in the RV industry for twenty-five years.

Available to all bookstores nationwide.
www.publishamerica.com